Teaching English as a Foreign or Second Language

A Self-Development and Methodology Guide

Third Edition

JERRY G. GEBHARD

University of Michigan Press
Ann Arbor

This third edition is dedicated to all the students I have taught throughout the years, especially to those students who have continued to develop their teaching beliefs and practices through systematic exploration.

I also dedicate this book to my nephew, Matt Gebhard, for his support and loyalty to family. I deeply appreciate his caring attitude toward family.

ISBN-13   978-0-472-03673-8 (paper)
ISBN-13   978-0-472-12369-8 (ebook)

Published in the United States of America
The University of Michigan Press
Manufactured in the United States of America

♾ Printed on acid-free paper

2020   2019   2018   2017   4   3   2   1

Contents

Acknowledgments

I sincerely thank Maria Saryuz Sarska, Dong Xu, and Tim Conrad for assisting me with research during the development of the first edition of this book. I also want to thank Tom McClaren for assisting me with research on technology, Theresa Tseng for her feedback and research into technology, and both Theresa and Qisi Zhang for helping me to update the appendixes on publishing companies and journals for the second edition. I also thank John Fanselow, Thomas Farrell, Pamela Friedman, Barbara Hill Hudson, Joe O'Connor, Judi Moy, and Lilia Savova for reading and commenting on the first edition of the book at different stages in its development, as well as Nancy Bell and Amy Minette for reading and giving thoughtful feedback on Chapter 3 in the second edition.

I thank the administration at the American Language Institute (ALI) at Indiana University of Pennsylvania (IUP) for their consent to observe and photograph classes; Mary Beth Mahler, Zubeyde Tezel, and Trikarti-kaningsih for inviting me into their classes; the students in their ALI classes for being so very cooperative. I also want to thank Tim and Kerry Conrad for their ongoing support.

I also thank the many graduate students in the Ph.D. Program in Rhetoric and Linguistics for commenting on chapters in the first edition, students in the Ph.D. Program in Composition & TESOL on chapters in the second edition, students in the MA TESOL Program for feedback on both editions, and students in the graduate and undergraduate programs in English Education at Pusan National University for ideas for this third edition.

Finally, I would like to thank Kelly Sippell for her support and patience as I recreated this book into second and third editions.

I'm an English Teacher!?

—Remark made by an underprepared teacher

Introduction:
A Self-Development and
Methodology Guide

This book is a teacher development and methodology book. It can be used by those of you who are learning to teach English as a foreign language (EFL) and English as a second language (ESL) as a part of your pre-service teacher education program. It can also be used as a teacher development text in in-service teacher development programs as a source for experienced EFL/ESL teachers who would like to refresh their knowledge and see their teaching differently. In addition, this book can act as an exploratory text for those who are simply curious about teaching EFL/ESL or by those who have accepted an EFL/ESL teaching position without the benefit of a formal teacher education program and are unprepared to take on all of the responsibilities of being a teacher.

The Purpose and Content of This Book

This book provides ways for you to work on the development of your teaching and classroom practices. It offers ways that you, as an EFL or ESL teacher, can develop your teaching through a process of exploration. This book also provides discussion on the different English teaching settings around the world and teaching issues associated within them. It also provides discussions, examples, and illustrations of how EFL/ESL can be taught as interaction among people; how classrooms can be managed; how teachers and students can make use of teaching materials, media, and technology; what digital technology includes and how it can be used; and the significance of culture for both students and teachers. In addition, this book shows how EFL/ESL teachers teach students to comprehend spoken English, to converse in English, to read for meaning, and to process writing.

This book is based on questions EFL/ESL teachers, including myself, have asked about teaching and learning over a number of years, and each chapter begins with a set of questions related to the content of that chapter. As such, one way to use this book as a part of your development is as a reference for ideas based on the questions posed at the beginning of each chapter and answered within it. This book also has a list of recommended sources at the end of each chapter and includes references to professional books and articles as well as EFL/ESL textbooks. The appendixes contain information on publishing companies and academic and practical journals on teaching EFL/ESL. These additional sources will help further your own development as an EFL/ESL teacher.

The end of each chapter includes a set of self-development tasks that are an integral part of this book. The purpose of these tasks is to offer opportunities to work on your development as an EFL/ESL teacher by observing, talking about, and writing about teaching. I encourage you to spend time on these tasks. I realize that finding the time to do these tasks is not necessarily easy because of busy schedules. However, I encourage you to find the time to systematically think about your teaching in new ways and to stretch your imaginations through the teacher development tasks.

I want to point out that this book is not, and was never meant to be, a book that neatly fits into what is known as "reflective teaching." I point this out because one reviewer (Rodgers 1998) mistakenly reviewed the first edition of this book alongside two other books that are clearly within the "reflective teaching" category. The reviewer took issue with the book; as she put it, "A reflective book it is not" (p. 611). As the title tag *A Teacher Self-Development and Methodology Guide* indicates, this book was created so that readers can work on their own development as teachers by understanding what other teachers, including me, believe about teaching and do in their classrooms. In short, reflection is an important part of learning to teach, and I do offer chances for teachers to reflect on teaching in this book. However, the focus of this book is much broader in scope than just reflection on teaching.

About the Third Edition

My approach to this edition was based primarily on feedback from readers, including those who took the time to write formal published reviews in journals, students in my TEFL/TESL Methodology class, and people I have met at conferences or online who offered feedback on the book. I have taken this feedback to heart, and I have done my best to incorporate what I have learned from you, the readers, into this edition.

The basic structure of the book has not changed. It still includes three parts. The first provides background to my understanding of self-development, as well as ways you, as teachers or prospective teachers, can explore teaching to work on your development. Part 2 still includes knowledge and experience related to teaching language, and Part 3 is about teaching language skills.

However, while maintaining the same three parts, I have used readers' feedback to make several changes in the book. To begin, I have added an additional chapter, Digital Literacy, Technology, and Teaching EFL/ESL (Chapter 7) to Part II. This chapter highlights how digital technology has impacted the field of teaching English as a foreign language (EFL) and English as a second language (ESL). It begins by defining digital literacy and goes on to discuss the kinds of digital technology that are available to EFL/ESL teachers and students, as well as provides examples of how teachers and students have used digital technology to facilitate language learning. As technology is changing very quickly, this chapter also addresses the exciting, yet uncertain, future of digital (or other advances in) technology that could impact teaching and learning languages. The chapter closes, like the other chapters in this book, by addressing some of the problems associated with the use of digital technology to teach EFL/ESL.

In addition, I have brought in additional discussion about and examples of the use of digital technology in Part III of this book on teaching language skills. However, I also emphasize that teaching and learning EFL and ESL depends on what happens between people inside and outside the classroom and that digital technology simply adds another means through which such interaction can take place. Further, I point out that digital technology is only one kind of technology. As I highlight in Chapter 6: EFL/ESL Materials, Media, and Technology, teaching technology can be placed on a continuum from low technology (e.g., writing with sticks in the dirt, chalk boards) to high technology (e.g., use of computer programs) to higher technology (e.g., digital technology that allows for synchronous interaction), and any form of technology can be used to facilitate learning. It is not what technology we use, but rather how we use the technology that is available to us that is important.

As with the first two editions, Chapters 1 and 2 introduce the concepts of exploring teaching. However, in Chapter 1, The Self-Developed Language Teacher, I provide three new-teacher scenarios, and unlike in the first two editions, in which I relied on my memory to recall the teaching lives of two EFL teachers, in this third edition I use classroom observation and research to show how three different teachers approached (or did not approach) development of their teaching beliefs and practices. Chapter 2, Exploration of Teaching, still highlights ways teachers can approach the development of their teaching; however, I have woven in different examples to illustrate how some teachers have worked on their development. Further, the third edition maintains the inclusion of teacher self-development tasks at the end of each chapter, some which I have revised or added.

I have also done my best to read extensively and talk with other professionals about teaching, as well as reflect on my own use of innovative ways to teach (especially in Korea and Hawaii), and I have used this experience to revise the content of the chapters in this book. For example, in

Chapter 4, Teaching Language as Communication among People, I have added a discussion on Task-Based teaching; and in Chapter 6, EFL/ESL Materials, Media, and Technology; I have added a detailed discussion on how teachers can select context appropriate textbooks, as well as a discussion on how teachers can discover websites that have teacher-created activities and games, many of which allow students to expand their study of English in a fun way inside and outside the classroom. I have also included a discussion on the value of corpus-informed textbooks.

Likewise, in Part 3 on teaching language skills, I have updated each chapter in regard to ways each skill can be taught. For example, in Chapter 10, Teaching Students to Speak in Class, I have added a detailed section on the use of student presentations, as well as how digital technology has added new means for students to expand their speaking opportunities. In Chapter 11, Teaching Students to Read for Meaning, I have brought in a discussion on the intermediate-level slump problem that readers face and ways to provide opportunities for learners to cope and make progress with their reading. I also updated my discussion on the use of reading strategies and have added a detailed discussion on the importance of teaching students to use metacognitive reading strategies, as well as how they can be taught to use them. In addition, I have added discussions on how teachers can teach vocabulary as well as use grammar to help students to comprehend text. Further, in Chapter 12, Teaching Students How to Process Writing, I have expanded my discussion of the writing process to include how students can get feedback on their writing. I also expanded on an earlier discussion (see Chapter 7) on using blogs and wikis as a way for students to write to a real audience and collaborate on writing projects. I have also added a detailed discussion on how teachers can teach grammar in their writing classes as well as why they should consider doing so. I also added a discussion on the problem of grading essays and how teachers can use a writing portfolio as a favorable way to evaluate what they have accomplished in a writing course.

This third edition also includes an updated Recommended Teacher Resources section at the end of each chapter, as well as updated appendixes on professional journals (Appendix A) and publishers (Appendix B) in the field. I have also updated the endnotes for each chapter to reflect current, as well as historical, theory and practice.

Part 1

Self-Development, Exploration, and Settings

1

Teachers themselves . . . must become the primary shapers of their own development.

—Lieberman 1992, vi

The Self-Developed Language Teacher

❙ *Does self-development make a difference?*
❙ *What factors are central to teacher self-development?*

Does Self-Development Make a Difference?

To emphasize the concept of self-development, I begin this book by illustrating its advantages. To do this, I invite you to enter three different classrooms.[1] The first is of an inexperienced teacher (Amy) who was beginning to work on the development of her teaching. The second is of a teacher (Kumiko) who had taken on the responsibility for her own development. The third is an experienced teacher (Soyoung) who had become complacent about her development. I stress that all three teachers can gain much by paying regular attention to their teaching.

AMY'S CLASS

The first example focuses on Amy, an inexperienced ESL teacher at the beginning of her development. Amy was in the last semester of her MA TESOL program at Indiana University of Pennsylvania and had an internship at the American Language Institute. Her particular job was to co-teach a conversation course to fifteen intermediate level students. As a part of the internship experience, the intern was mentored by a co-operating teacher, as well as by an internship supervisor. I was the internship supervisor. My job was to work with Amy on her development as a teacher, and I asked her to make short video recordings of a few of her lessons. I then viewed some of the recorded class and asked her to describe what was going on in the class. I suggested Amy pick her own parts of the lesson to describe and analyze, as well as to focus on her instructions and what students did just after she gave these instructions.

With my encouragement, Amy transcribed her instructions and what students did and said. When she met with me, I recall that she laughed and said, "The students really didn't understand my instructions, did they!" She had asked the students to form groups of four, read the role card she would be giving each of them, not to read other students cards, and then get ready to do a skit. The students looked at each other, moved their chairs slightly, not forming complete groups, and sat silently. Then, students asked each other – some in their native language – what they were supposed to be doing. Amy repeated the instructions as she handed out role descriptions on index cards, making sure to give the waiter a set of menus. Students looked at each other's cards and some took a menu to read. Amy told them not to do this, as she physically helped students move into groups of four students. The students read their cards in silence, and some students asked the teacher what they were supposed to do with the cards. Amy got the students' attention and explained that they were supposed to create a restaurant scene. The waiter should be standing and the customers should read the menus and do what is on the card. Examples of cards are:

Role 1: You are a waiter. Greet the customers. Give them menus. Give them time to read. Write down their orders.	Role 3: You are a customer. You are very hungry. Ask the waiter, "What do you recommend?"
Role 2: You are a customer. Study the menu. You have only eight dollars to spend.	Role 4: You are a customer. You don't eat meat. Ask the waiter, "What vegetarian food do you have?"

After six minutes of moving students into groups and explaining what they were supposed to do, the students started working on the role-play skit.

After the class, Amy and I talked. It was obvious to Amy that the students were confused about what they were supposed to do, and we talked about different ways to give instructions. Amy said that she could show them what to do by asking three students to help her with a demonstration. I added that she could write down the instructions and ask students to read them silently, as well as have a student paraphrase them. Since Amy was a talented artist, I suggested she could draw the instructions. She smiled. I also suggested she could give the instructions as a dictation. Amy pointed out that she also had trouble having students form groups, and we talked about different ways to do this. Students could count off, "one, two, three, four..." and Amy could instruct all number ones to form a group on the right, twos on the left, threes in the back, and so on. I also gave her one of my favorite ways of forming groups by giving students pieces of different flavored candy. Students with cherry-flavored candy are one group, lemon another, and so on. In the spirit of generating alternative ways of forming groups quickly, Amy smiled, eyes widening, as she expressed an idea to ask students to practice forming groups and maybe to have a contest on how fast they could form their groups based on her instructions.

KUMIKO'S CLASS

The second example centers on Kumiko, an experienced EFL teacher in Japan who consistently spent time working on her development. She believed that development of teaching is not something teachers just do when they are new to teaching, but should be a part of a career-long endeavor. In addition to joining JALT (Japanese Association of Language Teachers), attending their national and regional conferences and conducting workshops at these conferences, she decided to study for her MA TESOL degree at Teachers College, Columbia University, Tokyo campus. To gain entrance into this program, students had to be teaching. As such, students attended classes during weekends.

I taught at Teachers College during my sabbaticals from my university position in Pennsylvania, and Kumiko enrolled in my Speaking Practicum. As a part of this course, students were expected to visit each other's classes in small groups to observe classroom interaction, and three of us visited Kumiko's YWCA evening conversation class. In addition to having three observers jot down descriptive notes, short dialogues, and sketches of interaction, we audio-recorded the class.

After the class, the four of us went to a coffee shop to talk about the class. After each of us showed and explained our descriptive observation notes, Kumiko said she particularly was interested in the short dialogues one of the observers had jotted down. Here is an example:

[Chart on the wall with everyone's names and birthdates.]

Teacher: Look at the information on the chart about your class-mates' birthdays. Yuki, when is Toshinobu's birthday? January …?

Yuki: Birthday. January.

Teacher: Very good. When in January?

Yuki: November.

Teacher: Good. Very good. But, look at the chart. Here is Toshinobu's name and here is his birthday date. When is Toshi's birthday?

Yuki: Ano, January ten.

Teacher: Yes. Very good, Yuki.

This and other short dialogues raised questions about praising students, and we analyzed the way Kumiko praised students. We discovered that she used *good* and *very good* often, even when students did not answer questions correctly, such as when Yuki did not understand the teacher's question "when in January [is Toshi's birthday]?" and replied, "November." We then considered how the students might understand her praise, and we decided that it was likely ambiguous to the students. Because she praised them often, even when they gave wrong responses, we wondered if students knew she was praising them or if they were accepting the praise as an empty gesture or as a sign of encouragement. We then talked about the value of praising students and the how to use it to motivate students. We decided that genuine praise can be a motivating factor in students learning, especially if students know why they are being praised.

As a result of the observation and conversation, Kumiko decided to implement small changes in her praising techniques. For example, she monitored her use of praise and verbally expressed it only when she was genuinely impressed with a student's spoken and written English. When students submitted written work, such as written dialogues, she put happy-face stickers on it, but only when their work was considered outstanding.

After recording and analyzing her praise behaviors again, she knew that she used praise behaviors far less frequently and usually at times when students met her high expectations. She also looked at the quality of the students' written work, such as written dialogues, and she concluded that their work was genuinely improving. Some students even told her that they tried harder because they wanted to see a happy face on their written work.

SOYOUNG'S CLASS

The third example focuses on Soyoung, an experienced teacher who had become complacent about her development. Soyoung was an English Education major at a prestigious university in South Korea, and after graduating and passing the teacher exam, she began teaching middle school students and had done so for the next seventeen years. When she was a new teacher she attended a variety of teacher education workshops during winter and summer breaks, and she earned her MA in Education.

Relatively recently the Korean government incorporated The 7th National English Curriculum, which emphasizes the need to maximize the learner's opportunities for meaningful communication in English in the classroom.[2] This is a significant change as it points to a new direction of language teaching in the local scene. To accomplish this, the school system requires teachers to use specific textbooks that include chapters on different topics and a variety of readings, listening activities, and communication activities. Every three weeks the students are tested on the content of lessons.

I became interested in Soyoung's teaching as a result of directing one of my student's doctoral dissertation at Pusan National University.[3] The student had video recorded lots of interaction in one of Soyoung's middle school English classes, transcribed the interactions, and analyzed them. The student and I met often, and she described the patterns she saw in Soyoung's teaching. The same patterns happened over and over again; there was little change in the way she taught. Let's take a look inside one of her classes.

The scope of this 45-minute class was on Lesson 11, titled "I Hope We'll Arrive on Time" and tells a story of Mina's trip to New York. The general objective of this lesson is to learn the expressions needed for a trip. The specific objectives are to be able to ask a favor, inquire about factual information, reconfirm a fact, and express hope, as well as to use various grammatical structures, such as *to*-infinitive verbs.

Soyoung began the class by speaking Korean while reminding the students that their homework was to memorize a dialogue about being on the plane (from the textbook) and to use it to write their own announcements. She then called on a student to stand up and give the announcement. The teacher stood in front of the class. The other students looked down at their desks. The student stood while looking at his handwritten speech:

This is the captain speaking. Welcome aboard Hell, Hell Airline flight 444 bound for hell. It's, it's a pleasure to have you with us. Our flight time will be forever after takeoff. We hope you will enjoy the flight. Thank you.

The student had made four creative changes to the original announcement. Soyoung then asked four other students to stand up and give their announcements. They each made two changes.

Next, the teacher asked two students to stand up to read from the text. As each student read aloud, the others looked at their textbooks, following along. After reading, the teacher checked students' comprehension on the content. She asked each question in English, translated it into Korean, and then repeated it in English: "Where are they now? 지금 어디 있어요? Where are they now?" A student responded "Manhattan" with a heavy Korean accent. The teacher repeated it with her standard English pronunciation. She continued to ask comprehension questions in the same fashion, sometimes stopping to explain a point in Korean.

Next, the class moved to the usage of a grammar point, *to*-infinitive. The teacher advised the students in Korean not to care about the complex grammar term but when and how to use **to-infinitive** in speaking. She then asked the students to make up sentences using this grammar point, such as "I like to study English" and "I hope to go to New York." Soyoung corrected the students when they made grammar or pronunciation errors.

The students appeared to have fun making up sentences, and the teacher praised their efforts in English.

Soyoung basically taught from the textbook. She asked students to memorize passages, read aloud while other students followed along, translated English into Korean, explained most grammar and vocabulary meaning in Korean, praised students in English, and asked students questions from the text and sometimes related to the text in English. The students used English to read aloud, answer the teacher's questions, and do practice activities in the book. The teacher spoke much more than the students.

In addition to recording, analyzing and seeing interaction patterns in Soyoung's classroom, the doctoral student interviewed Soyoung. When asked what she did to reflect on a class, such as the one just observed, she replied that she was too busy to really think about a class when it was over. As long as the students were doing fine and doing well on tests, she felt satisfied.

A COMPARISON: AMY'S, KUMIKO'S, AND SOYOUNG'S TEACHING AS IT RELATES TO DEVELOPMENT

Amy was new to teaching. She was full of energy and likely anxious about how to teach. As such, she wanted to develop her teaching. Hopefully, Amy was not just learning about techniques she could use in the classroom, such as different ways to give instructions, but also learning about how she could approach her development through self-observation and collaborative talk with a more experienced teacher (me). She also had a positive attitude toward her development—one that could energize her to pay attention to how she teaches and the consequences this can have on classroom interaction and on student learning.

As I was trying to inspire within Amy, Kumiko, either through her own instincts or encouraging teachers in her past, had successfully captured the essence of developing herself as a teacher. She welcomed other teachers' observations and collaborative discussion, and she understood the power of doing these things as a way to consistently become more aware of her teaching and the influences it has had on the students. She also recognized the significance that description and analysis of teaching can have on creating alternative ways to teach, such as only praising students when they are doing terrific work instead of praising them all the time.

On the other hand, Soyoung, perhaps by no fault of her own, had never been instilled with the power to see her teaching differently or how to generate alternative ways to teach. As such, she become complacent and did not search out ways that would help the students to meet the new curriculum guidelines to communicate in English and develop communicative competence over time. Although she used a text that gave the pretense of teaching students to communicate in English, Soyoung used the book in a way that simply duplicated how she had always taught, a way that emphasized memorization, reading aloud, making up sentences, translation, and little real communication in English between all the members of the class.

With these three teachers in mind, I encourage you to be like Amy if you are new to teaching—open to new ideas—and the use of teaching techniques, but more important, open to learning how to develop your teaching through nonjudgmental observation, collaborative conversations with experienced teachers who are also open to see their teaching differently, and other ways to develop your teaching beliefs and practices. (See Chapter 2.) Or, if you are an experienced teacher, I encourage you to be like Kumiko, who approaches teaching with an open mind toward continuous development, as well as finding the time (unlike Soyoung) to work on your development.

What Factors Are Central to Teacher Self-Development?

Several factors affect teacher self-development. First, there is no doubt that development takes **time.** It takes time to observe interaction in our own classrooms and to visit other teachers' classes, and to talk to them about teaching. Pre-service teachers have an advantage in that the time factor is built into the teacher education program. Teachers in in-service programs or those working independently on their development have less time. Nonetheless, teachers such as Kumiko who believe that development is important need to make a commitment to devote time to their development.

In addition, for teachers who are in the first few years of their teaching career, time is needed to work through stages in their development.[4] Kumiko, for example, has apparently allowed herself to work through these stages. She was not always confident or able to create and re-create relevant, interesting lessons for the students. The developmental stages of a teacher include going from being dependent on outside sources (such as supervisors and the textbook) and concerned with self-survival ("What do I do tomorrow in class?") and with what kinds of techniques to use, to being concerned with student learning and able to make informed teaching decisions.

Second, development requires an **ongoing commitment.** Development is not something to do only in a teacher education program or at the beginning of a teaching career. Rather, even the most experienced teacher, such as Soyoung, can learn new things about teaching, and development is enhanced when the teacher makes a commitment to ongoing development.

Third, development is enhanced through **reflection,** which includes thoughtful and persistent consideration of teaching beliefs, attitudes, assumptions, and classroom practices.[5] Further, the more we explore, and the more we are able to see our teaching differently, the more we gain in our abilities to reflect-in-action and reflect-on-action.[6] As Amy was starting to realize, and Kumiko has found to be important, reflective practitioners look at their work in retrospect (**reflection-on-action**) in order to examine the reasons and beliefs underlying their actions and generate alternative ways to teach. Through such reflection-on-action experience, it becomes much easier to make spontaneous decisions in the classroom about how to adjust our teaching (**reflection-in-action**).

Just thinking about our teaching is not enough. There needs to be description, analysis, and interpretation our own and others' teaching to be truly reflective.[7] Chapter two shows you several ways to do this through self-observation, observing other teachers, keeping a teaching journal, and talking about teaching with other teachers.

Fourth, development is enhanced through **problem-solving.** When teachers recognize problems and work at solving them, they can discover new ways to teach and discover more about about their role as a teacher. For example, Amy discovered she had a problem with giving instructions, and she learned several possible ways to work on it.

Fifth, development is also enhanced through **exploration for exploration's sake.** Teachers can, indeed, discover much by exploring simply to explore, not just to solve a problem. Such exploration can be based on pure interest—for example, trying an approach that is the opposite of one you love simply to see what happens, or trying a new approach/technique simply because it sounds interesting.[8]

Sixth, development is enhanced by **paying attention to and reviewing the basics of EFL/ESL teaching.** Although Kumiko is experienced, she has continued to study ways to create opportunities for students to interact in English; ways to manage classroom behavior; and materials and media used to teach EFL. In addition, she undoubtedly considered ways to teach different skills, such as reading, writing, listening, and speaking. On the other hand, Soyoung needs to study such basics, especially because her previous basics were not based on teaching students to be communicatively competent.

Seventh, development is enhanced by **searching out opportunities** to develop. Kumiko talks with other teachers about teaching; she reads about teaching; she attends teaching seminars and workshops; and she participates in other activities that give her chances to see new teaching possibilities.

Eighth, self-development of teaching beliefs and practices requires the **cooperation of others.**[9] It takes others who are willing to observe us, listen to us, and talk with us about our teaching. We need administrators, students, other teachers, and friends to help us succeed with our development. Without their cooperation, self-development is very difficult as there is neither any source for feedback nor any stimulus for ideas.

TEACHER SELF-DEVELOPMENT TASKS

These tasks can be an integral part of your development as an EFL/ESL teacher. Although some can be done alone, it is to your advantage to gain the cooperation of others. If you are using this book as part of a pre-service or in-service teacher education program, it will be easy to attain the support of other teachers. If you are reading this book on your own, I encourage you to seek out others who will read this book and work on the self-development tasks with you. If you are not yet teaching and are using this book as a way to learn about the field, it will not be possible to do all of the tasks. However, there will still be many you can do.

Talk Tasks

1. What does self-development mean to you? What kinds of things do you believe you can do to work on your development as a teacher? Ask another EFL/ESL teacher these same questions. Discuss what self-development means and the steps you can take to work on your own development.

2. Read this quote from Maxine Greene's work. Do you agree? What does she mean? Talk with other teachers who have thought about her words.

   > If the teacher agrees to submerge himself into the system, if he consents to being defined by others' views of what he is supposed to be, he gives up his freedom to see, to understand, and to signify for himself. If he is immersed and impermeable, he can hardly stir others to define themselves as individuals. If, on the other hand, he is willing . . . to create a new perspective on what he has habitually considered real, his teaching may become the project of a person vitally open to his students and the world. . . . He will be continuously engaged in interpreting a reality forever new; he will feel more alive than he ever has before. (Greene 1973, 270)

3. Draw up a plan to work on your development as a teacher. Here are a few questions to get you started. Compare your plans with those of another EFL/ESL teacher who has made a plan. Would you revise your plan based on this discussion? If so, how?

   a. Are you ready to work on your teaching development? How strongly do you want to expand your knowledge of teaching and learn how to explore your teaching beliefs and practices?

   b. How much time are you willing to invest in your development as a language teacher? Can you make a tentative schedule of the time you can devote to this undertaking?

   c. Thumb through this book. Study the contents and the list of questions at the beginning of each chapter. What areas of teaching are you interested in developing right now?

d. How will you read this book? Will you selectively read chapters? Use the index? Use the questions at the start of each chapter as a way to decide what to read?

e. How will you get others involved in your process of development?

Journal Writing Tasks

1. Purchase a notebook that you can easily carry around with you and that has ample space for writing.

2. Write freely in your notebook about what self-development means to you.

3. Create in writing a plan for working on your development. What kinds of things do you plan to do to work on your development as a teacher?

RECOMMENDED TEACHER RESOURCES

Directory on Professional TESOL Preparation Programs

Directory of Teacher Education Programs in TESOL in the United States and Canada. Alexandria, VA: TESOL, 2005.

An Inspiring Book

Clarke, M. A. *A Place to Stand: Essays for Educators in Troubled Times.* Ann Arbor: University of Michigan Press, 2003.

ENDNOTES

1   I have changed the examples in this third edition from memories of classroom interaction in two classrooms to specific observations of interaction in three. I thank John Fanselow for his thoughtful nonjudgmental feedback that prompted this change.

2   See Chang (2009) for an historical account of The Ministry of Education's English Education policy changes over several decades, including the most recent change to student-centeredness, cultivating communicative competence, using English in an era of globalization, fostering creative thinking, and using activities and tasks.

3   See Nam (2011).

4   Early research by Bullough and Baughman (1993), Calderhead (1988), and Fuller and Brown (1975) shows that teachers need time to develop their teaching abilities. Research by Fuller (1969) and Fuller and Brown (1975) suggests that teachers move through stages from self-survival to making informed teaching decisions. More recent research is consistently noted throughout this book.

5   See Farrell (2015a, 2015b) for more on reflective teaching.

6   See Schön (1983).

7   Read Fanselow (1988, 1990, 1997).

8   Fanselow (1987, 2010) elaborates on how teachers can "try the opposite" as a way to explore their teaching. For example, if a teacher always teaches from the front of the classroom, she could try teaching from the back. If she always has students read aloud from the text, she could ask them to read silently.

9   See Edge (2002).

2

As we explore, rather than seeking prescriptions and judgments from others, rules [can be] broken that say we teachers must seek alternatives from those in charge, rather than ourselves or our peers, and that we must work alone within our autonomous but isolated and lonely classrooms, rather than with colleagues.

—Fanselow 1987, 7

Exploration of Teaching

I *What are ways to explore teaching?*
I *How can teachers explore teaching through self-observation?*
I *How can teachers explore their own teaching through the observation of other teachers?*
I *How can teachers explore teaching through talk?*
I *How can teachers explore teaching through a teacher journal?*
I *How does this book provide opportunities for teachers to explore teaching?*

What Are Ways to Explore Teaching?

Some of the ways we, as teachers, can explore our teaching beliefs and practices follow in Figure 2.1. In this section I briefly discuss these ways,[1] after which I go into more detail—the observation of other teachers, self-observation, talking to other teachers, and keeping a teacher journal.

One rather obvious way we can develop our teaching is to read professional books and journals on teaching and learning languages. Reading this book, for example, will help you gain knowledge about ESL and EFL teaching. In addition to single-author books, many anthologies are available, and a few are listed in the Recommended Teacher Resources section at the end of Chapter 4. These anthologies cover a variety of topics relevant to the field.

FIGURE 2.1: **Ways to Explore Teaching**

- Read journal articles and books about teaching and learning.
- Read teacher narratives.
- Attend professional conferences.
- Establish a mentoring relationship.
- Put together a teaching portfolio.
- Learn another language.
- Do action research.
- Do self-observation.
- Observe other teachers.
- Talk with other teachers.
- Keep a teacher journal.

For example, Celce-Murcia, Brinton, and Snow's book, *Teaching English as a Second or Foreign Language*,[2] includes chapters by different authors on such topics as communicative language teaching, teaching listening, speaking, reading and writing skills, teaching grammar and vocabulary, language assessment, lesson planning, content-based teaching and more.

Another way to work on development of our teaching and ourselves as teachers is to attend professional conferences. Thousands of ESL and EFL teachers attend the annual International TESOL Convention, which is usually held in a different major North American city each year. There are regional TESOL affiliates, too, and annual—or sometimes semiannual—local conferences are held. These are good opportunities to hear what teachers in your own area are doing in their classrooms, and good opportunities to present your own teaching experience or research. It is also possible to attend one of the worldwide affiliate conferences attached to TESOL International. These regional affiliate conferences vary in size from several thousand to a few hundred participants, depending on location. Likewise, the International Association of Teachers of English as a Foreign Language (IATEFL) hosts an international conference, usually in a European country. Participants who attend this conference come from more than 100 different countries. A smaller conference, but of very high quality, is held annually by the American Association of Applied Linguistics (AAAL). Those who attend are usually scholars (including teachers) who are interested in the multi-disciplinary field of applied linguistics. Presentations are on topics such as literacy, discourse analysis, language acquisition, language assessment, foreign and second language pedagogy, and language policy and planning. To learn more about the professional organization TESOL, go to www.tesol.org. To learn more about IATEFL, go to www.iatefl.org. To discover more about AAAL, go to www.aaal.org.

Another way to explore our teaching is through establishing a mentoring relationship with another teacher. Mentoring is sometimes thought of as a new approach to development for language teachers, but in fact, mentoring has a long history.[3] As Eisenman and Thornton point out, "mentoring actually goes back thousands of years to Homer's epic poem, the *Odyssey*."[4] The concept of mentoring has certainly changed from the days of a wise old sea captain giving guidance to Odysseus's son, Telemachus. As Bailey, Curtis, and Nunan define it, mentoring is "an interpersonal, ongoing, situated, supportive, and informative professional relationship between two (or more) individuals, one of whom (the mentor) has more experience in the profession, craft, or skill in question."[5]

A teaching portfolio is another additional way to explore and develop our teaching. Some ESL and EFL teacher preparation programs ask graduating students to put together a portfolio so that these teachers reflect on what they have learned in the program and have a collection of work that can be included with job applications. Karen Johnson points out that putting together a portfolio helps teachers make sense of what they have learned, provides chances for them to think about teaching and learning, demonstrates their competencies, and recognizes the complexities of learning to teach.[6]

There are, of course, a number of documents that can be included in a portfolio. Some include papers written for courses, class presentations, professional conference presentations, original teaching materials, reflective journal entries, personal narratives, video- or audiotapes of teaching, reflective observation reports, syllabi, letters of recommendation, reports on observations by others, evaluation reports, vitae, and a statement of teaching and learning philosophy.

Another way to explore our teaching as language teachers is to learn another language. Bailey, Curtis, and Nunan[7] point out several advantages to doing this: First, we can better understand the challenges that the learners face. Second, we can gain more insight into understanding language. Third, by assuming the role of learner, we can gain insight into ways of teaching that seem to work and don't work, at least within our language learning setting.

Another approach teachers use to explore teaching is action research, an approach that centers on problem posing. The cyclic process includes posing problems based on what goes on in the teacher's classroom, within a school, or beyond; systematically working to solve the problem by creating and initiating a plan of action; reflecting on the degree to which the plan works; and then posing a new problem based on the awareness generated from the previous inquiry.

During the past three decades, action research has become popular among language teachers.[8] This form of research allows teachers to investigate and pose problems in their teaching, to work at solving these problems, and generally to gain more awareness of teaching and classroom interaction. This is especially true when teachers have chances to talk about their action research. Ann Burns, for example, has created a forum for teachers to talk about and collaborate on their action research projects in Australia at the local, regional, and national levels.[9] She explains that teachers report they gain much awareness of their teaching after participating in such forums.

Observation is another way to explore and develop our teaching, including self-observation and observations of other teachers. Talking with other teachers about the teaching we observe is also a way to explore new possibilities in our teaching, as is writing about teaching in a journal. I write about each of these four ways to explore our teaching in the sections that follow.

How Can Teachers Explore Teaching through Self-Observation?

As teachers, we can explore through a process of describing, analyzing, and reflecting on our teaching. In this regard, I have been influenced by the work of John Fanselow,[10] whose ideas I have adapted and changed in my own pursuit to gain deeper awareness of teaching.[11] To achieve this aim, I have created the following cyclic process of observation: The first step in the cycle is to collect descriptive samples of our teaching that can be analyzed. This is followed by reflection and multiple interpretations. The next step is to consider how the same lesson could be taught differently and to draw up a teaching plan. Then, by implementing the new plan, the cycle returns to the collection of samples of teaching. Let's take a closer look at each stage in the cycle (see Figure 2.2):

FIGURE 2.2: **Process of Observation**

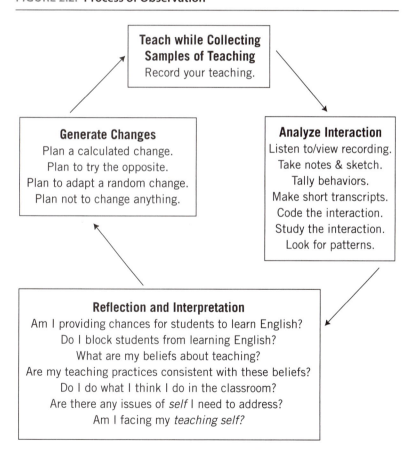

Teach while Collecting Samples of Teaching
Record your teaching.

Generate Changes
Plan a calculated change.
Plan to try the opposite.
Plan to adapt a random change.
Plan not to change anything.

Analyze Interaction
Listen to/view recording.
Take notes & sketch.
Tally behaviors.
Make short transcripts.
Code the interaction.
Study the interaction.
Look for patterns.

Reflection and Interpretation
Am I providing chances for students to learn English?
Do I block students from learning English?
What are my beliefs about teaching?
Are my teaching practices consistent with these beliefs?
Do I do what I think I do in the classroom?
Are there any issues of *self* I need to address?
Am I facing my *teaching self?*

COLLECTING SAMPLES OF TEACHING

When you collect samples of teaching, you have descriptions of what actually goes on in the classroom that focus attention on some aspect of your teaching. To give you an idea of areas of teaching that can be described, see Figure 2.3 listing some of the exploratory questions teachers have asked. On the left are the initial descriptive questions. On the right are the questions aimed at understanding what happens when a change in teaching behavior is initiated.

To collect samples of teaching that address an aspect of classroom behavior it is to our advantage to audio- or videotape classroom interaction. To do this, I suggest you use a small audio-recorder, camcorder, or your cellphone. The advantage of an audio-recorder is that it is easy to use. However, some teachers prefer to videorecord because it is easy to recognize who is talking and possible to study nonverbal behaviors.

At first the recorder may be a novelty, and some students will change their behavior because they are being recorded. But it really doesn't take long before students accept it and act normally. I have recorded many classes, and it is amazing how fast students accept the recorder, especially if it is treated as a natural part of the classroom setting.

How taping is done often depends on the goals of exploration. For example, if you are interested in the students' reactions to instructions or explanations, the audio- or videorecorder can be focused on the students. If you are interested in what happens during group work, it is logical to place the recorder with or on a group of students for a period of time. The idea is to think about the objective of your exploration and to consider how to record the class to obtain useful samples for later analysis.

ANALYZING THE SAMPLES OF TEACHING

The second stage is to analyze the collected samples of teaching, and analysis also depends on the objective of your exploration. For example, if you are interested in knowing the number of questions you ask, you can listen to or view the recording and tally each question you ask, as well as jot down examples of actual questions. You can do the same thing for the number of errors you treat, the number of times students speak English or their native language, and the seconds you wait for students to answer a question.

FIGURE 2.3: **Explanatory Questions for Teachers**

Initial Descriptive Questions	Questions: Further Exploration
■ How do I give instructions? What do students do after receiving the instructions? Start the task? Ask each other what to do? Ask the teacher to repeat the instructions?	■ What happens when I change the way I give instructions, such as when I dictate them? When students paraphrase them? When they read them?
■ How much time do I talk? How much time do students talk?	■ What happens if I talk less? If I don't talk at all?
■ How often do students speak their native language in class? When? What do I do when they use it?	■ What happens when I require students to only speak English? When they can't speak any English for ten minutes?
■ What is the content of my questions? About study of language? People's lives in general? Students' personal lives? Procedures? Other?	■ What happens when I increase the number of questions I ask about students' personal lives?
■ How long do I wait after asking a question to get a response?	■ What happens when I increase wait time?
■ How do I praise students? What words do I use? What nonverbal behaviors? What student behaviors do I praise? How often do I praise?	■ What happens when I don't praise students? When I only praise specific accomplishments?
■ How much time do students stay on task? What do they do when off task? What triggers going off task?	■ What happens when I add a time limit? Decrease time given to finish a task? Give no time limit?
■ What are usual seating arrangements in my class?	■ What happens when students sit in different seating arrangements?

A second way to analyze the collection of teaching samples is to make short transcripts from the recordings. Again, what you decide to transcribe depends mainly on the focus of your exploration. For example, if you are interested in learning how you treat language errors, you might make and study short transcripts of the times errors are treated. If you are interested in learning about the accuracy of the students' language during group work, you can transcribe and study short sections of interaction among students during group work activities.

While it is possible to have a particular focus when collecting and analyzing these descriptions, it is also possible to do the opposite, which I like to call "pure exploration." Such exploration does not focus on a specific observation objective. For example, it is possible to record a class, and while doing this, make one-minute transcripts of classroom interaction five, ten, and 20 minutes into the class. These transcripts could then be studied simply to study what is happening and when. I think of such exploration as being similar to going for a walk. Usually we have objectives when going for a walk, such as walking to the bank or the grocery store. However, sometimes we can simply take a walk, randomly taking side streets or alleys just to see what is there; when we do this, we often see new things.

INTERPRETING AND REFLECTING

After analyzing, we make sense of the descriptions of classroom interaction. To do this, we can focus on several questions. One set of questions I like to ask includes: *How does the interaction in this class provide chances for students to learn the language?* and *How does the interaction possibly block students from learning the language?* Of course, I can narrow the question based on a particular interest. For example, if I am interested in error treatment and have analyzed the patterns of interaction around the treatment of students' oral errors, I can ask, *How does my way of treating students' language errors possibly provide chances for them to be more accurate in their use of English?* and *How does my way of treating their errors possibly hamper their accuracy?* Likewise, if my interest is in understanding classroom behavior with regard to student talk and questioning behavior, after analyzing the patterns of interaction in the class between the students and me, I might ask, *How does my interaction with students possibly provide chances for them to talk in class, initiate interaction, and ask questions?* and *How does my interaction with them possibly interfere with students' chances to talk, initiate interaction, and ask questions?*

I also ask this set of questions: *What are my beliefs about teaching?* and *Are my teaching practices consistent with these beliefs?* Although it is not necessarily easy to answer these questions, it is well worth the effort. It is possible to give a comprehensive answer to the first question, taking into consideration theory and research in different fields, such as in second language acquisition, intercultural communication, and sociolinguistics. It is, of course, also possible to narrow the questions to specific aspects of teaching. For example, we can ask, *What are my beliefs about treating students' language errors?* and *Are my teaching practices consistent with my beliefs?*

Reflection can also include this question: *Do I do what I think I do in the classroom?* I have found that most teachers are surprised by the answer to this question. It is not until they have had a chance to describe their teaching and think about it that they realize that what they believe they are doing does not always match what they think they are doing. For example, later in this chapter (pages 28–29) I give an example of how my teaching partner and I realized that the students in our team-taught class were not aware that we were treating their oral errors although we thought that we were!

Finally, I like to ask this set of questions: *Are there any issues of* self *I need to address?* and *Am I facing my* teaching self? There are a wide range of issues that teachers might not want to face, more than I can possibly write about here. One example is that some teachers avoid certain issues that trigger negative feelings, such as disciplining students or becoming personally involved in troubled students' lives. Another example is a teacher who struggled in facing the realization that not all students appreciate or accept his friendly, highly personal way of interacting with them.

Jersild points out in *When Teachers Face Themselves* that to gain knowledge of ourselves, we need to find the courage to seek it, as well as the humility to accept what we discover.[12] Such exploration of the self is not easy for some teachers. But, such exploration can be well worth the effort.

DECIDING ON CHANGES IN TEACHING BEHAVIOR

The next stage in the exploration cycle is to decide which changes we want to make in our teaching through such questions as: *What do I want to continue to do?* and *What small changes do I want to make in my teaching behavior?* Here I agree with John Fanselow, who has observed that small changes can have big consequences.[13]

One reason to change the way we teach is to solve a problem: Students don't talk; instructions aren't clear; students speak their native language a lot. For example, if some students aren't talking during whole-class discussions, the teacher might try group work to see if these students will talk with classmates. If the teacher discovers that students are not understanding instructions when they are given orally, the teacher might write them on the board.

Problem-solving is the usual way that teachers make decisions about what to change in their teaching. However, it is also possible to explore teaching simply to see what happens. This could include doing the opposite of what we usually do or trying something we have never tried before. For example, even if the students understand the oral instructions, it is still possible to write them down and let students read them just to see what happens. If most of our questions are from the text, we can ask questions that are not in the text. There are endless opposite possibilities![14]

Based on the changes we decide to make, whether calculated to solve a problem or be creative by trying the opposite, the idea is to continue the cycle of exploration while again collecting samples of teaching through audio or video recordings.

WHAT TEACHERS HAVE DONE: EXAMPLES OF THE OBSERVATION PROCESS

The first example is from my own teaching. While teaching an American literature course in Hungary, I wondered about the way I used questions in class. To better understand my questioning behaviors, I designed a tally sheet (see Figure 2.4). I audio-recorded my class and using a tally sheet, I kept track of the targets of my questions (e.g., to an individual student or the whole class) and the content of each question (e.g., about students' lives, about people and places in general, about language, or about the content of the reading selection). The tally sheet in Figure 2.4 shows what I found.

During my analysis, I discovered that I asked 28 questions during a 25-minute time period; that most of my questions were addressed to the whole class; and that 12 of my questions were about general places and people, 8 about language, and 6 directly about the content of the reading.

FIGURE 2.4: **Tally Sheet: Content and Target of Teacher Questions**

Content of Questions	To Individual	To Whole Class
Questions: Student lives	II	
Questions: People & places		JHT JHT III
Questions: Language	I	JHT II
Questions: Material content		JHT I

Upon reflection, I was not surprised that I asked mostly whole-class questions. However, I was surprised that I averaged more than one question per minute. This discovery was very useful. First, it gave me the chance to reflect on my questioning behavior. As a part of my reflection, I thought about how discussions go on outside classrooms, how all the participants not only answer questions but also ask them and react to each other's responses. Second, I was able to see that my questioning techniques dominated class discussion and prevented students from raising their own questions and reacting to responses. Third, I was able to systematically modify my questioning behavior. In the next seminar, while audiorecording, I consciously asked fewer questions and attempted to achieve more discussion based on a single question. Also, after a student responded to one of my questions, I remained silent or said *uh-huh* in an encouraging way while looking at the other students. If no one reacted or asked a question, I paraphrased what was just said.

After audiorecording and analyzing this second seminar, I discovered that I asked fewer questions, that students asked each other questions, and that students reacted to the responses of others. In short, I was able to achieve my objective—to have students discuss a reading selection in their foreign language.

The preceding examples illustrate how I worked through problem areas in my teaching, but this next example shows how a teacher explored her teaching simply to explore.[15] The teacher, a native Japanese speaker, was teaching an introductory class in Japanese as a Foreign Language to American university students. She was interested in exploring her teaching simply to discover patterns in her teaching behavior, so she audio-recorded her class, transcribed short segments of the class, and studied them for recurring patterns of interaction.

She discovered certain patterns of interaction in her classes. She found that most of her teaching consisted of drills and that she followed a lock-step way of teaching. In short, class was teacher-centered: She asked all the questions, the students responded, and she reacted to these responses. She also reflected on the fact that she asked display questions (e.g., questions for which she already knew the answers) and that the content of the lessons mostly concerned the study of language (i.e., learning about language rather than using language for a communicative purpose).

Based on the patterns of interaction reflected in her classroom, the teacher decided that students did not have ample opportunities to communicate in their foreign language in class. As such, she decided to make a small change in her teaching by doing the opposite of what she usually did. Instead of drilling students on language points, she planned to ask them questions about their lives. She knew that some students were going on a trip to a nearby city, and she decided to ask them about their trip in the foreign language. As an afterthought, she brought a map of the city to class. She then audiorecorded her teaching while posing these "life-personal" questions in Japanese and then transcribed parts of the class.

Classroom interaction changed dramatically. Students asked each other questions and reacted to each other's comments. The teacher and students asked questions that they did not know the answers to before asking them. This type of query was not evident in the interaction in the earlier class.

What brought about this change in the interaction? The teacher's purpose was to do the opposite of what she normally did, to ask personal questions to see if the interaction would change in her class, and she did begin her lesson by asking personal questions about where a student went on spring break. According to her analysis, this change was most likely a part of the reason why student interactions changed. However, she also had students show her exactly where they went by using the map. This map also had the apparent consequence (which the teacher was surprised to discover) of allowing the interaction to shift from asking and answering personal questions to studying the map itself. In short, the teacher interpreted the reason for the emergence of student questions and reactions to be the combination of asking personal questions and using the map. It is interesting that the teacher had not predicted that the map itself would contribute to this change in the pattern. This discovery was quite incidental, and such discoveries are one reason to explore teaching.

My purpose in giving these examples of self-observation has been to demonstrate how as teachers we can explore our own teaching. However, exploration does not have to be limited to looking at what goes on in one's own classroom. It is also possible to explore teaching by observing other teachers' classrooms, the topic of the next section.

How Can Teachers Explore Their Own Teaching through the Observation of Other Teachers?

At first the idea that we can explore our own teaching by observing other teachers may seem contradictory. However, as John Fanselow points out, we can see our own teaching in the teaching of others. When we observe others to gain knowledge of self, we have the chance to construct and reconstruct our own knowledge. Fanselow articulates this in another way: "I came to your class not only with a magnifying glass to look carefully at what was being done, but with a mirror so that I could see that what you were doing is a reflection of much of what I do."[16]

While observing other teachers, it is possible to collect samples of teaching in a variety of ways. We can take fast notes, draw sketches, tally behaviors, and note short transcript-like samples of interaction. As with collecting samples in our own classes, it is possible to audio- or videorecord other teachers' classes and photograph interaction. These recording can be used later to analyze classroom behaviors. I want to point out that I encourage observers and the observed teacher to meet to look at photos, listen to or view recordings, study short transcripts, and talk about the class. By doing so, exploration is enhanced for all. The examples that follow and my later discussion on the value of talking about teaching should clarify this point.

OBSERVING OTHERS TO EXPLORE ONE'S OWN TEACHING: SOME EXAMPLES

This first example involves collaboration between my teaching partner and me. My partner showed consistent interest in error treatment and wanted to gain more awareness of how she treated students' errors. As such, I audiotaped her class and transcribed short segments that centered on how she treated students' language errors. Here's one of these short transcripts:[17]

Student: I have only two sister.

Teacher: Uh-huh.

Student: I have no brother.

Teacher: Two sisters?

Student: Because my mother she dead when I was three years old.

Teacher: She died when you were three?

Student: Yes. She dead when I was three years old.

My partner and I later met to talk, and she was delighted (and a little surprised) to see the way she treated errors. She used rising intonation (i.e., when she asked, "Two sisters?") or asked questions while emphasizing the word she was correcting (as in "She DIED when you were three?"). After appraising her treatment techniques, she decided that the students most likely did not know she was even treating their errors. Instead, they focused on meaning. As a part of our discussion, she also raised a concern over whether or not treating errors was useful. However, at the same time, students were asking her to treat their language errors, and she wanted to comply. As such, she decided that if she did treat the errors, she could at least do so in a way in which the students were aware of being corrected. She read about and discussed error treatment, and subsequently designed and implemented alternative ways to treat errors.

My partner obviously gained awareness from more clearly seeing her way of treating errors, and through the process of observing (and talking) with my partner, I also had the chance to reflect on my own beliefs and techniques for treating errors. I was able to see my teaching in hers; I realized that I often treated errors similarly, and that most likely, students were not especially aware that I was treating specific language errors. By recording and analyzing my teaching, I was able to reconfirm this reflection and develop new ways to treat students' errors.

The second example of the value of observing others teach involves a teacher in Japan who wanted to explore the use of photography as a way to observe teaching.[18] He and I were invited to observe a class at a private language school for young children, and he decided to take his camera. He was able to move freely around the classroom while the students and teacher went about their lesson; as a second observer, I was impressed by the way he was able to fit into the natural flow of the classroom interaction in an unobtrusive way. Surprisingly, after the first few snapshots, the children hardly paid any attention to him.

Later, he created a photographic essay of the classroom interaction, and while looking at the photos with the teacher, he was able to reflect on his own teaching. For example, he noticed how spontaneously the children spoke up in English and wondered how he could get students in his high school EFL class to do this. As a second observer, I was also able to see my teaching in that of the photographed teacher; as I studied the photos, I was impressed by the great number of activities the teacher did with the students, each leading naturally into the next, and I wondered how I could design lessons to do this in my own classes.

How Can Teachers Explore Teaching through Talk?

Talking about teaching can offer chances to learn about and reflect on our own teaching. Talking can indeed be useful. Unfortunately, talking about teaching is not something that normally goes on among EFL/ESL teachers, and when it does, it seems to take on a face-saving nature. As Paul Arcario[19] points out, the way conversations about teaching normally take place begins with the observer giving an opening evaluative remark, such as, "I liked your class." This is followed by a three-step evaluative sequence. In the first step of the sequence a positive or negative evaluation is made, such as "I think the students are talking a lot" (positive) or "Maybe the students don't have enough chances to speak" (negative). These comments lead to a second step, justification (explanation of why the comment was made), and then to the third step, prescriptions about what should be done in the class to improve teaching, such as, "You should do more group work." Arcario points out that this last prescriptive step is more obvious when a negative evaluation is made because there is a perceived problem to be solved.

This usual way of talking about teaching is not especially productive. It is also not necessarily easy to change. But change can be made, especially if we take the time and effort to prepare for the discussions and follow agreed-upon rules that aim at nonjudgmental and non-prescriptive discussion. This was evident from an experience in Japan where I had the pleasure of teaching 12 experienced American, Canadian, and Japanese EFL teachers, all of whom taught in different settings (Japanese public and private schools, corporations, and language schools). We planned for and visited some of the teachers' classes in small groups of three or four. After observing, we talked about the class over lunch or coffee. We found both the observations and discussions to be highly stimulating and informative.

We also established rules about how to talk about the teaching we observed. We came to an agreement to stop ourselves from making positive and negative judgments about our own and others' teaching. We made this agreement because judgments take attention away from description of and toward feelings about what is going on. We also agreed not to seek prescriptions about teaching, in other words, what we should do in the classroom. Rather, we worked at generating alternatives based on descriptions of teaching. We looked for possibilities to try out, not best ways to teach. The teachers and I found these two sets of rules to be very powerful. We gained lots of description of teaching, were able to generate alternative techniques for the classroom, and, by the end of our experience together, became far less judgmental in our attitudes toward teaching.

As we did in Japan, I encourage you to talk to other teachers about teaching. To do this, I invite you to plan observation visits, meet to talk about your observations in non-prescriptive nonjudgmental terms, and generate alternative approaches to teaching. However, I also encourage you to talk about issues in teaching, media and materials, technology, and mutual problems, such as with student motivation, unreasonable administrative demands, and working conditions.

How Can Teachers Explore through a Teacher Journal?

We can explore teaching by writing in a journal.[20] The purpose is to have a place to record our observations of what goes on in our own and other teachers' classrooms, write about our discussions, consider teaching ideas, and reflect on our teaching. However, journals are also a place for us to raise doubts, express frustrations, and raise questions. With this in mind, here's a list of what some teachers include in their journals:

- Quickly written descriptions of classroom interaction collected in their own and other teachers' classrooms, as well as analyses and interpretations of these descriptions
- Tally sheets, transcripts, sketches, and coding as a part of their description and analysis
- Photos (snapshots) and descriptions of what goes on in each photo
- Summaries and reflections on discussions with other teachers
- Lists of alternative ways to teach aspects of a lesson (e.g., different ways to give instructions)
- Stream-of-consciousness writing (to let ideas flow)
- Reflections on language-learning experiences
- Thoughts on beliefs about teaching and learning
- Questions about teaching and learning
- Answers to their own questions
- Summaries and critiques of journal articles and books
- Lesson plans and teaching ideas

Those of us who have maintained teaching journals know how time-consuming it can be. As such, I suggest you only try to keep a journal from time to time. For me, a few weeks a year seems just about right. I also encourage you to carry a journal with you and take the time to write down ideas when they emerge. Along with these inspired entries, I encourage you to write entries soon after teaching, while the experiences are fresh. Finally, at the end of a period of time, I encourage you to take the time to read your entries thoughtfully, look for patterns in your teaching and thinking about teaching, and write an entry on this analysis.[21] Taking time to review past entries is important, since it is through this kind of reflection that we can see ourselves as teachers and view our teaching differently.

How Does This Book Provide Opportunities for Teachers to Explore Teaching?

Since observation as a way to explore teaching can be empowering, in this book I provide a number of opportunities to explore teaching through observation. This book contains descriptions of teaching based on my observations of lessons taught by EFL/ESL teachers and on my own self-observations. By reading this book, you are considering a variety of different observation reports on what EFL/ESL teachers do in their classrooms.

In addition, the Teacher Self-Development Tasks section at the end of each chapter provides a variety of different observation tasks. The purpose of these tasks is to teach a nonjudgmental process of looking at what goes on in your own and others' classrooms. Some of these tasks ask you to audio- and videorecord teaching, tally behaviors or make short transcripts, and analyze teaching. The goal of doing these observation tasks is for you to see your teaching differently. It is through awareness of your own and others' teaching that it is possible to see new possibilities.

As you perform these observation tasks, I also encourage you to work through the reflective exploration cycle by collecting samples of your teaching, analyzing these samples, interpreting and reflecting on the analysis, deciding on changes, and implementing these changes while again collecting samples of your teaching for analysis and continuation of the cycle. Throughout this cycle, I encourage you to explore and solve problems in your teaching, as well as to explore for exploration's sake, simply to see what happens.

The tasks in each chapter provide chances for you to talk about teaching. For discussion with other teachers, I offer topics related to the content of each chapter, and I also provide chances for you to generate your own topics based on your interests and needs. I remind you that talk about teaching is enhanced if done in a nonjudgmental, descriptive, and alternative-generating way.

Finally, at the end of each chapter I provide opportunities for you to write in a journal about your teaching experiences, ideas, observations, and beliefs about teaching. Although I give a variety of writing tasks related to the content of each chapter, I also encourage you to go beyond my suggestions.

As highlighted in Chapter 1, it is through the combination of reading, observing, talking, and writing about teaching that you will gain the kind of knowledge that frees you to raise new questions and ideas about your teaching beliefs and practices, as well as to search for answers to your questions and discover and rediscover the teacher that lies within you.

TEACHER SELF-DEVELOPMENT TASKS

Talk Tasks

1. Review the list of Ways to Explore Teaching in Figure 2.1. Talk with other teachers about this list. Which ways capture your attention? Why? Which ways have you already experienced? What was this experience like? Did you discover new things about yourself as a teacher?

2. Answer these questions:

   a. What is a judgment? What words indicate that a judgment is being made? Why do I suggest teachers avoid making judgments about the teaching they observe?

   b. What is a prescription? What words indicate a teaching prescription is being made? (For example, "You should. . . ." indicates prescription.) Why do I think prescriptions of teaching are not useful?

   c. What is an alternative? What is the value of generating alternative teaching ideas (over prescriptions)?

3. Talk about your experiences as a language learner. How did your past language teachers teach? What did you like or dislike about the way they taught? How do you think your language learning experience has influenced you as a teacher?

Observation and Talk Tasks

1. Arrange to visit a friend's class with at least one other teacher.

   a. Prepare to observe the class by asking the teacher what aspects of teaching he or she wants you to observe. (You might want to study the list of topics given in Figure 2.3.) Also consider how you will go about collecting descriptions of teaching that will capture aspects of it. (For example, will you write quick notes, draw sketches, jot down dialogue, tally behaviors, audio- or videorecord, photograph?)

   b. Observe the class.

   c. Meet after the class over coffee or lunch to talk about the class. Monitor your way of talking about the class so that your conversations about teaching are nonjudgmental and nonprescriptive. During your conversation, generate a list of alternative ways the teacher could teach aspects of the same lesson differently.

2. Audiorecord or videorecord interaction in your class. Listen to or view the recording. Select interaction that interests you. Make short transcriptions of the interaction in dialogue form (using a new line when the speaker changes). Then, meet with another teacher. Together study and talk about the transcripts by working through these steps:

   a. Analyze the interaction. What is going on? Is there anything in the interaction that captures your attention? What?

   b. Interpret the teaching. Are opportunities provided for students to learn English? Are opportunities possibly blocked?

   c. Decide on a small change. What are alternative ways to teach? Which would you like to try?

   d. Design a new lesson that includes a small change. Implement this change while taping and again analyze what happened.

Journal Writing Tasks

1. Write about your experiences as a language learner. How did your past language teachers teach? What did you like or dislike about the way they taught? How do you think your language learning experience has influenced you as a teacher?

2. Write about your observation and conversation experiences (from doing the Observation and Talk Tasks). Take time to reflect on the experience. What did you learn about teaching? What ideas do you now have about your own teaching? What did you learn about observation and talking about teaching in a nonjudgmental descriptive way?

3. Carry your journal with you. When a teaching idea or reflection comes to you, write it down.

4. The idea of this task is to experience writing about a class over a period of time. Pick one of your classes. Make sure you have a break soon after the class. Just after the class, each time you have taught it, take 15 minutes to write about this class. Use a stream- of-consciousness approach to your writing. In other words, just let the ideas flow. Feel free to add sketches, anything that works for you. After a few weeks, find a place where you can concentrate. Read all your entries. Then, take time to write about what you have learned about yourself as a teacher and how you teach.

RECOMMENDED TEACHER RESOURCES

Readings on Ways to Explore and Develop Teaching

Bailey, K.M. "Classroom Research, Teacher Research, and Action Research in Language Teaching." In *Teaching English as a Second or Foreign Language, 4th ed.*, eds. M. Celce Murcia, D. M. Brinton, and M. A. Snow, 601–12. Boston: Heinle Cengage, 2014.

Bailey, K. M., A Curtis, and D. Nunan. *Pursuing Professional Development.* Boston: Heinle & Heinle, 2001.

Burns, A. *Action Research in English Language Teaching: A Guide for Practioners.* New York: Routledge, 2011.

Fanselow, J. F. "'Let's See': Contrasting Conversations about Teaching." *TESOL Quarterly 22* (1988): 113–20.

Farrell, T. S. C. *Teacher Reflection in Second Language Education.* New York: Routledge, 2015.

Gebhard, J. G. "Reflective Development of Teaching through Self-Observation: Learning To See our Teaching Differently." *International Journal in English Language Teaching and Research 3*, No. 1 (2014): 50–64.

Gebhard, J. G. and R. Oprandy. *Language Teaching Awareness: A Guide to Exploring Beliefs and Practices.* New York: Cambridge University Press, 1999.

Richards, J. C. and T. S. C. Farrell. *Professional Development for Language Teachers.* New York: Cambridge University Press, 2005.

Schön, D. A. *Educating the Reflective Practitioner: Toward a New Design for Teaching and Learning in the Professions.* San Francisco: Jossey-Bass, 1987.

ENDNOTES

1 Sources with suggestions for exploration of teaching and professional growth are also in Bailey, Curtis, and Nunan (1998, 2001); Gebhard (1992, 2014); Fanselow (1987, 1988, 1992, 2010); Farrell (2015a); Gebhard and Oprandy (1999); Richards and Farrell (2005).

2 See Celce-Murcia, Brinton, and Snow (2014).

3 See Bailey, Curtis, and Nunan (2001).

4 Discovered in Bailey, Curtis, and Nunan (2001, 207). See Eisenman and Thorton (1999, 80–81) for the original quote and full article on the topic.

5 See Bailey, Curtis, and Nunan (2001, 207).

6 See Johnson (1996).

7 See Bailey, Curtis, and Nunan (2001).

8 Those who discuss the process of doing action research in ESL/EFL classes include Bailey, Curtis, and Nunan (2001); Burns (1998, 2004, 2011); Crookes (1993); Gebhard (2005a, 2005b); Gebhard and Oprandy (1999); Nunan and Bailey (2009); and Wallace (1998).

9 See Burns (1996).

10 As a doctoral student at Teachers College, Columbia University, I studied with John Fanselow. I especially appreciate his nonjudgmental descriptive approach to looking at teaching, his use of multiple interpretations of a description, and his creative way of categorizing knowledge and generating alternative teaching behavior. I suggest teachers and teacher educators read his work (1977, 1983, 1987, 1988, 1992, 1997, 2010).

11 See Gebhard (1992, 2014), Gebhard and Oprandy (1999), and Gebhard and Ueda-Montonaga (1992).

12 See Jersild (1955).

13 See Fanselow (1987).

14 Fanselow (2010) gives many ways to try the opposite.

15 A more detailed account can be found in Gebhard and Ueda-Motonaga (1992).

16 See Fanselow (1992, 2).
17 This transcript was originally published in Gebhard (1990).
18 The observer-photographer was Yutaka Yamauchi, who at the time was a gradu-
    ate student in the MA TESOL program at Teachers College, Columbia University
    (Tokyo) and a private high school EFL teacher.
19 See Arcario (1994). Also see Bailey (2006) and Fanselow (1988).
20 Research has shown that teachers use journals as a way to change their percep-
    tions of themselves as teachers (Brinton and Holten 1989), address teaching issues
    (Gebhard 1999; Holten and Brinton 1995; Yahya 2000), understand common con-
    cerns and pressing needs (Numrich 1996), develop a sense of critical reflection
    (Farrell 1998; Richards and Ho 1998), and discover the value of keeping a collabora-
    tive journal (Gebhard and Nakamine 2005).
21 Bailey (1990) emphasizes that reviewing entries and looking for salient features in
    our teaching is crucial to a successful journal experience.

3

The number of English language learners worldwide is up to 1.5 billion.

—Knagg 2014

EFL and ESL Teaching Settings

I *What is an EFL teaching setting? What is an ESL teaching setting? Why are these two terms, EFL and ESL, not always adequate to describe English teaching settings?*

I *What are examples of EFL and ESL teaching settings?*

I *How are different teaching settings woven into this book?*

What Is an EFL Teaching Setting?
What Is an ESL Teaching Setting?
Why Are These Two Terms, *EFL* and *ESL*, Not Always Adequate to Describe English Teaching Settings?

EFL is an acronym for English as a Foreign Language and is studied by people who live in places where English is not a first language, such as in Italy, Saudi Arabia, and Vietnam. ESL is an acronym for English as a Second Language. People who study ESL speak other languages, such as Spanish, Arabic, Chinese, or Swahili as their first or native language. However, they live in places where English is used as the first or native language, such as Australia, New Zealand, Canada, the United Kingdom, and the United States.

Although I am at risk of overgeneralizing, it is possible to point out a few other differences between EFL and ESL settings. To begin, student populations differ. In many EFL contexts, the population is homogeneous in many ways, for example, all sharing a similar history of being Korean, German, or Egyptian. ESL settings, however, for the most part are quite heterogeneous. Students from a great variety of countries can be found in the same ESL classroom. For example, I recently observed an ESL class with students from Italy, Costa Rica, Japan, Korea, Malaysia, Thailand, Bangladesh, the United Arab Emirates, and Turkey.

Further, in EFL settings there are fewer chances for students to use English outside the classroom. Quite often the only understandable English some EFL students experience is in the classroom, although this has been progressively changing due to the spread of technology, such as the Internet and satellite television. In contrast, when ESL students leave the classroom, they can enter any number of situations in which they can hear and use English.

In addition, the goals of learning EFL and ESL are often quite different. In many countries where English is a foreign language, a dual goal for teenagers studying in the educational system is to pass English entrance exams to enter good high schools and universities and, more recently, to be able to use English as an international language. However, the goal is often quite different for young people studying ESL in countries where the medium of communication is English. The purpose is often tied to literacy. The aim is being able to read, write, and interact in English in culturally defined ways.

Of course, there are individuals in EFL settings who want to be literate in English and need to learn English to communicate effectively with others, including those interested in living abroad, doing international business, working as translators, and working in the tourist industry. Subsequently, to meet this need English language programs and teachers provide language-rich experiences for learners within countries that are traditionally thought of as EFL settings. Such programs often offer students lessons on adapting to other cultural contexts while using English and gaining strategies to develop English throughout their lifetimes. Likewise, there are those who study in ESL settings who need to pass entrance exams, for example, students at language institutes who have to pass TOEFL® (Test of English as a Foreign Language) to gain admittance into an American university and ESL students in K–12 settings who have to pass standardized tests given to all students in the public school system.

Such examples certainly illustrate the inadequacy of considering all learners within an EFL and ESL setting as having the same goals and of considering all language programs within these settings as alike. Such overgeneralizations can be quite misleading, even to the point of stereotyping all EFL learners as having certain language learning experiences and all ESL learners as having other experiences.

It also is important to point out, so as not to oversimplify things, that not all English fits neatly into the category of EFL or ESL. This is especially clear when focusing on those populations of people around the world who use an institutionalized second-language variety of English.[1] Such populations use English on a day-to-day basis alongside one or more other languages. Such institutionalized varieties of English are also called **New Englishes** or **varieties of English**,[2] which function as intranational languages, or languages "other than the mother tongue, which is used by nationals of the same country for communication."[3] A New English develops through the educational system where it is often used as the medium of instruction, and within various other institutions, such as government offices. However, the mother tongue is used in most other contexts, such as in interaction with friends and family members.

Such Englishes have especially developed in countries in Africa (e.g., Ghana, Kenya, Nigeria, Tanzania, Zambia) and Asia (e.g., Bangladesh, India, Pakistan, Philippines, Singapore, Sri Lanka), where there was a need for an official language. Some countries developed English after colonial rule. For example, Kenya was a British colony from 1920 to 1963; English was the official language for several years, but Swahili has since replaced it. Nonetheless, English was maintained, adopted more widely, and has become one of the New Englishes. Another example is in Singapore, where English was introduced as a "unifying medium" alongside Chinese, Malay, or Tamil.[4] As New Englishes developed in each of these countries, they tended to take on some of the language features unique to the users' native language or languages, such as pronunciation, choice of words, and syntactic features. For example, the English used in Singapore has syntactic (i.e., word order), phonemic (i.e., pronunciation of vowel sounds), and lexical (i.e., word choice) features of Chinese and Malay, so much so that it is difficult for many outsiders to comprehend this variety of English when they first encounter it.[5]

What Are Examples of EFL and ESL Teaching Settings?

In this section I consider settings in which EFL and ESL learners study English. EFL settings include public schools (K–12), universities, public language schools, and private language schools. ESL settings include public schools (K–12), university language programs, and refugee/literacy centers. I also consider two settings that do not fit neatly into either an EFL or ESL setting.

EFL TEACHING SETTINGS

English is presently taught to EFL students in **public schools** worldwide, and in recent years the trend has been to offer English to younger and younger students.[6] For example, in the past, English was introduced to most Japanese students at the age of 13, when they entered junior high school. However, the Ministry of Education established an English curriculum for the public schools that includes teaching English to elementary school students through music, games, and other engaging activities. Other examples include Italy's School Reform Bill that shifted the start of English to the elementary level and Saudi Arabia's reform to do the same.

Students' experience varies from country to country. For example, in elementary school in South Korea, teachers devote 40 minutes twice each week to English. My recent experience teaching English teachers at Pusan National University and observing school English classes showed me that teachers attempt to teach English through integrative skills of reading, writing, listening, and speaking. They do this by having students experience games, songs, and reading activities, but they also rely on traditional "repeat after me" and simple grammar manipulation activities. In junior high school the time increases to four days each week, and in many of these settings teachers are required to use approved textbooks. The goal also shifts to passing the college entrance exam, with emphasis placed more on teaching distinct skills of listening and reading.

As in South Korea, fourth graders in public schools in Saudi Arabia study English two days each week, and increase this to four 45-minute classes each week. However, textbooks are designed under the supervision of the Ministry of Education; these texts observe the Saudi traditions of Muslim values and emphasize having students learn to read, write, listen, and speak English. Since English is not tested on the university entrance exam, the junior and senior high school curricula is not geared toward teaching students to pass entrance exams (except for prospective English majors), but rather more toward comprehension and communication.[7]

University EFL settings offer a variety of different English programs. Most universities worldwide require students to take several semesters of a foreign language, and English is either a choice among other languages or required. Many non-native English speakers teach reading and grammar-related courses, while native or near-native speakers (often nationals who have studied abroad) are often asked to teach conversation because of a widely held (and often misinformed) belief that only native English speakers can teach students to converse.

Some universities in EFL settings offer **English for Specific Purposes (ESP)** courses to fill a need within a particular major. For example, students majoring in Hotel Management might be required to take a course on Tourism and English, and a student majoring in pre-med, a course on reading medical journals written in English. Universities in EFL settings also offer programs for English majors, and there are a variety of different specializations that English majors can pursue. For example, Eötvös Loránd University in Budapest has different English departments, including American Studies, English Applied Linguistics, English Linguistics, and English Studies (Literature).

The number of **public language schools** in EFL settings has greatly increased in recent years. Some of these schools have an assortment of English programs and classes, while others are smaller and more specialized. It is also worth pointing out that although there are some well-established excellent language schools, there are also, unfortunately, a number of schools that have no solid theoretical foundation and hire unqualified teachers.

One well-established school is the American University Association Alumni Language Center in Thailand, better known as AUA.[8] Established in 1952, it grew over the years to include four branches in Bangkok and 13 branches throughout the country. AUA has a choice of three main programs: The Regular Program (15-level multi-skill course), the Intensive Academic English Program (to prepare students to study abroad), and Special Courses, such as TOEFL® Preparation.

In addition to language schools with a variety of programs and courses, there are also schools that have a single program designed to meet a specific need. For example, in Japan there are a large number of cram schools that students attend in the evening and on weekends. The schools specialize in preparing high school students to pass college entrance exams in such subjects as English. One of the most famous of these schools, Yoyogi Seminar has branches throughout Japan. These students usually arrive after having spent a full day at school or arrive on a weekend morning.

Unlike public language programs where anyone who can pay the tuition can attend, only particular groups of people can attend a **private language program.** These programs are usually established to meet the English language needs of people who work in government positions, such as diplomats and embassy personnel, or the private sector, for example, those who work in the tourist industry (hotel clerks, tour guides), the airline industry (pilots, flight attendants, check-in clerks), oil industry (engineers, technicians on oil rigs), and business (managers headed overseas, those doing international business).

Here's an example of a private language program based on my own experience. Some years ago I worked for Heuristic Associates, a small firm that contracted with Japanese companies, such as Mitsubishi Corporation, to teach small groups of businesspeople (five male students in each class). We taught each group of students four hours daily for 11 months, five days each week. Our goal was not only to see improvement in the accuracy and fluency of these businessmen as they gained communicative competence, but also to prepare them to interact with people from different backgrounds in culturally appropriate ways depending on the context. To accomplish this, we read and talked about cultural beliefs, values, and behaviors, did role-play and culturally based problem-solving activities, and carried out simulations.

ESL TEACHING SETTINGS

A wave of immigrants to English-speaking countries such as Australia, Canada, and the United States has created a challenge for the **public school systems** to educate children who are just beginning to learn English. For example, there are close to five million English language learners in the U.S., about 9 percent of total public school enrollment.[9] These students arrive with varied educational backgrounds. As Helene Becker points out in *Teaching ESL K–12: Views from the Classroom*, "Some have had extensive schooling in their native countries and are well prepared for the academic challenges ahead. Others arrive underprepared for grade-level schoolwork having had (little) formal education."[10]

Another population in public schools includes Generation 1.5 students. These students are long-term residents of the United States, Canada, Britain, New Zealand, and Australia, and they are usually quite fluent in spoken English. However, many of these students still have language problems, especially with writing and occasionally reading. A problem is that many of these Generation 1.5 students do not want to be labeled as ESL students, and many tend to avoid being grouped with recent immigrants. This often results in a predicament for content-area teachers who do not know how to teach students who have native-like proficiency in spoken English but have ESL features in their writing.[11] (See Chapter 12 for suggestions on teaching writing to Generation 1.5 students.)

School districts have responded to the needs of K–12 students in a variety of ways. Some have been overwhelmed by the growing presence of students with not only language and cultural adjustment needs, but also in some cases perceptual awareness needs related to the concept of literacy and schooling. Their response sometimes has been to place immigrants in low-track or remediation programs. Unfortunately, remediation and putting students in low-level classes is the exact opposite of what many of these students need. Such placement simply puts limits on their opportunities to gain the interaction, language, and skills they need to be successful in the new school. Another option is to create **newcomer** schools or programs. A list of different programs appears in Figure 3.1.[12]

A separate program that addresses students language and academic needs is the **pullout model** in which ESL specialists pull students out of their grade-level classroom for ESL lessons. Pulling students out of their

FIGURE 3.1: K–12 ESL Programs

Newcomer: Used when ESL students first arrive, faculty and students join efforts to make the ESL and minority students feel welcome, offer personal-social support, give an orientation to the school, assess language skills, provide survival English for those who need it, and provide cultural adjustment advice.

Pullout: ESL specialists pull students out of their grade-level classroom for ESL lessons.

Inclusion: ESL specialist goes into the classroom to work with the ESL students, either as a small group or individually, during classroom instruction.

Team-Teaching: Also known as a co-teaching model, the ESL teacher and grade-level teacher team-teach the class. As equal partners, they plan and take turns teaching both native and ESL students.

Subtractive Bilingualism: The bilingual teacher begins with using the students' native language while developing their second language. As students develop the second language and begin to shift away from identity with the home language and culture, more and more emphasis is placed on using the second language.

Additive Bilingualism Program: Unlike subtractive bilingualism, which is criticized because the goal is to take cultural identity away from the child, additive bilingualism aims at providing students with the opportunity to become fully literate in both their native and second languages.

classrooms has certain benefits. Time can be used to address content needs, review lessons to clear up language and concept problems, bond with a person who cares, and provide survival-level oral English and reading instruction for beginning level students. However, pullout program with little direct connection to what students are studying in their grade-level classroom could be an ineffective way to facilitate success in school. Indeed, success is more probable if there is continuing communication between the ESL instructor and the grade-level teacher.

Another approach is the **inclusion model** in which the ESL teacher goes into the classroom to work with the ESL students, either as a small group or individually, during classroom instruction; there are certain benefits from this approach. To begin, the inclusion gives the ESL teacher direct access to what is going on in the classroom, the assignments that are being done, and the kinds of challenges these assignments might have for the ESL student, such as fully comprehending the instructions or using the library. In addition, the ESL students can voice their problems and concerns with language and content while class is in process, and the ESL teacher can immediately address these problems.

Unfortunately, it is not always possible for the ESL specialist to be in the classroom, especially if he or she is expected to be with other students in other classrooms or even other schools. Another problem is that of embarrassment. Some ESL teachers working in high school inclusion programs, for example, have told me that some of these older students don't want to draw attention to themselves and their language limitations in front of classmates.

A third approach to teaching ESL students is a **team-teaching model.** Also known as a co-teaching model, the ESL teacher and grade-level teacher team-teach the class. As equal partners, they plan and take turns teaching both native and ESL students. One benefit of the team-teaching model is that the ESL teacher can use ESL teaching strategies to present material to the students. Another benefit of using team-teaching, as Helene Becker puts it, is that the ESL students "perceive themselves as 'students' rather than 'ESL students'; they are not singled out as 'different.'"[13]

Some public schools also offer **bilingual programs,** including what researchers call **subtractive bilingualism** and **additive bilingualism programs.** Subtractive bilingualism begins with using the students' native language while working at developing the second language. As students develop the second language and begin to shift away from identity with the home language and culture, greater emphasis is placed on using the second language. Unlike subtractive bilingualism, which is criticized because a goal is to take cultural identity away from the child, additive bilingualism aims at providing students with the opportunity to become fully literate in both their native and second languages. So as not to oversimplify things, it is important to point out that bilingual programs can vary a great deal and do not adhere exactly to one model or another."[14]

An example of an innovative additive bilingual class is Kerry Conrad's[15] dual-language Spanish/English science class in Utah. Through the support of parents and teachers, Kerry has been able to create a dual-level middle school class consisting of half Mexican immigrants and half native English speakers. This class is taught in a dual-language immersion approach with Spanish and English as medium of instruction alternating daily. What happens inside this classroom is especially interesting. Children not only listen to short lectures by the teacher and read materials in either English or Spanish, they also interact with each other as they ask and answer each other's questions and work on science projects. Kerry has been able to create a supportive trusting learning environment both inside and outside the classroom for these students, who became enabled to explore and learn from their difficulties in cross-cultural, cross-lingual communication as they studied science together in an activity-based, cooperative-learning classroom.

Another group of ESL students are those who travel abroad to study at universities in English-speaking countries. In the United States alone there are close to 900,000 international students enrolled in universities each year.[16] Not all of these international students enroll in degree programs; rather, some first take classes in a **university ESL institute** before going on to a degree program, and some simply come to study at the institute and then return home. Some institutes are quite large, attracting hundreds of students and including numerous kinds of English language programs, while smaller, lesser-known colleges and universities attract a more modest number of students to a single program that aims at meeting their academic and social needs.

A survey of university language institutes in the United States shows a variety of English language programs.[17] The list of English programs in Figure 3.2 at language institutes shows brief descriptions of programs. The most sought-after program, and one offered by all the universities I surveyed, is the intensive **English for Academic Purposes (EAP) program**. The EAP program is designed to meet the academic and social needs of both undergraduate and graduate students who are seeking admission or are conditionally admitted.

ESL is also taught in **refugee and literacy centers** where, depending on the political climate, learners come from a variety of nations and backgrounds. They often include doctors, nurses, teachers, businesspeople, construction workers, electricians, soldiers, secretaries, housewives, farmers, and migrant workers, among others. However, many have one thing in common: They are unable or unwilling to return to their country

FIGURE 3.2: **English Programs at Language Institutes**

English for Academic Purposes (EAP) Program: This program usually lasts a full semester. Students study 20 to 25 hours each week in one of several levels (or in mixed levels), in such courses as reading, writing, listening, oral communications, grammar, pronunciation, English online, vocabulary building, and intercultural communication. At beginning levels the goal is to develop basic language skills; at higher levels students turn to TOEFL® preparation and more academic subjects, including courses in listening to lectures, research writing, and classroom communications.

English for Business: This program is usually designed for international students who want to gain entrance into an MBA program or business professionals who want to further develop their English.

TOEFL® Preparation: Some of the larger language institutes have separate programs just for students who want to raise their TOEFL® score.

Advanced Academic Preparation: Some of the larger institutes offer short (5- to 7-week) programs for advanced learners who will begin their studies at an American university.

Bridge Program: This program offers students the opportunity to be a part-time student in a university degree program while taking support classes at the language institute.

English for Visitors: A short-term program that provides learners with survival English for the purpose of travel and meeting people who speak English.

English for Law: A few language institutes offer English for legal professionals and pre-law students.

---

because they have a strong fear of being persecuted based on their race, religion, nationality, or association with a particular group. They have been forced to flee their homeland, and they find themselves living in another country.

Some refugee programs are non-profit organizations that rely on volunteers. One such refugee program is the Colorado Refugee ESL volunteers (CRESL). This program has served the adult refugee community in Colorado[18] for many years. Refugees in this ESL program have come from Bhutan, Bosnia, Sudan, Somalia, Ethiopia, Congo, Iraq, Iran, Mayanmar, Vietnam, Russia, and the Ukraine. The purpose of the program is primarily to provide literacy instruction and job readiness, as well as help refugees with acculturation.

I have categorized refugee and literacy programs together because there is some overlap. While literacy programs are usually larger in scope than refugee programs, they are concerned with the literacy of people born in the country, as well as immigrants. The Greater Pittsburgh Literacy Council, which advertises itself as "a national leader in adult education and family literacy," clearly defines what a literacy center does: "to ensure that adults and families acquire reading, writing, math, English language, workforce skills and computer skills so they may reach their fullest potential in life and participate productively in their community."[19] As such, a literacy center is concerned with the refugee population in Pittsburgh, but it does not concentrate only on the needs of refugees, and their concern goes beyond simply providing ESL lessons to these students.

Related to ESL teaching, literacy centers and refugee programs are similar in some ways. They both provide classes designed to meet the needs of the students, such as classes in survival English for those who cannot communicate in the language. They also train and depend on volunteer tutors. The Greater Pittsburgh Literacy Center advertises: "Volunteer tutors, who are specially trained in English as a second language methods, work with students to improve their English skills. Beyond simple language practice, students have the opportunity to work with tutors who can help with cultural concerns that are not addressed in a classroom setting. Tutors offer valuable insights into the inner workings of our culture to help students deal with the day-to-day issues they confront."

As a participant teacher in the refugee program in Hawaii and an observer of several refugee programs and literacy centers, I have gained a great deal of respect for volunteers and regular ESL teachers in both settings. They are usually very devoted and caring, work long hours, are often quite talented at teaching, and work as volunteers or for low wages. But, most say it is worth it! These people experience the hopes and dreams, the struggles and successes of individuals and complete families.

OVERLAPPING SETTINGS

Not all settings fit neatly into an EFL or ESL setting. One such setting is the **international school (K–12).** These schools offer all classes in English to expatriates, nationals who have returned home from living in English-speaking countries, and others. Most of the international schools attract students from a variety of cultural and language backgrounds. As such, walking through the hallways, it is possible not only to hear conversations in English, but also in Japanese, Korean, German, Italian, French, Arabic, Chinese, and other languages, depending on the population of students at the school.

What makes such schools interesting from an EFL/ESL perspective is that within the walls of the school, it is more of an ESL setting in which English is used as a medium of communication. However, within those same walls there are also subcultures and multiple languages being spoken, and outside the school English is often not spoken very much at all, as is characteristic of an EFL setting.

Another setting that does not fit neatly into either EFL or ESL is the **university within traditionally EFL contexts** where students with strong English skills can take most of their classes in English. Most of these degree programs are international. However, in many cases the majority of students are natives from the country. In such programs, students are expected to do all coursework in English and interact in English while in the classroom and outside the class (at least with students from other countries). However, although English is used within the walls of the university much like in an ESL setting, students who are from the country will leave the university and speak their native language, something that happens in EFL settings.

One example is Tokyo's Sophia University, which has more than 1,150 foreign students from 602 countries.[20] In addition, Sophia maintains a policy of inviting researchers from around the world to teach, head research projects, and give invited lectures in English. As such, Japanese, as well as international students, are within an ESL context within the university, but the Japanese students usually find themselves in an EFL setting when they leave the walls of the university.

Finally there is the digital teaching and learning setting, and this setting can take on many forms. Students can study English at home through video, as is the case with video-based distant education programs for adult immigrants.[21] Teaching and learning within EFL and ESL settings can be done through virtual classrooms with synchronous (students and teacher communicate in real time) and asynchronous (not in real time) systems, as well as across settings, in which students in classrooms in any setting can connect with students in classrooms around the world. Further, students worldwide can connect on the broader web-based "e-learning for all" (UNESCO's motto) by making use of chat rooms, blogs, twitter, wikis, and other technology that opens up the world for learners.[22] (See Chapter 7 for more on digital literacy and language teaching and learning, as well Part 3 on teaching language skills.)

How Are Different Teaching Settings Woven into This Book?

Understanding different settings is important, to remind you that teaching English is context dependent. How and what we teach depend very much on the setting. For example, the goals of teaching ESL to immigrant children in an elementary school in the United States are quite different in many ways from those of teaching EFL to elementary school children in Japan. In the U.S. setting, the goal is to fully integrate children into the academic and social system. In Japan, the goal is most likely to give children an appreciation of English, the concept of communication in another language, and a basic understanding of grammar and vocabulary.

Throughout this book, I weave in examples, even sections, on how the principles and teaching techniques and strategies are relevant to the different teaching settings I have introduced in this chapter. For example, in Chapter 4 on teaching English as interaction, I give an example lesson from a beginning-level junior high school class in Hungary to illustrate how a Hungarian EFL teacher was successfully able to include communicative activities in her high school class. Likewise, in Chapter 5 on classroom management I include a section on guidelines for facilitating learning in K–12 ESL settings. In short, I include a great variety of illustrations throughout this book, some from my observations of what colleagues do, some from journal articles and books, and some from my own experience, and I have intentionally drawn these illustrations from across many different settings.

TEACHER SELF-DEVELOPMENT TASKS

Talk Tasks

1. I describe a number of EFL and ESL teaching settings. Which settings are you familiar with? Find to be most interesting? Least interesting? Why? If possible, meet with others who have read about these settings. What answers do they give to these questions?

2. Find a friend. Together, go to and talk about the website for TESOL International: www.tesol.org. Spend some time exploring what TESOL International is and what the organization can offer you as an ESL or EFL teacher or prospective one. After you are familiar with the organization, locate the Interest Sections part of the website. Study the Interest Sections Overview. Select several Interest Sections from the list (e.g., Higher Education, Elementary Education, Intercultural Communication, Adult Education, ESL in Bilingual Education, Video, Computer-Assisted Language Learning, English as a Foreign Language). Consider how each of the Interest Sections might be a part of different ESL/EFL settings.

3. ESL students who have recently arrived in the United States sometimes complain if they walk into a classroom to find that their teacher is a non-native English speaker. I have seen this happen at language institutes, refugee programs, and K–12 programs. However, there are obvious advantages that these newly arrived students have overlooked. Why do you think some ESL students complain about having a non-native English speaker as a teacher? What would you say to the ESL students who are complaining? [23]

Observation and Talk Task

1. If possible, visit one of the settings written about in this chapter. Talk with those who work or study there. If possible, observe a class. Then, if possible, get together with others who are reading this book. Talk about what you learned about that teaching setting.

Journal Writing Tasks

1. If you were able to visit and talk about one of the teaching settings, as given in the observation and talk tasks, write about your experience in your journal.

2. Reflect on the language learning settings you have experienced as a teacher or learner. As you write, also consider what it must be like to learn a language in settings that you have not experienced but have read about in this chapter.

3. Write about what you learned from studying the different interest sections on the TESOL International website. How might the different interest sections help inform you about different EFL and ESL teaching settings?

RECOMMENDED TEACHER RESOURCES

Resources on Teaching EFL Abroad

Boas, I. V. and K. Cox. *Teaching English in a Binational Center in Brazil*. Alexandria, VA: TESOL, 2015.

Corrales, K. A., E. F. Arizia, and R. Paba. *Teaching University Level English in Columbia*. Alexandria, VA: TESOL, 2015.

Hartse, J. H. and J. Dong. *Teaching English at Colleges and Universities in China*. Alexandria, VA: TESOL, 2015.

Hastings, C. *Teaching English for Specific Purposes in Saudi Arabia*. Alexandria, VA: TESOL, 2015.

McConnell, D. L. *Imparting Diversity: Inside Japan's Jet Program*. Berkeley: University of California Press, 2000.

Poirier, S. *Teaching English in Korea*. Seoul: Darakwon Press (Also Amazon Digital Press), 2011.

Shearan, B. *Get a Job Teaching in Japan*. Tokyo: Subtle Frog Press, 2013.

Snow, D. B. *More than a Native Speaker: An Introduction for Volunteers Teaching English Abroad*. Alexandria, VA: TESOL, 2006.

Takeda, N. *Teaching English at an NGO in Cambodia*. Alexandria, VA: TESOL, 2015.

Resources for K–12 ESL Teachers

Dormer, J. E. *What School Leaders Need to Know about English Learners*. Alexandria, VA: TESOL, 2016.

Pèregoy, S. F. and O. F. Boyle. *Reading, Writing & Learning in ESL: A Resource Book for K–12 Teachers, 7ᵗʰ ed*. New York: Pearson, 2017.

Olson, C. B., R. C. Scarcella, and T. Matuchniak. *Helping English Learners to Write: Meeting Common Core Standards Grades 6–12.* Alexandria, VA: TESOL, 2015.

TESOL. *Pre K–12 Language Proficiency Standards.* Alexandria, VA: TESOL, 2006.

ENDNOTES

1   I have learned about the complexity of Englishes from reading the work of Kachru (1986, 1989), Sharma (2012); Trudgill and Hannah (2008).

2   See Platt, Weber, and Lian (1984, 2–3), McKay (1992, 89–95), and Sharma (2012).

3   See Smith (1983, 14), discovered in McKay (1992, 90).

4   See Crystal's (2003) book, *English as a Global Language,* for an historical account of how English became a language of use in countries around the world.

5   See Wong (1992) for a detailed linguistic analysis of Singapore English.

6   Much of the information about English language curricula in different countries was obtained through interviews with teachers and school administrators from each country. I would like to thank Theresa Tseng for assisting me with these interviews. Clark and Park (2013) and Jung and Norton (2002) have also done very useful research. I also found a document published by the Korean Ministry of Education (2010) to be quite useful.

7   See Alrashidi and Phan (2015) for an overview of English teaching and learning in Saudi Arabia.

8   The American University Alumni Association website is worth looking at: www. auathailand.org.

9   See Jacobs (2016).

10   See Becker (2001, 69). Also Pèregoy and Boyle (2007).

11   Harklau, Losey, and Siegal (1999) and Thonus (2003) write about serving the writing needs of Generation 1.5 students, including pedagogical practices that have proven to be effective.

12   Dwyer (1998) explains experiences of students with limited English proficiency placed in low-track high school sections. Many of these students did not reach the more advanced science and math classes. They experienced less challenging academics and scored lower on standardized tests. Hull, Rose, Fraser, and Castellano (2002) also provide a deeply disturbing understanding of remediation as a social construct.

13   See Becker (2001, 64).

14   See Pèregoy and Boyle (2017). Also see Lessow-Hurley (1996) and Reyes and Kleyn (2010) for discussion on bilingual education programs and issues attached to them.

15   See Conrad (2000) for a detailed description of this dual-level Spanish-English classroom. Also see Conrad and Conrad (2002) for a class memory book done in this class.

16   This information was obtained from the Institute of International Education: www. iie.org. See Institute of Higher Education (2014).

17 I surveyed Language Institutes at the following universities in the United States: Columbia University, New York University, University of Pittsburgh, Fairleigh Dickinson University, Indiana University of Pennsylvania, San Diego State University, Loyola University, the University of Pennsylvania, Marshall University, the University of Tennessee, University of Southern California, California State University, the University of Michigan, and Wichita State University. Also see Orlando (2016).

18 To learn about this refugee program, go to: www.refugee-esl.org

19 To learn more about the Greater Pittsburgh Literacy Center, log on to www.gplc.org.

20 These numbers are based on figures for 2015. To learn more about Sophia University, go to www.sophia.ac.jp.

21 See Ramirez and Savage (2003).

22 See Bloch and Wilkinson (2014) and Sokolik (2014).

23 See Llurda (2006) for discussions on non-native language teachers' perceptions, challenges, and contributions to teaching a second or foreign language. See Medgyes (1991) for his classic discussion on the value of non-native English teachers.

Part 2
Principles of EFL/ESL Teaching

4

Language and learning and teaching can be an exciting and refreshing interval in the day for students and teacher. There are so many possible ways of stimulating communicative interaction, yet, all over the world, one still finds classrooms where language learning is a tedious, dry-as-dust process, devoid of contact with the real world in which language use is as natural as breathing.

—Rivers 1987, 14

Teaching Language as Communication among People

I *What is the main goal of a communicative classroom?*

I *How do EFL/ESL teachers provide opportunities for beginning students to communicate in English?*

I *How do EFL/ESL teachers provide opportunities for more advanced students to communitcate in English in meaningful ways?*

I *What makes a classroom communicative?*

I *What problems do some EFL/ESL teachers face when teaching language as communication?*

What Is the Main Goal of a Communicative Classroom?

The primary goal of a communicative classroom is student development of *communicative competence* in English. At a basic level, this includes development of students' ability to comprehend and produce written and spoken English in communicatively proficient and accurate ways.

Influenced by the thinking of Dell Hymes,[1] Michael Canal and Merrill Swain,[2] and Sandra Savignon,[3] communicative competence has four inter-related components—grammatical, discourse, socio-cultural, and strategic competency.

To have **grammatical competency** means to be able to recognize sentence-level grammatical forms, including **lexical items** (vocabulary/ words), **morphological items** (smallest units of meaning, such as *re-* meaning again as in *remind*), **syntactic features** (word order), and **phonological features** (consonant and vowel sounds, intonation patterns, and other aspects of the sound system).

Communicative competence also includes **discourse competency,** or the ability to interconnect a series of utterances (written or spoken) to form a meaningful text (letter, e-mail, essay, telephone conversation, formal speech, or joke). This includes being able to use both **top-down** (knowledge based on experience and context) and **bottom-up** (knowledge of grammatical forms) processing. (See Part 3 of this book for more discussion on top-down and bottom-up processing.) According to Sandra Savignon, discourse competency also includes text coherence and cohesion. She defines **coherence** as "the relation of all sentences or utterances in a text to a single global proposition (or topic)."[4] While coherence establishes a global meaning or topic, **cohesion** provides the smaller structural links between individual sentences, such as in the use of *first, second, next,* and *after this.*[5]

The third component of communicative competence is **socio-cultural competency,** which is the ability to use English in social contexts in culturally appropriate ways. When do people compliment each other? How often? What kinds of things do they compliment? What kind of verbal and nonverbal behaviors do they use? The same kinds of questions can be asked about other functions of language, such as when apologizing, complaining, interrupting, asking for permission, requesting, and turning down an invitation. Developing socio-cultural competency means being able to adapt the use of English to the ways people in any culture interact. For example, if an Egyptian were living in Toronto, then he or she would need to adapt to the socio-cultural rules for using English in Toronto. However, if this same person moves to Tokyo, the socio-cultural rules when using English change. Socio-cultural competency becomes most interesting when people from different cultures, such as people from Taiwan, Korea, and Thailand, interact in a context outside any of their own native cultures, as in rural western Pennsylvania. Do they follow the rules used by Americans in rural western Pennsylvania? Or do they create their own rules based partly on the common features of their cultures?

Finally, communicative competence includes **strategic competency,** or the ability to cope with breakdowns in communication, to problem- solve in unfamiliar contexts when communication fails, and to draw on strategies that help restore communication. Examples of such strategies include knowing how to explain directions by drawing a map, knowing how to ask someone to repeat what she said in different words, and paraphrasing to check understanding.

How Do EFL/ESL Teachers Provide Opportunities for Beginning Students to Communicate in English?

Some EFL/ESL classes are taught in a teacher- and text-centered fashion. Recall Soyoung's class in Chapter 1. Interaction is dominated by the teacher and textbook. However, to provide chances for students to gain communicative competence, other EFL/ESL teachers see value in getting students involved in interacting in English and in this section, based on a classic framework provided by Littlewood,[6] I discuss how this can be done.

Some teachers who aim at having a communicative classroom begin lessons with what Littlewood calls "precommunicative activities." Used primarily with beginning- and intermediate-level students, precommunicative activities allow the teacher to isolate specific elements of knowledge or skill that compose communicative ability, giving students opportunities to practice them without having to fully engage in communicating meaning. Littlewood discusses two types of precommunicative activities—structural and quasi-communicative. **Structural activities** focus on the grammar and vocabulary of English, while **quasi-communicative activities** focus on how the language is used to communicate meaning. Quasi-communicative activities are often in the form of dialogues or relatively simple activities in which students interact under highly controlled conditions.

Here are illustrations of these two types of precommunicative activities in a beginning-level class I observed in Hungary. The teacher's goal was to teach students how to ask about food likes and dislikes. The teacher first taught a grammatical item, the use of the auxiliary verb *do* when used in a yes-no question (a structural activity). She began by giving several examples, such as this one:

Statement: You like (to eat) cake.
Question: Do you like (to eat) cake?

She then led students in a vocabulary-building activity (another structural activity) in which she put large pictures of food items on the wall and matched them with the names of food items she had written in big bold letters on separate pieces of paper. She gave students chances to read the names of food items, say them aloud as a whole class, and copy the names while drawing their own pictures of each item.

In order to work up to a communicative activity, the teacher gave students the sample precommunicative activity handout shown in Figure 4.1. Then the teacher held up a picture of each item (e.g., of a piece of cake), and as she did this, she asked the whole class, "Do you like to eat cake?"

FIGURE 4.1: A Pre-Communicative Activity Handout

Do you like (to eat) cake?
bananas?
fish?
ice cream?
apples?
toilet paper?
pie?

The students then shouted out "Yes!" or "No!" depending on their own preference. There was lots of laughter, especially when she asked, "Do you like to eat toilet paper?"

The teacher then handed out a dialogue that combined grammatical and vocabulary items and added a little new language:

> *A.* Do you like cake?
>
> *B.* Yes, I do.
>
> *A:* Do you like bananas?
>
> *B:* Yes, very much.
>
> *A:* How about fish? Do you like fish?
>
> *B:* I don't know. Maybe.

The teacher read the dialogue out loud, asked students to repeat it after her, and asked students to practice it in pairs.

Next, the teacher did another quasi-communicative activity by dividing students into pairs and placing a set of pictures of different food items face down on their desks. The students took turns picking a picture from a pile, and, using the picture as a cue, asked each other about their likes and dislikes. The teacher included a few comical items, such as a picture of soap, and a few students made up their own comical items, such as chicken ice cream.

Some teachers follow up precommunicative activities with what Little-wood calls **communicative activities.** To illustrate what communicative activities are and how they are used to follow precommunicative activities, let's return to my observation on food items and preferences. After the structural and quasi-communicative activities, and reviewing basic letter-writing formatting, the teacher asked the students to write short letters to students in one of her other classes. Although the teacher encouraged the students to ask about what food they liked, she also encouraged them to express themselves freely.

There are many other possible examples of precommunicative and communicative activities teachers can have students do in classrooms, and I provide more examples in Part 3 of the book. The point here is that, as teachers, we can create lessons or use textbook activities designed to move students from precommunicative to more communicative abilities.

How Do EFL/ESL Teachers Provide Opportunities for More Advanced Students to Communicate in Meaningful Ways?

If you are teaching students beyond a basic level, it's okay to skip the pre-communicative activities. If we begin with communicative activities, students can begin with a task, such as writing and producing their own play, giving oral and written presentations on topics they researched through interviewing and library research, and solving problems in small groups. As students work on these tasks, their attention will sometimes shift to language use—for example, they might ask the meaning of a word or how to express an idea—but the thrust of the lesson is for students to communicate with the teacher and each other in meaningful ways.

One way to approach having students interact more with each other and the teacher in meaningful ways is through **task-based teaching.**[7] The principles underlying this approach include (1) focusing on students developing an ability to communicate in English through the use of English rather than having students study about English -- Students learn by doing; (2) providing chances for students to focus attention on their learning processes, something they can continue to develop and use as they strive for higher levels of English ability; (3) providing chances for students to bring in their own personal experiences; (4) exposing students to authentic listening and reading texts; (5) providing opportunities for students to link in class learning to what they are doing or expected to be doing outside the classroom.[8]

Tasks can be focused or unfocused.[9] Although the **focused task** is not specifically designed to give students practice on a particular grammar point, it does have a particular grammatical form in mind, one that will be needed to complete the task. One focused task I have used is to have groups list places each student has visited. I narrow the choices of places based on the context. For example, for ESL students in the U.S., I might narrow the choice to include just states or places within the local community, depending on my knowledge of the students in the class. After the groups make their lists, I ask each group to report on the places their group members have visited and find out who else in the class has been to the same places. The reason this is a focused task is because I knew the students would use the present perfect tense while interacting, such as *I have been to San Francisco*, or *I have shopped at Macy's* and *Have you ever been to an American football game?*

An **unfocused task** is one that does not have a grammatical form in mind, and in Part 3 I provide many examples of unfocused tasks, such as having students solve a problem by listening and reading, put together a strip story in groups, read a short story and create a group ending, write, produce, and act out their own short plays, produce a news show, and generate a class newsletter which requires them to interview, photograph, write, and edit. All these tasks have a process of discovery and a product in mind, and students have to interact with each other and the teacher to complete the task.

One particular kind of task I like is the **project-based task.** These tasks take longer to complete than simpler tasks. Depending on the teaching setting and goals of the course, a project-based task might take a week or even a complete semester. Students might work on the project one class period each week or continuously throughout a period of time. Here is an example of such as task I have done over the years with students in EFL and ESL settings[10]: The class decides on a place they would like to visit. For some classes, they make it a real place and then visit that place. For example, an ESL class studying at the American Language Institute (ALI) at Indiana University of Pennsylvania (IUP) decided they wanted to learn more about the Amish, a traditional conservative society within America that settled in Pennsylvania and Ohio. With this in mind, the class broke into groups. Using online research tools and tourist literature, one group researched the history and culture of the Amish; another group looked into places near IUP where the class could visit, such as an Amish country store and an Amish farm open to visitors. Another group looked into places to eat, menus they could print out and study, and traditional Amish food. Each group reported on what they learned to the class, and we created a trip schedule. We then used the ALI van to go to a local Amish place, after which students talked and wrote about their experience.

What Makes a Classroom Communicative?

Four closely related factors contribute to making classrooms communicative are:

- reduction in the centrality of the teacher
- an appreciation for the uniqueness of individuals
- chances for students to express themselves in meaningful ways
- choices, both in relation to what students say and how they say it.

The first factor is reducing the central (and traditional) position of the teacher. However, this does not mean that teachers have to give up control of the class. The teacher can maintain control of what goes on in the classroom while still giving students freedom to initiate communication among themselves and with the teacher.[11]

Genuine communication is enhanced if there is an appreciation for the uniqueness of individuals in the class. Each student brings unique language-learning and life experiences (both successful and unsuccessful) to the classroom, as well as feelings about these experiences (including joy, anxiety, and fear). As teachers, we need to be sensitive to each individual's background and affective state. To create a classroom atmosphere conducive to communication, we need to understand and accept each student as he or she is, and sometimes this is harder than one might imagine.

Also, providing chances for the students to express themselves in meaningful ways contributes to a communicative classroom. Students need chances to listen to each other, express their ideas in speech and writing, and read each other's writing. Negotiation of meaning needs to become the norm; while negotiating, students need chances to ask for and receive clarification, confirm their understanding, ask and respond to questions, and react to responses. If true negotiation of meaning is going on, students will be fully engaged in using English to understand the meaning intended by others, as well as to express their own meaning as clearly as possible. Negotiation of meaning also implies that students have choices as to what they want to say, to whom they want to say it, and how they want to say it. Throughtout this book I provide a variety of classroom activities that promote such interactions. For example, in Chapter 10 I discuss how students can use games, buzz groups, stories, and problem-solving activities to promote communication. In Chapter 12 I discuss writing activities that do this, too.

What Problems Do Some EFL/ESL Teachers Face when Teaching Language as Communication?

Beginning with this chapter, one section of each subsequent chapter addresses the kinds of problems EFL/ESL teachers report with an aspect of EFL/ESL. Here, it's the problems teachers have related to interacting with students. Suggestions on how teachers might resolve these problems are provided.

Problems some EFL/ESL teachers face include:

- the bandwagon problem
- the overly anxious problem
- the engagement problem.

THE BANDWAGON PROBLEM

One problem of teaching language as interaction between people can occur in EFL/ESL classrooms when teachers jump on the latest methodological bandwagon. For the phrase *to jump on a bandwagon, Roget's Thesaurus* gives the alternatives "to float or swim with the stream; to join the parade, go with the crowd." With this in mind, as Mark Clarke points out, bandwagons are "the 'latest word,' the trendy, the fashionable, the most up-to-date in methods, materials, technique."[12]

As Earl Stevick stated some years ago at a TESOL conference, bandwagons provide confidence, the company of others who believe in the same thing, and useful techniques.[13] Those who are new to teaching often welcome a method of teaching that provides these things. This is only problematic if teachers cannot see beyond the "in way" of teaching, cannot accept the bandwagon as simply other people's prescriptions about teaching based on their personal set of beliefs about the relationship between teaching and learning. If we blindly follow a certain method because it is said to be the best way to teach, we become impervious to other creative ways we can interact with our students, and students with each other. As discussed in Chapter 1 and 2, teachers can be liberated to make our own informed teaching decisions, if we know how to become aware of teaching behaviors, analyze their consequences, and generate new teaching behaviors based on the awareness. Reflecting on our teaching through classroom observation, talking with other teachers, and writing about teaching are far more important to teachers than jumping of the latest bandwagon. While bandwagons provide us with ideas about teaching possibilities, confidence, company, and techniques, they may not liberate us to be able to make our own informed teaching decisions, and they could stop us from genuine interaction in the classroom.

THE OVERLY ANXIOUS PROBLEM

Tom Scovel believes anxiety is a state of apprehension and a vague fear.[14] H. D. Brown adds that anxiety includes feelings of self-doubt, apprehension, and worry.[15] There are many reasons for teachers to think about why students might be anxious:[16]

- inability to pronounce sounds and words
- not knowing the meaning of words or sentences
- inability to understand and answer questions
- reputation of the language class as a place for failure
- peer criticism
- not knowing or understanding course goals or requirements
- testing, especially oral testing
- previous unsuccessful language-learning attempts
- encountering different cultural values and behaviors.

High levels of anxiety can inhibit students from interacting with the teacher and classmates. I have observed particularly high levels of anxiety in many different teaching settings, but especially in EFL settings where students do not have much experience interacting in English, as well as in K–12 ESL settings where language learners are expected to speak English in front of native speakers. In fact, anxiety can create so much apprehension that some students cannot function normally. Most of us have experienced such debilitating anxiety. The teacher asks a question in the new language; all we can do is sit, hearts slightly racing, mouths slightly open, staring at the book or the teacher, nothing coming to mind. Facilitative anxiety, in contrast, can create just the right amount of tension to bring out the best in us. This is what happens to some actors and public speakers before they appear onstage. It can also happen to students before taking a test, and to EFL/ESL students in situations where they are given a chance to use English.

If students in our classes have high degrees of anxiety that are limiting them, there are things we can do to possibly reduce this. For example, they do not need criticism on their language performance. Rather, we must show understanding: When a student expresses an idea, we can use an "understanding response"[17] by really listening to the student and paraphrasing back what he or she said. Paraphrasing not only can provide a way for the student to reflect on his or her own language in a non-critical way but can also improve understanding. When we consistently and sincerely work at trying to understand students' meaning without expressing verbal or nonverbal judgment of the language used, a positive, trusting relationship between the student and teacher can develop, one that also reduces anxiety about being in a language classroom.

Tom Farrell, who taught university students in Korea and Singapore, suggests that students analyze their own propensity for anxiety through the use of personal diaries. If the student sees value in writing about his or her feelings in a journal addressed to the teacher, the topic of the student's anxiety could be pursued by the teacher or even initiated by the student. As Farrell points out, "This use of a diary can show the students that they are not totally alone in times of emotional distress."[18]

THE ENGAGEMENT PROBLEM

As previously mentioned, promoting interaction in the classroom requires the teacher to step out of the limelight and yield to the students so that they feel free to interact with the teacher and each other. However, this is not easy for some teachers. As Wilga Rivers puts it, "Never having experienced an interactive classroom, [teachers] are afraid it will be chaotic and hesitate to try."[19] Adding to this problem are the students' attitudes. Students quite often come into our classrooms with little experience in initiating and participating in interaction in English. As such, they will also hesitate to interact, afraid that things will become out of control, frenzied, or embarrassing.

To avoid this half-engagement problem, it is our responsibility as teachers to provide an atmosphere conducive to interaction. As teachers, we need to show emotional maturity, sensitivity to the students' feelings, and a perceptiveness and commitment that interaction in English is not only appropriate but also expected and necessary for the students if they want to learn to communicate in English. As Wilga Rivers, one of the pioneers of the TESOL field, has said, "when a teacher demonstrates such qualities, students lose their fear of embarrassment and are willing to try to express themselves."[20]

TEACHER SELF-DEVELOPMENT TASKS

Talk Tasks

1. The point of this task is to learn about the language learning history of an EFL/ESL student.

   a. Talk to an EFL/ESL student at an intermediate/advanced level. Find out about his or her language-learning background. What kinds of language-learning experiences has he or she had? What kinds of classroom activities does he or she prefer and not prefer? Why?

   b. Get together with other teachers who have talked with students. Explain what you have learned. Listen to what other teachers have learned.

2. Some EFL students complain that it is difficult to learn to be communicatively competent in English because everyone in the class speaks the same native language (e.g., Spanish, Japanese, Vietnamese). These students say it feels awkward to interact with classmates in English in meaningful ways. Some say classmates make grammar, word choice, and pronunciation errors, and they cannot become accurate English speakers because of this. If students told you this, how would you respond?

3. As language teachers we are expected to take on a number of roles. We are expected to be language authorities, cultural informants, needs assessors, classroom managers, text adapters,

model English speakers, and even entertainers. Select three different roles and consider what they mean in relation to being an ESL/EFL teacher. Which roles interest you the most? Which roles are challenging for you?

Observation and Talk Tasks

1. This task gives you a chance to reflect on your teaching. It involves four steps, and you will need the cooperation of at least one other teacher.

   Step 1: Audiorecord or videorecord a class you teach or another teacher teaches.

   Step 2: Listen to or view the recording. As you do, take descriptive notes, draw sketches, and jot down samples of interactive dialogue. Avoid making judgments about the teaching as being good or bad. Simply describe the activities the students do.

   Step 3: Reflect on the experience. List three things you learned about yourself as a teacher and about teaching. List one or two new things you would like to try out in your teaching.

2. The point of this observation is to consider what happens in the classroom from the student's perspective.

   Visit a class. Sit next to a student. Draw a line down the center of your notepad to make two columns. On one side write everything the teacher does, including what the teacher asks that student to do. On the other side write what the student does. For example:

WHAT THE TEACHER DOES	WHAT THE STUDENT DOES[21]
Tells students to open their books to page 103.	Opens book to page 33.
Calls on a student to answer Question 1.	Searches page 33 for Question 1. Looks at classmate's book. Sees she is on wrong page. Flips pages. Is silent. Looks at page. Looks at teacher.
Teacher calls on another student.	

At the end of the observation, consider the class from the student's point of view. Meet with other teachers who have done the same task. Talk about what some students experience in EFL classrooms.

Journal Writing Tasks

1. Reflect on the kinds of roles ESL/EFL teachers play in the classroom. Make a list of roles. Which roles do you like to play? Which roles are you not comfortable playing? What do you need to learn to play some roles more professionally? What additional roles could you play?

2. Consider the list of problems teachers face discussed earlier in this chapter. Write about some of your experiences related to these problems. If you have had chances to talk with others about these same problems, write about what they feel and think about the problem and possible solutions.

3. Reread the first section (pages 57–59) on communicative competence. Write your thoughts on what competence includes.

RECOMMENDED TEACHER RESOURCES

Teaching Methodology Books: Theory and Practice

Brown, H. D. *Principles of Language Learning and Teaching, 6th ed.* White Plains, NY: Pearson Education, 2014.

Brown, H.D. and H. Lee. *Teaching by Principles: An Interaction Approach to Language Pedagogy.* White Plains, NY: Pearson Education, 2015.

Burns, A. and J. Richards, eds. *The Cambridge Guide to Pedagogy and Practice in Second Language Teaching.* New York: Cambridge University Press, 2012.

Celce-Murcia, M., D. Brinton, and M. A. Snow, eds. *Teaching English as a Second or Foreign Language, 4th ed.* Boston: Heinle Cengage, 2014.

Larsen-Freeman, D. and M. Anderson. *Techniques and Principles in Language Teaching, 3rd ed.* New York: Oxford University Press, 2011.

Littlewood, W. *Communicative Language Teaching.* Cambridge, U.K.: Cambridge University Press, 1981.

Richards, J. C. and T. Rodgers. *Approaches and Methods in Language Teaching, 3rd ed.* New York: Cambridge University Press, 2011.

Rivers, W., ed. *Interactive Language Teaching.* New York: Cambridge University Press, 1987.

ENDNOTES

1   See Hymes (1971, 1972).
2   See Canale and Swain (1980).
3   See Savignon (1997, 2001).
4   See Savignon (2001, 17).
5   See Halliday and Hasan (1976).
6   See Littlewood (1981).
7   See Doughty and Long (2003), Ellis (2003), Larson-Freeman and Anderson (2011, Chapter 11), Nunan (2004, 2014), Richards and Rodgers (2011), and Thomas and Reinders (2015) for historical, theoretical, and practical uses of task-based teaching.
8   My list is adapted from Doughty and Long (2003) and Nunan (2014).
9   See Ellis (2008) and Nunan (2014).
10 I first learned about using this project-based task from reading Melvin and Stout (1987). They wrote about having students "Discover a City" through the use of authentic materials.
11 Stevick (1978, 1980) and Curran (1976) influenced my teaching related to teacher control and student initiative
12 The dictionary definition was discovered in Clarke (1982). The quote is also from the same source (p. 439). Clarke has very much influenced my thinking in regard to making my own informed decisions. I highly recommend his original 1982 article, as well as his more recent 2003 book and his 2002 book chapter with Sandra Silberstein.
13 See Stevick (1982).
14 See Scovel (1978, 135).
15 See Brown (2014).
16 See Ohata (2004) and Oxford (1999).
17 See Curran (1978).
18 See Farrell (1993, 17).
19 See Rivers (1987, 10).
20 See Rivers (1987, 10).
21 This activity was originally designed by Robert Oprandy.

5

Success [in learning a language] depends less on materials, techniques, and linguistic analysis, and more on what goes on inside and between people in the classroom.

—Stevick 1980, 4

Classroom Management

I *What is classroom management?*
I *How can EFL/ESL teachers use knowledge of classroom management to create opportunities for students to interact in English in meaningful ways?*
I *What can K–12 teachers do to create a positive learning setting for ESL students?*
I *What problems do some EFL/ESL teachers have managing classroom interaction?*

What Is Classroom Management?

Classroom management refers to the way teachers organize what goes on in the classroom. As the most powerful person in the classroom, the teacher has the authority to influence the kind of interaction that goes on in the class, and this interaction is created from a combination of many related factors—such as how much the teacher talks and what the teacher says, and how the teacher gives instructions, keeps students on task, and makes language comprehensible to the students. The goal of classroom management is to create a classroom atmosphere conducive to interacting in English in meaningful ways so that students can make progress in learning English.

How Can EFL/ESL Teachers Use Knowledge of Classroom Management to Create Opportunities for Students to Interact in English in Meaningful Ways?

I emphasize throughout this section that classroom management is a personal and creative endeavor in which a complex set of factors are combined and constantly tested through classroom use.

TEACHER TALK

When asked to audiorecord their teaching, listen to the recording, and total the amount of time they talk, teachers are generally surprised to discover they spend much more time talking than they had imagined. Some teachers will say that too much talk is bad and should be avoided. But this is not necessarily true. When it comes down to it, it is not how much time we spend talking, but rather *the way we use talk* to promote meaningful interaction that is significant. Certain uses of teacher talk lack this purpose and are therefore not productive. Other uses seem purposeful and potentially productive.

Some EFL/ESL teachers mindlessly think aloud in the classroom. Although some students might gain something positive from this authentic language experience, it can confuse students, so some students might stop listening even when the teacher has something important to say. Or, if the teacher gives long explanations about language or long-winded speeches on abstract ideas, some students will become passive learners, accepting English as a subject in which the teacher lectures, sometimes in abstract terms that are beyond comprehension. However, we can elect to use English selectively and purposefully to answer students' questions, give instructions, demonstrate useful reading processes, explain homework assignments, relate an amusing story that students can comprehend, participate in daily interpersonal communications with students in English, and use teacher talk as part of the students' planned listening comprehension experience, such as a dictation.

THE TEACHER'S QUESTIONS

Teachers ask a lot of questions. For example, I observed six expatriate teachers who were all teaching in different contexts in Japan and found they averaged 52 questions every 30 minutes during teacher-initiated activities. Since teachers do ask many questions, understanding questioning behaviors can benefit those who want to stimulate students to communicate in English in meaningful ways.

One way to focus on our questioning behaviors is to consider the purposes of questions (see Figure 5.1).[1] For many teachers, one purpose is to ask students to "display" their knowledge. For example, when a teacher holds up a large paper clock and asks, *What time is it?* the teacher is asking students to show they know how to tell time in English. And when the teacher asks, *What is the past tense of* to do? the teacher wants to see if they know this grammatical point.

Another purpose for asking questions is to learn things about students and their knowledge through *referential questions.* Such questions can stimulate interaction and show genuine interest in the students. For example, if the teacher forgot his or her watch and wants to know the time, he or she would use the referential question, *What time is it?* The same is true if the teacher asks, *Who has been to a museum?*—to know who has and who has not been to one because of genuine interest.

Many of those who advocate an interactive approach to EFL/ESL teaching favor the use of referential questions over display questions. My

FIGURE 5.1: The Purpose of Teachers' Questions

Display Question	A question in which the teacher already knows the answer and wants the student to display knowledge. *(What color is your shirt?)*
Referential Question	A question in which the teacher does not know the answer. *(What is your favorite color?)*
Comprehension Check	A question to find out if a student understands. *(Who can tell me what I said?)*
Confirmation Question	A question to verify what was said. *(You said you got up at 6:00?)*
Clarification Check	A question to further define or clarify. *(Did you say you got up at 6:00 or 7:00?)*

own belief is that both have a place in the language classroom. Referential questions provide a means through which to bring real questions into the classroom. They can also be engaging for students because the questions are aimed at communicating with them, not testing their knowledge. However, display questions offer a way to practice language or to drill students, something some students both like and need, and when students find display questions to be engaging, this is meaningful to them.

Another purpose of teachers' questions is to check students' comprehension; to do this, teachers often ask, *Do you understand?* Such comprehension checks are not as common outside as they are inside classrooms, and I wonder what real value they sometimes have. Much of the time, if asked, *Do you understand?* students will reply that they do, even when they do not. Perhaps a question such as, *Who can tell me what I just said?* is more valuable because it not only shows student comprehension, but also gives the student practice in paraphrasing.

Two other purposes of asking questions are to confirm and clarify understanding. For example, *We'll meet at 6:00. Right?* asks the listener to confirm something that the asker believes is true, while *Did you say you like strawberry or chocolate ice cream?* and *I'm a little confused. What time are we going to meet?* aim at clarification. I encourage teachers and students to confirm and clarify often, if for no other reason than to have more natural, and hopefully meaningful, conversations inside classrooms.

In addition to focusing on the purpose of questions, we can consider the content of our questions (Figure 5.2).[4] Questions can include three possible content areas: study, procedure, and life. I have observed that many of the questions in EFL/ESL classrooms are about *study,* often on the study of language, such as on some aspect of grammar or vocabulary. Less often, teachers ask questions about content other than language, such as questions about movies, trees, food, or anything that is not about language itself. Questions can also be about *procedures,* such as questions used to take attendance, return papers, and ask about schedules.

Besides study and procedure, content of questions can be about *life.* As Fanselow points out, questions can be general to a group of people (life-general content) or specific to one person (life-personal content). Two examples of life-general questions are *How do people greet each other in*

FIGURE 5.2: **The Content of Teachers' Questions**

Study of Language	Questions that ask students about aspects of language. *(What is the past tense of* eat? *What does the word* acculturation *mean?)*
Study of Subjects	Questions that ask students about content other than the study of language. *(How big is the Little Prince? How many countries are there in the world?)*
Procedure	Questions that ask students about procedural matters. *(Did you do your homework? Would you like the test to be on Thursday or Friday?)*
Life-General	Questions about the lives of groups of people. *(Do Japanese women generally like hot tea in the summer? How do Nigerians celebrate birthdays?)*
Life-Personal	Questions about the lives of individuals. *(Do you like to drink hot tea in the summer? How do you celebrate your birthday?)*

Vietnam? and *What music is popular among teenagers in France?* Examples of life-personal questions are *What is* your *favorite kind of music?* and *What did* you *do at the picnic?*

Some teachers believe that when we include study (not about language), life-general, and life-personal questions in our classroom interaction, we can provide greater opportunities for meaningful interaction than when our questions focus exclusively on the study of language and procedures. Study questions can involve students in using language to learn about a topic, rather than simply studying about the language itself. Likewise, life-general and life-personal questions can involve students in talking about their culture and themselves.

Finally, as teachers, we can consider "wait time" in relation to creating chances for students to engage in meaningful interaction. On average, teachers wait less than one second for a student to answer a question before calling on this student again or on another student. In addition, teachers tend not to wait after a student gives a response, reacting very quickly with *Very good!* and the like. As a result, a usual pattern of classroom interaction emerges: The teacher ends up asking many questions, only students who can respond quickly do so, and the teacher ends up reacting to the students' responses. However, if teachers wait a little longer (three to five seconds) and offer polite encouragement through nonverbal behavior, this pattern can change. When teachers extend their wait time after asking a question, student participation may increase in these ways:[3]

- The average length of students' responses might increase.
- Students could ask more questions.
- Students may react to each other's comments.
- The number of correct responses could go up.
- Students might make more inferences.

I encourage you to increase your wait time, but I also caution that simply increasing wait time will not necessarily create changes in classroom interaction. The teacher needs to be sincere in waiting; he or she has to genuinely want to hear the student's answer and what other students think about it.

SETTING UP CLASSROOM ACTIVITIES

In order to manage and promote interactive classrooms, we also need to know how to arrange a variety of classroom activities. We can choose to have students work (1) alone, (2) in pairs, (3) in small groups, or (4) as a whole class.

Look at the example of different seating arrangements in Figure 5.3, which shows that we have choices as to how we have students sit in the class. These arrangements also imply that we have choices about the activities students do in class. They can sit in a traditional seating arrangement or in a semi-circle during teacher-class discussions or lectures. They can stand up and walk around as they study, for example, to memorize lines in a poem. They can move their chairs to sit alone or in groups while working on a task. They can sit face to face, for example, as they interview each other; back-to-back as they simulate a phone conversation; across from each other as they practice a dialogue; in circles as they solve a problem or discuss an issue; or next to each other as they study a reading selection, plan a party, or collaborate on a piece of writing. They can also move around the class as they practice skits or role plays. The point here is that we do not have to limit the students to traditional seating. If our goal is to

FIGURE 5.3: **Seating Arrangements: Possibilities**

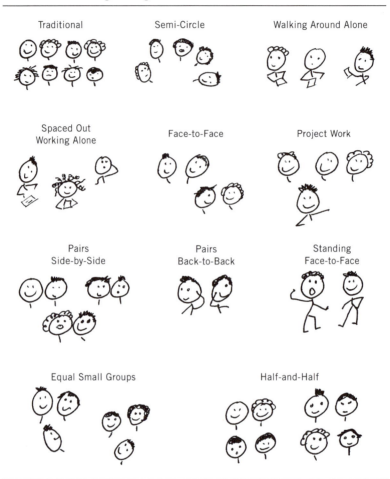

provide lots of chances for students to use English to communicate mean-ing, we need to feel free to create seating combinations that make this possible.

Another aspect of setting up classroom activities is how we group students, and there are a variety of ways to do this. One way is to select students in advance of the class based on personality characteristics or abil-ities and experience. For example, shy students can be matched with shy or talkative students, fluent students with those who are or are not fluent (see Figure 5.4).

FIGURE 5.4: **Ways to Group Learners**

Selectively by the Teacher in Advance
The teacher can group students with the same or opposite characteristics or mix them. For example, shy students could be grouped together or shy and outgoing students grouped.

By Ability and Experience	**By Personality Factors**
Fluent/Not fluent	Shy/Outgoing
Use English at work/Do not use it	Front-sitters/Back-sitters
Can cook/Cannot cook	Talkers/Non-talkers
	Early-risers/Late-sleepers

Randomly in Class

By Characteristics	**By Lottery**	**By Location**
Favorite color,	Same flavor candy,	Same side of room,
music group, or	same colored dot,	proximity, number
types of books read	same end of string,	after counting
	same number, same	(1, 2, 3, 4; 1 . . .)
	piece of picture, same coin	

Other Ways
Students self-select
Pick-up teams

Students can make their own decisions about which group to join, or they can be grouped according to different characteristics, such as month of birthdate, or color of hair, etc. We can also randomly group students, for example, by having them count off—one through four—and having all the ones form a group, the twos another, and so on. Students could be given pieces of paper with colored dots and grouped by the color of the dot they receive. The same thing is possible with pieces of candy, coins, or anything that can be used to distinguish members of a group. Teachers can also cut pictures or proverbs into pieces like a puzzle, hand the pieces out randomly, and have students locate others who have the sections of the same picture or proverb. This way of forming groups can also be an icebreaker, a way to reduce students' anxiety about speaking in English.

If the goal is to form pairs, we can simply have students sitting next to each other pair up or have students pair up on their own. We could also have students randomly pair-up through a pairing technique, such as having each student find the person with the other half of a picture. I find students are amused by a pairing technique in which the teacher holds up a set of strings (half the number of strings as there are students in the class), letting the ends dangle. Each student grabs an end. The students holding the ends of the same string form a pair.[4]

GIVING INSTRUCTIONS

The way we give instructions is another aspect of managing a classroom. It is worth taking time to consider how we can make our instructions clear and at the same time provide opportunities through the instructions for students to interact in meaningful ways.[5]

Some ways to give instructions include:

- writing instructions and giving them verbally
- giving instructions verbally and role-playing them, showing the students what they are to do
- asking a student to read the instructions and then having a student or two paraphrase them to the class
- writing the instructions, letting the students read them silently, and then asking them to tell you what you expect from them
- dictating instructions and then asking the students to check each other's dictations
- miming the instructions as students guess what they are supposed to do
- whispering the instructions as students lean forward in their seats and then asking students to repeat the instructions to the person next to them in a whisper.

KEEPING STUDENTS ON TASK

Teachers can group students, provide activities, and explore ways to give instructions, but this is not always enough to keep students on task. In addition, some teachers believe that keeping students on task is an important part of providing students with opportunities for meaningful interaction. However, this is not always easy, even when the students know what to do. For example, as a great number of experienced EFL/ESL teachers can point out, while working on tasks in small groups, students will sometimes have their own discussions on matters unrelated to the task. Personally, I have no problems with this, especially if their discussions are in English and they come back to and are able to complete the task. (Perhaps they even benefit more from their own discussion than from working on the task.) However, students will sometimes use their native language during group or pair work to work through the task or talk about something else. And the students are very clever about this! Groups might use their native language while the teacher is on another side of the room and switch back to English as the teacher gets closer.

There are things we can do to keep students on task. The instructions themselves can be important. Some educators believe that students tend to begin working on a task sooner and work toward its completion when it is clear to them what the task involves. Setting a reasonable time limit for the students to accomplish the task may also keep them on task. If students know they cannot possibly finish the task, for example, if you ask them to answer 20 questions on a long reading selection in 30 minutes, they might stop working on the task.

One thing that works for me is to require an oral or written report as a part of the task. For example, if a group task was assigned to identify the traits of a good student, each group of students would be required to write these traits on the board toward the end of the lesson. If the task was to write a dialogue, the students would be expected to act it out or read it to the class.

Finally, the teacher needs to stay out of the way, letting the students work on the task. This is not always easy to do! Some teachers talk to students while they work. I have seen some teachers, including myself, circling, listening, and finally interrupting students in groups to make a comment or ask a question. Sometimes this keeps students even more intently on their task. But, it can also do the opposite. By the time the teacher leaves, students can be totally off task.

In summary, here are some suggestions for keeping students on task:

- Give clear instructions. Make sure the students know what the goal of the task is.
- Let students know that you expect them to stay on the task.
- Ask students to work on tasks that they can accomplish in a set amount of time. Let students know how much time they have left to complete the task as they work on it.

- Give tasks that have a product as an outcome.
- Appoint students to take on specific roles—for example, as recorder, timekeeper, or discussion leader.
- Let the students work on the task. Do not interrupt without first considering your purpose.

MAKING LANGUAGE COMPREHENSIBLE TO STUDENTS

As EFL teachers, we can also work at providing opportunities for meaningful interaction by making language comprehensible to the students. If the language used by the teacher or in materials is not comprehensible, students can lose interest, become anxious or frustrated, and sometimes become passive or inattentive. As such, it makes sense to work at making language comprehensible, but how can this be done? I suggest three ways to make language comprehensible to students:

1. Simplify speech.
2. Add visuals, sounds, and non-verbal behaviors.
3. Negotiate meaning.

First, we can attempt to make language comprehensible by simplifying our speech. This includes clear pronunciation, facial expressions; slower speech rate; frequent uses of pauses, gestures, and sentence expansion. Also, realize that speaking louder will likely not help. We can also simplify materials, as some writers of texts do. They present students with authentic materials (notes, newspaper articles, textbook excerpts, crossword puzzles, maps, letters, advertisements, etc.), but they also simplify the language to their estimate of the students' level of comprehension.

Second, we can add visuals (pictures, objects, realia), sounds (bird chirps, the sound of water flowing, the sound of the wind in the trees, etc.), and non-verbal features (gestures, eye contact, touch, distance/use of space, etc.). For example, if the students are to read an authentic restaurant menu and the text is too difficult for them, the teacher and students can bring in or draw pictures of the food on the menu, bring in real food items for students to taste and smell, write a short description of different foods, or act out how a particular food is eaten, such as how to eat a plate of spaghetti with a spoon and fork or Japanese ramen with chopsticks.

Third, we can work at making language comprehensible to students by negotiating meaning. The teacher can open up communication by asking questions that aim at clarification and confirmation. These same types of questions are useful for negotiating meaning for both the teacher and students; when the students work at clarifying and confirming meaning, language can become more comprehensible to them.

MANAGING AN INTERACTIVE CLASSROOM: QUESTIONS TEACHERS CAN ASK

To conclude this section on creating opportunities for interaction, I suggest you ask yourself these questions:

- How much do I talk in the classroom? What function does my talk serve? Does my talk seem to be productive? Unproductive? Are there times when I do not need to talk?
- What are the purposes of my questions? Do I mostly ask students to display their knowledge, or do I also ask questions to discover and learn about what the students know and do? Do I ask questions to clarify and confirm understanding of what students have said?
- How long do I wait after asking a question for the student to respond? If my wait time is short (about a second), can I expand the time I wait? What happens when I do this?
- What is the content of my questions? Are the majority of my questions about the study of language? Do I also ask life-personal and life-general questions? Questions about the study of things other than language itself? What consequences do questions with different content have on classroom interaction?
- What seating arrangements do I use? Have I explored a variety of arrangements? What happens when I try out different seating arrangements?

- Do the students stay on task during group work? If students go off task, what do they talk about? What language do they use? What are different ways to keep students on task? What happens when I use these ways?

- How do I make language comprehensible to students? Do I simplify my speech? If so, in what ways? Do I add media? How? Do I negotiate meaning? How? What happens when I try different ways to make language comprehensible to students?

- How do I group students? What creative ways of grouping students would I like to try? What are the consequences of different ways of grouping students?

- How do I give instructions? Are my instructions clear to the students? How can I give instructions differently? What happens when I give instructions differently?

What Can K–12 Teachers Do to Create a Positive Learning Setting for ESL Students?

I have been asked by a number of K–12 teachers to suggest ways they can create a flourishing learning atmosphere for ESL students. In response, I decided to include my answer to the question posed above. However, before answering this question, allow me to summarize research findings and teacher observations on how K–12 teachers tend to interact with ESL students.[6]

Most K–12 teachers are at a disadvantage in that they have not had the chance to study stages of second language acquisition and development[7] and are not fully aware that it takes time, opportunities to interact, and much encouragement for ESL students to move from a beginning level to a fully communicatively competent and literate user of English.

Those who have studied the interaction between elementary and secondary teachers and ESL students have also discovered that K–12 teachers without ESL training unintentionally tend to prohibit interaction opportunities for ESL students.[8] They tend to ask ESL students fewer questions than the other students, and when they do ask questions, they are more likely to be about procedures (for example, *Do you understand what you are to do with the paper and paste?*) or questions about facts, rather than asking high-level cognitive questions that provide opportunities for students to think, such as questions in which students have to make inferences by relating two pieces of information. Uninformed teachers tend to underestimate ESL students' abilities to produce extended utterances and are concerned about the amount of time it might take an ESL student to answer a question. In addition, teachers tend to want to protect the ESL students from being embarrassed. Given all these concerns, teachers tend simply not to call on the student.

A concern in terms of teaching ESL students in a public school is that some administrators place ESL students in lower-track classes. They do this because they assume that these classes will be easier for ESL students so they will have time to develop their language skills. Once they have improved their English, they can be placed in higher-level classes, according to these administrators. However, as Linda Harklau points out, this is the opposite of what most bright ESL students need.[9] Her observations show that interaction in lower-track classes relies heavily on teacher-directed activities and individual seatwork, rather than on interaction-fostering activities that promote comprehension and development of communicative competence. In addition, higher-level classroom students are exposed to a variety of supplemental reading materials, in addition to the required text. In the lower-track classes, teachers tend to focus exclusively on the text, thus limiting content exposure for ESL students.

A list of some basic things that K–12 teachers can do to manage their classroom behaviors to accommodate ESL students follows. Keep in mind that these suggestions are not prescriptions about how we should teach, but ideas based on research, experiences of K–12 teachers, and my own thoughts.

- Pay attention to the social and emotional needs of the new ESL student.
- Adjust speech. When you know that the ESL student's English comprehension is still developing; reduce sentence and word choice complexity; and increase repetition, pausing, and use of gestures. Speaking more loudly will likely not help comprehension.

- When possible, use realia, photos, and drawings while explaining concepts.

- Take time to check if the student comprehends. Go beyond simply asking, *Do you understand?* Instead, ask specific questions. For beginners, it helps to ask questions that require a *yes, no,* or a single answer. For example: *Let's review. When we mix red paint and yellow paint, we get purple paint. Right? No. Really? Then what color? Orange! That's right!*

- Include ESL students in class discussions. Get to know each student and his or her language abilities. Take calculated risks by asking questions that require extended answers, if the student seems ready to answer such questions.

- Assign each ESL student a mentor or even a small group of mentors whose job it is to get to know and coach the student and to explain assignments, concepts, and other classroom interactions when needed. Meet with the mentors periodically to talk about problems, successes, and needs.

- Engage students in interaction-fostering activities, such as group work and task-based activities. Encourage the native-speakers to include the ESL students as viable members of the group.

- Encourage administrators to place capable ESL students in higher-track or age-appropriate classrooms. Also encourage them to set up an *inclusion* program that includes an ESL teacher. If a *pullout* program is used, try to arrange for students to leave the classroom during lessons that are not highly relevant. (See Chapter 3, the section on teaching K–12 ESL classes, to learn more about *inclusion* and *pullout* programs.)

What Problems Do Some EFL/ESL Teachers Have Managing Classroom Interaction?

Problems some EFL/ESL teachers face include:

- The "how do I get students to use English in class?" problem
- The "name remembering" problem

THE "HOW DO I GET STUDENTS TO USE ENGLISH IN CLASS?" PROBLEM

I have met EFL/ESL teachers who strongly believe in an English-only policy. Some believe that to learn English, students need to interact only in English. When the goal is to get students to use English much of the time—a problematic goal—teachers have tried a number of things. Some put up signs that say, for example, "This is an English-only zone!" Others point at the student and say, "Speak English!" Others initiate a system in which students can cash in poker chips at times they want to use their native language. Still others create a fund in which students give a coin toward a class party each time they speak in their native language.

Personally, I believe these techniques have minimal effectiveness for most teachers who face classroom English-use problems. If students are not motivated to use English in the classroom or are pressured by peers to follow a hidden set of classroom rules that includes interacting in the students' native language, then these more or less superficial techniques to compel students to use English can become novelties that will likely wane in their effect quickly.

If we truly believe that students need to use English to learn English but they are not doing so, we need to negotiate with them why it is important to use English in class. It is important to gain their trust and commitment. They need to want to use English in class because they see value in doing so. We then are more likely to be successful in implementing techniques that focus their attention on using English to learn English.

THE "NAME REMEMBERING" PROBLEM

To my embarrassment, I never could remember my students' names. Names are important; learning a student's name shows that a teacher is interested enough to know his or her name. I asked people who are good at remembering names what they do, and I read *The Memory Book*.[10] First, I discovered that people who remember names really listen to the name and use it as soon as they hear it. They also study the person's face and match the name to the face, making mental notes: "This is Jacinta from India, with long black hair and black eyes."

Surprisingly, simply paying attention to the name and face worked wonderfully for me when meeting individuals. But when faced with three or four classes of new students, I still had problems. So I decided to create ways to learn whole classes of students' names. I had students complete information sheets about themselves and draw their pictures on the sheets. I could then study the sheets and match the drawings with their names. An alternative is to use digital photo sheets.[11]

My initial exploration into better remembering students' names inspired me to develop a number of activities for the first day of each class that focus on learning the names of the students. One activity is to have students interview each other in small groups (or pairs), and I join each group. We meet to learn each other's names and at least three things about each other. We then form a new group to interview each other. After several switches, we form a large circle and list what we learned about each person in the class.

Another activity is a "cocktail party."[12] I ask each student to write a variety of information on a large nametag. The information might include, for example, the student's name in the center; a favorite food in the top right corner; a word recently learned in the bottom right corner; a hobby in the top left corner; and, in the remaining corner, the name of a person, dead or alive, whom the student would like to meet. We then walk around the classroom reading each other's nametags and striking up conversations. As I do this, I pay particular attention to the person's name and face.

TEACHER SELF-DEVELOPMENT TASKS

Talk Tasks

1. Study the list of questions in the section Managing an Interactive Classroom: Questions Teachers Can Ask. Put a check next to the questions that interest you. Then study the ones you checked. Choose three questions you would like to explore. Meet with other teachers. Who has similar interests to yours?

2. Study the seating arrangements given earlier in this chapter. Meet with other teachers. Design a lesson (on the content of your choice) that makes use of at least five different seating arrangements.

3. Study the list of ways I provide to give instructions. How many additional ways can you think of to give instructions?

4. Study the ways to group learners. Talk about which ones you like. Can you add other ways to group learners?

Observation and Talk Tasks

1. Ask a friend if you can observe his or her class. Remember that your purpose is not to judge his or her teaching or the students but to collect descriptions of how he or she manages classroom interaction.

   a. Before observing, consider what aspect of classroom management you will observe: for example, the teacher's questioning behaviors, the teacher's way of giving instructions, or the teacher's wait time and its consequences on students' behavior.

   b. After deciding on an area of classroom management to focus on during the observation, consider how you will collect descriptions of teaching (see Chapter 2). For example, will you tally behaviors? Jot down sample dialogue? Sketch?

   c. Observe the class, collecting descriptions. Meet with the teacher (just after the class, if possible). Talk about the class, focusing attention on descriptions of teaching you collected. Avoid making judgments, the good teaching/bad teaching trap.

   d. Reflect on what you have learned. Were you able to see your own teaching in this person's teaching? What does this teacher do that you would like to do? What do you think this teacher might do differently?

Journal Writing Tasks

1. Answer this question: What is the value of observing other teachers and of talking about the observation? If possible, base your discussion on your own experience in observing other teachers and then talking with the teacher about the class you observed.

2. Write what you learned from doing the Talk Tasks in this chapter.

3. Write about your observation experiences from the first observation and Talk Task in this chapter. Include discussion on what you learned about how to go about studying your own teaching.

4. Select one or two aspects of classroom management you find interesting. Using stream-of-consciousness writing, reflect on your way of managing classroom interaction.

5. Reflect on how past (or present) language teachers managed classroom interaction. What did you like about the way they managed interaction? As a learner, what did you dislike?

RECOMMENDED TEACHER RESOURCES: OTHER WAYS TO UNDERSTAND CLASSROOM MANAGEMENT

Farrell, T. S. C., ed. *Classroom Management.* Alexandria, VA: TESOL, 2008.

Giannotti, J. *Voices of Experience: How Teachers Manage Student-Centered ESL Classes.* Ann Arbor: University of Michigan Press, 2015.

Holliday, A. "Teachers' and Students' Lessons." In *Enriching ESOL Pedagogy*, eds. V. Zamel and R. Spack, 17–43. Mahwah, NJ: Lawrence Erlbaum, 2002.

Lewis, M. "Classroom Management." In *Methodology in Language Teaching: An Anthology of Current Practice*, eds. J. C. Richards and W. A. Renandya, 40–58. New York: Cambridge University Press, 2002.

Quirke, P. *Managing the Language Classroom.* Alexandria VA: TESOL, 2015.

ENDNOTES

1   The work of Barns (1975), Brinton (2014), Long and Sato (1983), Brock (1986), Zohrabi, Yaghoubi-Notash, and Khiabani (2014), and Fanselow (1987) has influenced the way I understand the purpose of teachers' questions.

2   My ideas on the content of teachers' questions have been adapted from Fanselow (1987) and a personal communication with Fanselow.

3   See Rowe (1986).
4   This idea comes from Maley and Duff (1982).
5   I thank John Fanselow for sharing his way of giving instructions.
6   A number of ESL teachers/researchers have looked closely at the interaction between K–12 teachers and ESL students. Ryan (2004) researched how teachers without any formal ESL training interact with ESL children at an elementary school in a rural southern U.S. setting. Harklau (2002) researched the differences in interaction in ESL and regular high school classrooms, as well as differences in the kind of interaction ESL students experienced when placed in low-track and high-track classes. In addition, there are interesting and useful accounts of ESL students' experiences in mainstream classrooms, including those of Pèregoy and Boyle (2017), Bérubé (2000), and Becker (2001).
7   See Brown (2014).
8   See Harklau (2002) and Ryan (2004).
9   See Harklau (2002).
10 See Lorayne and Lucas (1974).
11 See Delaney (2008).
12 I adapted this activity from Wright, Betteridge, and Buckby (1994).

6

EFL/ESL Materials, Media, and Technology

■ *Who creates the materials available to EFL/ESL teachers?*

■ *How can teachers select context-appropriate textbooks?*

■ *What are authentic materials? What types are available?*

■ *How do EFL/ESL teachers use authentic materials and media?*

■ *What kinds of technology do EFL/ESL teachers use?*

■ *What problems do some EFL/ESL teachers have with materials, media, and technology?*

Who Creates the Materials Available to EFL/ESL Teachers?

Basically, materials used in EFL/ESL classrooms are created by four groups of people: publishing companies, government agencies, curriculum development teams at the school level, and classroom teachers.

If you teach in a private language school, ESL K–12 program, business, or other settings, you might be using commercial materials such as EFL/ESL texts accompanying workbooks, companion website activities (from the publisher), and computer programs. In fact, a large number of commercially made texts and other materials are on the market for teaching reading, writing, listening, speaking, grammar, survival English, K–12, vocabulary building, cross-cultural communication, pronunciation, English for business, TOEFL® preparation, vocational skills, literature, and more. In addition, publishing companies are producing full series of texts for beginner through advanced proficiency levels. (See the list of publishers in Appendix B.)

If you teach in a public school in a country with a centralized educational system, you might find yourself teaching with materials produced (or selected) by a government education agency or committee. Some countries establish special committees that either produce their own texts or solicit proposals from teachers to produce texts. After being approved by this central committee, these texts are produced and used in the schools. For example, the Ministry of Education and Training (MOET) in Vietnam mandated English as a compulsory subject with the emphasis on English being "instrumental to the access of world science and technology as well as world culture."[1] It describes the aims for English teaching at the secondary school level as enabling students to: (1) "use English as a means for basic communication both in spoken and written channels"; (2) master basic and relatively systematic knowledge of English suited to their levels of proficiency and ages"; (3) gain "some general understanding of the people and cultures of some English-speaking countries and develop a positive attitude toward the people, cultures and language of these countries"; and (4) "cultivate the pride in, love for and respect to the Vietnamese culture and language."[2]

If you teach at certain universities, well-established private language schools, some ESL K–12 schools, and corporations with language programs, you could find yourself teaching with locally designed texts and materials. Teachers who have some EFL/ESL teaching experience usually produce these in-house materials. Sometimes the writers of the materials are also members of a team who design the curriculum for the language program. As a result, classroom teachers are sometimes given a day-by-day lesson plan, which includes goals of each lesson, steps in implementing it, and the materials needed to teach it.

There are also teaching contexts, such as university language courses, public language schools, and tutoring programs, in which the teacher selects a textbook and other materials. I can also add that if you are among the teachers who are not completely satisfied with a textbook selected for you, you probably can adapt the text or design lessons with materials you create yourself. Examples of such materials are illustrated later in this chapter and throughout this book.

How Can Teachers Select Context-Appropriate Textbooks?

When we, as teachers, have a voice in the selection of a textbook, it helps to have knowledge through which we can make more informed decisions. In this section I discuss criteria I have developed over the years for doing this, including questions I ask.[3] To begin, the textbook needs to fit into the overall curriculum of the program. For example, when asked to teach a university second semester conversation course for English majors at Pusan National University, I asked, "What are the stated curriculum goals of this course? What were the stated goals for the first semester course, and is this one a continuation of that course? What are the overall goals of the English major curriculum in regard to students abilities to converse in English?" I also asked, "Are there example syllabi available that include textbooks other teachers have used? Who taught the course before? Is this person available for me to consult?"

I approached the department chair to ask about the curriculum and the course. She gave me a copy of a document in Korean that described the English Education major curriculum, the goals of each course, and more. She was nice enough to verbally translate the goals of the course I would be teaching. In short, the three basic goals were to strengthen students' abilities to use everyday English in conversation, discuss current issues, and to gain skill in giving oral presentations. I discovered that there was no official syllabus available, but the department chair gave me the name and contact information for the person who had previously taught the course. He gave me his syllabus and the even loaned me the one of the textbooks he had used. The book was titled *Small Group Discussion Topics for Korean Students: Political, Environmental, Economic, Social Issues Facing Korea in the 21st Century,*[4] and he pointed out issues in the book that students liked and those they didn't, as well as gave me advice about introducing some of the topics. He also told me about problems students had with the book. This was very useful to me.

This text looked promising, so I thought I would read it carefully while also considering other criteria that would help me in my textbook selection decision. I also thought I would search for other books online and at bookstores.

In addition to meeting the goals of the curriculum, I believe a textbook should address the needs of the students, and for me, considering their needs was quite difficult, as I had not yet met the students I would be teaching and had not taught in the teaching context before. But, I had taught many students from Korea in the United States, and I could approximate their needs. I also knew that students have their own perceived needs, that is, what they believed they needed to learn, and these perceived needs do not always match the teacher's understanding of what they need in relation to the course goals. I could guess at their perceived needs (i.e., more grammar, larger vocabulary, practice speaking with a U.S. speaker), as well as mentally assess what I thought they needed in relation to the course goals (i.e., more practice talking in public, more practice with and feedback on interacting with others in English). As such, while searching for course texts, I continually asked:

- Do the aims of the book correspond closely with the needs that students believe they have?
- Do the goals of the textbook address the students' actual needs as I understand them?

I also knew that the content and design of a textbook needed to interest the students. As such, I asked these questions as I reviewed books for the course (see also Figure 6.1):

- Is the content of the textbook going to interest the students?
- Might the content be offensive to any of the students?
- Is the content age-appropriate?
- Will the students be attracted to the design of the textbook?

FIGURE 6.1: **Questions on Textbook Selection**

Questions related to course and curriculum goals	■ What are the goals of the course in which the textbook will be used? ■ How does the text help meet the larger goals of the curriculum?
Reflective questions about past experience	■ What experiences have I had with teaching this course or ones like it? ■ What textbooks have I used previously? ■ How well did that work out for the students and me? ■ Did the text provide opportunities for students to learn? ■ Was the text too difficult? ■ How do other texts compare to the text(s) I have used in the past?
Questions related to students' perceived and actual needs	■ Do the aims of the book correspond closely with the needs that students believe they have? ■ Do the goals of the text address the students' needs as understood by the teacher?
Questions related to students cultural backgrounds and interests	■ Is the content of the text going to interest the students? ■ Might the content be offensive to any of the students? ■ Is the content age-appropriate?
Questions related to comprehensibility and usefulness	■ Do explanations in the text help the learners to understand? ■ Do the tasks in the text include enough variety? ■ Meet the different learning styles of students? ■ Does the text have complementary supporting online resources for students who want them?
Questions related to selection of grammar and vocabulary	■ Has the grammar and vocabulary been thoughtfully presented? ■ Is the book corpus-informed?
Questions related to the teacher's preference	■ Is the text comprehensible to me, the teacher? ■ Is it easy to use? ■ Is it easy to adapt if necessary? ■ Is the text aesthetically pleasing to me? ■ Does the book have a useful teacher's manual?

I also wanted to assess the book in regard to comprehensibility and usefulness by asking these questions:

■ Do explanations in the textbook help the learners to understand?

■ Do the tasks in the textbook include enough variety?

■ Do the tasks address the different learning styles of students?

■ Does the textbook have complimentary supporting online resources for students who want them?

Another criterion for selecting a textbook is whether or not the grammar and vocabulary in the book is **corpus-informed**. In brief, corpus-informed knowledge comes from **corpus linguistics,** an area of linguistics that studies large collected samples of naturally occurring English (or any language). These samples are analyzed through the use of corpora, programs that analyze and categorize grammar and vocabulary patterns based on different questions. Here are some of the questions that have been addressed: What are the most frequent words and phrases in English? What differences are there between spoken and written English? What tenses do people use most frequently? How do people use words like *can*, *may*, and *might*? What are common adverbs of degree (i.e., *very, really, quite*), and how frequently are they used? Of course, there are an endless number of questions that can be explored.

In relation to my search for a textbook to teach second semester conversation to English Education majors at Pusan National University, I asked:

- Has the grammar and vocabulary been thoughtfully presented?
- Is the book corpus-informed in terms of including useful vocabulary for Korean English Education majors?
- Is the grammar corpus-informed in terms of being at the intermediate level of the students?

A number of corpora have been developed over the past two decades. One of the most popular is Corpus of Contemporary American English (COCA), the largest free corpus of English. You can learn more about COCA on youtube.com. Type "Introduction to COCA," and then look for COCA01: Introduction to using the corpus of contemporary American English. I also recommend these books: *Corpus-Based Approaches to English Language Teaching*,[5] *Using Corpora in the Language Classroom*,[6] and *Using Corpora in the Language Learning Classroom*.[7]

Many textbook writers and publishers now use corpora to make decisions about the grammar and vocabulary they will include in their textbooks, so study textbook introductions and chapters to understand whether the book is corpus-informed and if so, in what ways. For your interest, some examples of textbooks that are corpus-informed are included in the Recommended Teacher Resources section at the end of this chapter.

In addition, I am the one who will be teaching from the book, so I wanted to make sure I would be comfortable using it throughout a semester. In this regard I asked myself:

- Is the textbook comprehensible to me, the teacher?
- Is it easy to use?
- Is it easy to adapt if necessary?
- Do I like the design?
- Does the textbook have a useful teacher's manual?

My search did take some time, but I was happy with the textbooks I selected. I did select the book used by the previous teacher, *Small Group Discussion Topics for Korean Students*, as it met much of the criteria I used to select a book, but I also decided to add a book titled *Present Yourself 2*.[8]

What Are Authentic Materials? What Types Are Available?

To move beyond a text, many EFL/ESL teachers adapt or create authentic materials and media. But what are authentic materials, and what types of authentic materials are available to us? Basically, authentic materials include anything that is used to communicate. To give you an idea of the scope of what I mean, here is a partial list of some authentic materials EFL/ESL teachers have used.

AUTHENTIC LISTENING/VIEWING MATERIALS

silent films; TV commercials, quiz shows, cartoons, news, comedy shows, dramas, movies, and soap operas; radio news, dramas, and ads; professionally audiotaped short stories and novels; pop, rock, country, film, and children's songs; home videos; professionally videotaped travel logs, documentaries, and sales pitches

AUTHENTIC VISUAL MATERIALS

slides; photographs; paintings; sketches; drawings by children; stick-figure drawings; wordless street signs; silhouettes; calendar pictures; pictures from travel, news, and popular magazines; ink blots; postcard pictures; wordless picture books; stamps; x-rays

AUTHENTIC PRINTED MATERIALS

newspaper articles, cartoons, advertisements, movie advertisements, astrology columns, sports reports, obituary columns, and advice columns; travel magazines; science, math, and history books; short stories; novels; books of photographs; lyrics to popular, rock, folk, and children's songs; restaurant menus; street signs; postcards; currency; cereal boxes; candy wrappers; tourist information brochures and guidebooks; university catalogs; department store catalogs; phone books; world, city, and relief maps; calendars; TV guides; driver's licenses; comic books; greeting cards; business cards; bank checks and deposit forms; grocery coupons; hotel registration forms; pins with messages; bus, plane, train, and jitney schedules; teletext subtitles for the hearing impaired

REALIA USED IN EFL/ESL CLASSROOMS

dolls, puppets, currency, key rings, scissors, folded paper, toothpaste, toothbrushes, combs, stuffed and toy animals, wall clocks, balloons, walkie-talkies, candles, fly swatters, string, thread, chewing gum, glue, rulers, tacks, paper clips, rubber bands, trains, aprons, plastic forks and spoons, dishes, glasses, bowls, umbrellas, wallets, purses, balls, phones, fishing reels, furniture, people, cars, bug collections, play money, stones, plants, sand, clay, ink, sticks, jars, coffee cans, chalk, credit cards, hats, Halloween masks, mannequins

Using authentic materials and media has disadvantages and advantages. One disadvantage is that it takes time and effort to locate authentic materials. It is also difficult to make authentic materials and media comprehensible to the students. Also, some students will not accept some authentic materials and media as being a valuable learning source. For example, students will sometimes reject TV comedy or games as a learning source because they consider them entertainment but view learning as a serious enterprise.

Nevertheless, there are reasons to use authentic materials and media. They reinforce the direct relation between classroom lessons and the outside world. In addition, they offer a way to contextualize language learning. When lessons are centered on comprehending a repair manual, a menu, a TV weather report, a documentary, or anything that is used in the real world, students tend to focus more on content and meaning than on language. This offers students a valuable source of language input, since they can be exposed to more than just the language presented by the teacher and the text.

How Do EFL/ESL Teachers Use Authentic Materials and Media?

Some teachers use authentic materials to get beyond the limitations of a text. They begin with an idea in a text and, based on their understanding of students' needs and interests, locate authentic materials, as well as create additional activities that make use of them. Here is an example of how one EFL teacher did this. While engaged in a textbook activity, students in a functional English class expressed interest in learning how to describe people. So, the teacher pulled together photos from his private collection and from magazines that showed groups of people. He then photocopied them, divided the students into groups, gave one student in each group a photo, and told that student not to show it to group members. That student then was asked to select one person in the photo. The other students then asked the photo-holder questions, such as, "Is the person male or female?" and "What color is her hair." After finishing, the group looked at the photo and tried to identify the person who was described.

As this teacher's activity illustrates, it is possible to adapt lessons to a text using authentic materials. However, some teachers also see the need to go beyond the text and to create their own lessons based solely on authentic materials and media. There are many examples of how EFL/ESL teachers have done this. Garber and Holmes, for example, used authentic video as a means to have students in their French as a foreign language classes write and produce their own commentaries.[9] They prepared four five-minute video segments on everyday themes, showed them to the students without a soundtrack, and asked them to write a commentary based on the video segment of their choice. The commentaries were corrected by the teachers and audiorecorded by the students. After more teacher feedback, students rerecorded their soundtracks. They then watched the original video segments with sound and compared their versions with the original.

Another way to use authentic materials is to include them on reading boards. A reading board looks similar to a bulletin board, but it is purposefully designed to promote interaction between the reader and the text. It can include quick quizzes, problems to solve, quotes from famous people, cartoons and jokes, and news items. Teachers who have created reading boards have used advice columns in which the problem is given without solutions (blank space is provided for readers to write in their own advice). Some teachers have used advertisements that ask readers to compare prices and select the best buy on a product, as well as cartoons with blank bubbles, cultural quizzes, crossword puzzles, and funny pictures or photos of classmates under which readers can write in possible captions. Although the original idea was to place these reading boards on classroom walls, modern technology now also allows us to create them using computer technology and put them on a class website.

There are many ideas online about how to use or create your own materials. For example, using a program (www.eslgamesword.com), I created a Jeopardy™-like challenge for a student I was tutoring. I based content on the student's interest and achievements with the present perfect tense, her problems with using the past continuous tense, what she had been learning about writing, some of the errors she had made, and just for fun, my interest in seeing what she would do with hypothetical use of English. The challenge begins with the student selecting a value and category, for example, ten points on writing. That particular window is opened by clicking on it. The student then completes the task.

A sample gameboard is shown in Figure 6.2.

What Kinds of Technology Do EFL/ESL Teachers Use?

When you hear the word *technology,* what comes to mind? For many of us the words *computer, website, satellite,* and web 2.0, e-readers, wiki, blogs, *email* do. But, in reality, technology is much more than this. Technology is scientific and industrial know-how or expertise. Every culture uses technology, for example, to run the transportation system, the communications systems (such as the telephone), the agricultural system, and other systems that provide people with the means to live. Some countries have advanced technology, with very efficient trains and buses, digital enter-

FIGURE 6.2: Jeopardy™-Like Game

Value	Present Perfect Tense	Writing	Hypothetical and the Future	Correct these Sentences	Past Continuous Tense
10 points	♪	Write down a sentence with exactly 8 words.	♪	♪	♪
15 points	O	O	O	O	O
20 points	♯	♯	♯	♯	♯
25 points	✪	✪	✪	✪	✪

tainment wired into homes or beaming in from satellites, and modern computerized machinery in the factories. Other countries have quite the opposite technology, with slow-moving trains and buses, and labor-intense factories. Of course, there are some countries that are developing, some quite fast, and they have very advanced technology and very old technology within the same country.

We can carry this same idea of technology into a discussion of technology as it is used to teach English around the world. Some teachers have access to high technology, such as computers that can surf the Internet at lightening speed, while other teachers will only have access to chalk and a blackboard.

Before going on to map out and illustrate examples of technology, using a continuum from low to high technology, it is important to emphasize that technology is only one aspect of culture. In addition to having a technological system, every culture has a social system, a human communication system, and an ideological system. Even though people in a culture might not have access to advanced technology, they can still be a highly developed culture in other ways. For example, although some Laotian villagers do not have modern technological conveniences, through centuries of experience with Theravada Buddhism, they now have highly developed ideological and social systems.

The technology continuum in Figure 6.3 shows examples of low through high technology used by EFL/ESL teachers. At the one end is some of the most basic technology—those things naturally around us that can serve as teaching tools. For example, when living in a village some years ago in rural northeast Thailand, I made friends with Buddhist monks. They were interested in learning English, and I was interested in learning Thai and about Theravada Buddhism. We taught each other whenever time allowed and in no particular place. We looked at clouds and asked, "What do you see?" We taught each other how to write by using sticks and the earth, and we spelled words in the air. I treasure this experience, not only because of the wonderful friends I made, but because I learned that even the most simplistic of things can be useful as teaching technology.

FIGURE 6.3: **A Technology Continuum**

Low Technology				High Technology
Sticks Earth Air Clouds	Chalk Blackboard Crayons Paint Kazoo Scissors Paper	Overhead Projector Slide Projector Filmstrip Projector Audiocassette Recorder Radio Telephone VCR Video Camera 35 mm Camera	Computer Web 1.0 Email Chat Webpages Bulletin Boards	Web 2.0 Blogging Twitter Wikis Digital storytelling

Moving across the continuum to such usual items as whiteboards, paper, and pencils, most teachers simply smile. These are familiar to all experienced teachers. However, teachers are often surprised to learn that they use the board in quite limited ways. See Jeannine Dobbs' *Using the Board in the Language Classroom*,[10] in which 130 board activities are provided.

Most older teachers are also familiar with the overhead projector, film-strip projector, slide projector, audiocassette recorder, video camera, and VCR.

One useful technology that is sometimes overlooked by teachers is the radio. However, as a group of elementary school children in Israel discovered, learning to be amateur radio operators cannot only open up our understanding of the world, but also can be an interesting way to develop speaking skills in English.[11] The radio has also been used as a traditional way to conduct long-distance education in some parts of the world. Although video and computers are now used frequently in long-distance English education programs, radio still plays a part in more remote and less technologically advanced areas of the world.

Another technology sometimes overlooked is the telephone. Here's an example of how a teacher used the telephone in a creative way. The teacher, Magdolna Lehmann, was teaching English to a group of employees who need to use English at work. Most of the students were confident, but one student was particularly shy, especially about using English in public and on the phone. Magdolna noticed that every time someone spoke English, she handed the receiver to her colleague, saying, "Moment, please." So, Magdolna decided to create lots of chances for this student to speak English on the phone. She not only had the student practice simulated phone calls, but she also designed rather tricky lessons at the office. On a number of occasions, Magdolna asked the shy student's colleagues to leave the office. She then had a friend call the office. At first, the shy student responded, "Please call later." However, the speaker insisted on leaving short messages, and this forced the shy student to communicate with the caller. Of course, after several days, Magdolna and the others confessed that all was not as it seemed! However, the student was not upset and found it easier to answer the phone.[12]

At the other end of the continuum is high technology, which includes both web 1.0 and 2.0 technologies. I discuss these technologies in more detail in Chapter 7, so here I will simply say web 1.0 technologies include the use of email, chat rooms, webpages, and bulletin boards, and web 2.0 include more interactive technologies, including blogging, twitter, wikis, Digital Storytelling, and more. Since I weave a variety of examples of how teachers use both web 1.0 and 2.0 digital technology into other chapters, especially in Chapter 7 and those on teaching language skills, I won't go into great detail here. However, I would like to draw attention to a few examples of how technology has been used creatively to teach English.

My first example is how two teachers, Kerry and Timothy Conrad, made use of computer technology (web 1.0) to have students create their own Class Memory Book at the end of the school year. This project not only provided language learning experiences for a class of K–12 ESL students, but also promoted a feeling of belonging for a group of low-income students who do not fit neatly into the mainstream school culture, helped build students' self-esteem, enhanced computer literacy skills, as well as gave the students something they can treasure for years to come. To accomplish this, they began early in the school year by introducing the students to the concept of a memory book. They also encouraged students to use a digital camera inside and outside the classroom. During the year, they discussed and practiced using computer technology to transfer photos, used different computer software programs, and finally processed the Memory Book. The Conrads report that the results of the project surpassed their expectations. The ESL students not only had great satisfaction and enjoyment in creating the book and writing in each other's copies at the end of the year, but they also were able to feel more a part of the larger school community, recognized by the fact that non-ESL students asked for copies of the Memory Book.[13]

My second example is about the use of digital video technology at the Marzio School, a private language institute in France. One task of the teachers at the Marzio School prepares employees to do business abroad. Although students were able to increase their abilities to communicate within the classroom walls, they were having difficulties with authentic

English when talking with people in such places as London, New York, and Texas. With this problem in mind, a team set off for several English-speaking countries, digital video camera in hand, to collect authentic oral materials that students at a beginning level could use to prepare for travel abroad. The team collected a database of 850 authentic language scenes representing 90,000 lines of speech. Although they had difficulties selecting video clips that were authentic and still comprehensible, they were able to categorize and create listening lessons on a great variety of topics such as greetings, weather, jobs, and family. Related to the use of technology, there were benefits to the fact that digital video was used, allowing students to use the computer program to maneuver quickly as they make decisions about what scenes they want to experience. For example, in lesson 10—"What's your job?"—students can click on any of 13 interviews. In addition, unlike with traditional video, it was much easier for students to listen again and again to the same sentence, skip ahead or go back to segments, and go back and forth between different interviews.[14]

What Problems Do Some EFL/ESL Teachers Have with Materials, Media, and Technology?

Problems some EFL/ESL teachers face include:

- The "I am required to teach from the book" problem
- The "let the textbook do the teaching" problem
- The "how do I locate useful websites?" problem
- The "the technology I planned to use isn't working" problem

THE "I AM REQUIRED TO TEACH FROM THE BOOK" PROBLEM

Some EFL/ESL teachers are required to follow a particular text, and they find that the administration's policy is stringent. Sometimes, actual lesson plans are provided, and supervisors make sure they are followed. When this happens, teachers can feel helpless in the face of being creative with materials and media. Unfortunately, some teachers give in under the pressure and simply follow the prescribed lessons.

However, other teachers find ways to incorporate additional materials while adapting to the prescribed lesson. They might bring in photos or pictures that correspond to the required reading to make it more vivid. They might have friends record a one-minute natural conversation based on language in a dialogue in the text. Or they might have students spend the last ten minutes of class using Scrabble® letters to spell out words found in their text and make up original sentences from these words. Some teachers also set aside days during a semester to do activities that are not related to the textbook.

Whether adapting a lesson or creating a special day every so often, the possibilities for making small changes are endless, and the changes can ultimately have big consequences on the way students interact with each other and the teacher in English.

THE "LET THE TEXTBOOK DO THE TEACHING" PROBLEM

Following a textbook has certain advantages. It saves time, and novice teachers can learn something about teaching by following a textbook closely, studying the accompanying teaching manual, and using materials from companion websites. But adhering to a textbook without considering the effects on the students—for example, whether or not they are negotiating meaning with each other and the teacher—can trivialize the experience for the students.

Of course, not all teachers accept the constraints imposed on them by the textbook. Some teachers want to be more than technicians, doing more than mindlessly following a book and its accompanying materials. They realize that textbooks are not meant to be blindly plodded through and that teaching guides are only other teachers' ways to teach lessons, which might not be appropriate for all students. They also might want to make their own informed decisions about how to teach a particular, always unique, group of students.

THE "HOW DO I LOCATE USEFUL WEBSITES?" PROBLEM

Many websites can be used to develop teaching, locate materials and lessons, and be recommended to students. These websites might be useful:

- www.breakingnewsenglish.com (Breaking News English)—Created to provide free interactive and printable English lessons on a wide variety of news stories for student Levels 1 through 7. Also includes speed-reading activities dictations, and speed-listening exercises.

- www.eslcafe.com (Dave's ESL Café)—Includes interactive resources, including the ESL Graffiti Wall, ESL Question Page, ESL Idea Page, ESL Message Exchange, ESL Quiz Center, ESL Links Pages, ESL Help Center, ESL E-mail Connection Pages, ESL Discussion Center, and the ESL Job Center.

- www.eslpartyland.com (Karin's ESL PartyLand)—Designed for ESL students and teachers, there is a student section and a teacher section. Students can find a variety of interactive quizzes, discussion forums, a chat room, and interactive lessons on a variety of topics. Teachers can find lesson plans, reproducible materials, discussion forums, ideas for communicative practice activities, a chat room, a job board, and links.

- learnenglish.britishcouncil.org/en (British Council Learn English)—Includes free video and audio lessons, grammar tasks, games, video lessons on teaching writing, and much more.

- www.onestopenglish.com (One Stop English)—Created for EFL/ESL teachers with quality content on teaching methodology and on teaching language skills, teaching grammar, teaching vocabulary, teaching children and teenagers, etc. The website is updated frequently with new resources.

- iteslj.org (The Internet TESL Journal)—This site includes an abundance of knowledge for teachers including articles on a variety of topics (e.g., teaching children, culture, grammar, learner autonomy, materials development, teaching conversation, reading, listening), lesson plans and materials, classroom activities, and more. This site is a goldmine for a new and innovative teachers.

THE "THE TECHNOLOGY I PLANNED TO USE ISN'T WORKING" PROBLEM

Here's a problem I had in Korea with technology I planned to use in the classroom: The English Education majors in their advanced communication class had spent weeks working on a research project in and outside the classroom and prepared to present what they learned to their classmates and me. The students' presentations included PowerPoint slides, video clips, and more, all of which were dependent on the classroom computer and overhead projector. But, the computer would not activate the overhead projector lamp.

Problems like this happen often in classrooms that depend on technology, and the problem is often defined by the type of task the teacher and students are working on. Sometimes the problem occurs because the network cannot handle increased traffic, or because the website server goes down, or because students cannot log onto the chat room that you planned to use. Other times it's because students didn't follow instructions. For example, even though I emphasize that students should always use a thumb drive, external hard drive, or the cloud to back up their work, I still get students who approach me in panic, "My work disappeared! The computer ate my paper!" These kinds of problems can be frustrating, and students often look to the teacher, who might or might not know what to do to solve the problem.

My advice to teachers is to expect technology to fail sometimes and to have a back-up plan. To start to solve a problem, knowing the basics might be enough. If the computer won't start, see if it is plugged in. If the overhead projector won't turn on from the computer, check to see if it has been manually turned off at the lamp or if the bulb is burned out. Simply rebooting the computer is often useful. If the basics don't work, and you are not savvy with modern technology or are simply stumped, remember that you have a classroom full of students, some who are very experienced at solving technological problems and like to help with such matters. Or, you can use Google to try to find a solution. However, if none of this works, or time is of the essence, then I recommend having a Plan B (see Chapter 2) to work out an alternative plan on the fly.

In terms of the communication class presentation day, the problem turned out to be a burned out overhead project lamp. I hadn't anticipated this, and I had no Plan B. I asked the students to give their presentations anyway by using the white board and any other resources that they might have. Some of the students became nervous and asked to postpone the presentations, especially students who relied heavily on the overheads to draw attention away from them, and used memorized lines to go along with each overhead slide. Nevertheless, we went ahead, and most of the students found that they were able to explain their project research and what they learned without the visuals. Further, when a student was not understood, some students asked clarification questions, at my encouragement. At the end of the class, I praised the students for a job well done. They had met the challenge of speaking without overheads, were truly communicative, and had learned not to depend on technology as the center piece of their communication.

TEACHER SELF-DEVELOPMENT TASKS

Talk Tasks

1. Locate three different EFL or ESL textbooks. Study the introduction and a chapter or two in each. What are some of the obvious differences in the goals of each book? In other words, what does the author/publisher of each book intend for the students to learn through the use of the book? What kinds of activities are provided? After studying the books, meet with a friend who has also reviewed a few texts. Take turns showing the text materials and discussing the goals of each book.

2. Study the lists of authentic printed, visual, and listening materials given earlier in this chapter (pages 98–99). Which do you personally find interesting? Select a combination of three or four items from the lists. Note ideas for a lesson that might use this combination of authentic materials and media. Then meet with another teacher and talk about your ideas for lessons using authentic materials.

3. Review Figure 6.3. Which kinds of technology have you used or would you like to use? How might you use this technology in your teaching?

4. Go to at least three of the websites for EFL/ESL teachers described earlier. Which sites do you find to be most interesting? Why? Talk with other teachers about the sites.

Observation and Talk Tasks

The point of this task is to consider how language-learning materials and use of technology can provide or block opportunities for students to learn English. First, pair up with another teacher. Listen to the recording of one of your classes. As you do, transcribe the interaction in the class when students are focused on using materials and/or technology. Study the transcription. Together, list several things you notice about the interaction and answer the following questions: How does the use of the material and/or technology seem to provide opportunities for the students to learn English? How does the use of the material and/or technology seem to block students? How could you use the same materials and/or technology differently?

Journal Writing Tasks

1. Write lesson ideas in which you use a variety of authentic materials and media.

2. Write your reflections on your experiences as a language learner related to the materials you have used. What kinds of materials did you study as a language learner? How did these materials seem to help you to make progress in the language you were studying? How did they possibly hinder progress?

3. Write what you learned from doing the observation and talk task on materials and/or technology and classroom interaction.

4. Do you agree that there is no best technology to teach EFL/ESL and that teachers need to select technology based on the teaching situation? Or are there learning limitations placed on teachers and students who do not have access to high technology? Write your thoughts.

RECOMMENDED TEACHER RESOURCES

Resources on Course Design and Materials & Media

Copeland, F. and S. Mann. *Developing Materials: Inside and Outside the Coursebook*. Tokyo: ABAX, 2012.

Harwood, N. *English Language Teaching Materials: Theory and Practice*. New York: Cambridge University Press, 2010.

Man, S. and F. Copeland. *Materials Development*. Alexandria, VA: TESOL, 2015.

Mishan, F. and I. Timmis. *Material Development for TESOL*. Edinburgh: Edinburgh University Press, 2015.

Murphy, J. and P. Byrd, eds. *Understanding the Courses We Teach: Local Perspectives on English Language Teaching*. Ann Arbor: University of Michigan Press, 2001.

Tomlinson, B. *Applied Linguistics and Materials Development*. London: Bloomsbury Academics, 2013.

Tomlinson, B. *Developing Materials for Language Teaching, 2nd ed.* London: Bloomsbury Publishing, 2014.

Wright, A., D. Betteridge, and M. Buckly. *Games for Language Learning, 3rd ed.* Cambridge, U.K.: Cambridge University Press, 2006.

Select Corpus-Informed ESL/EFL Grammar and Vocabulary Textbooks

Folse, K. S. *Clear Grammar 3, 2ⁿᵈ ed.* Ann Arbor: University of Michigan Press, 2015.

Folse, K. S., D. Gordon, and B. Smith-Palinkas. *Grammar for Great Writing* (Intermediate). Boston: National Geographic Publishing, 2017.

McCarthy, M. and F. O'Dell. *Academic Vocabulary in Use: Vocabulary Reference and Practice, 4ᵗʰ ed.* Cambridge, U.K.: Cambridge University Press, 2016.

McCarthy, M. and F. O'Dell. *English Vocabulary in Use.* Cambridge, U.K.: Cambridge University Press, 2014.

Reppen, R. *Grammar and Beyond* (Level 1). New York: Cambridge University Press, 2012.

ENDNOTES

1 See Ministry of Education and Training (MOET) (2006:5). Also see Minh (2007) for a history of English textbook development in Vietnam and an evaluation of textbooks presently being used.

2 From MOET (2006). Discovered in Minh (2007).

3 My knowledge about selecting a text comes out of my own extensive teaching experience, studying other teachers' syllabi and textbook selections, as well as reading and using ideas from such teacher-scholars as Graves (2000) and Munby (1981). Mann and Copland (2015).

4 See Martire (2001; 2011).

5 Compoy, Bellés-Fortuno, and Gea-Valdor (2010).

6 Reppen (2010).

7 Bennett (2010). Other corpora are listed in Appendix 1 of Bennett's book.

8 See Gershen (2015).

9 See Garber and Holmes (1981).

10 See Dobbs (2001).

11 See Freund (1997).

12 For a fuller account of this telephone lesson, see Gebhard, Fodor, and Lehmann (2003).

13 See Conrad and Conrad (2002) for a fuller account.

14 See Marzio (2000) for a more detailed account of the digital video project.

7

One temptation teachers face when they discover a new technology is to consider the technology first ("How can I use Facebook in my classroom?") rather than first evaluating which technology will best fit the nature of literacy.
—Bloch and Wilkinson, 2014, 3

Digital Literacy, Technology, and Teaching EFL/ESL

▌ *What is digital literacy?*

▌ *What kinds of digital technology are available to EFL/ESL teachers and students?*

▌ *What are examples of how EFL/ESL teachers and students have used digital technology?*

▌ *What is the future of digital technology and teaching EFL/ESL?*

▌ *What problems are associated with the use of digital technology?*

What Is Digital Literacy?

Can you attach a photo to an email? Can you upload a video and share it on YouTube? Create your own blog? Remix a video with a sound track? Do you know what a *wiki* is? What is the difference between *asynchronous* and *synchronous* technology? What is a *blogroll*? What does *trackback* mean? What is the difference between *trackback* and *pingback*? If you can answer these questions, then you are likely digitally literate, and if you were born into the digital age, you probably know quite a lot even if you don't know the technological words in my questions. But, stay with me as I discuss how it can be used in the EFL/ESL classroom, my thoughts on the future of digital technology, and the kinds of problems that are associated with the use of digital technology.

Digital literacy[1] includes skills, knowledge, and behaviors that we use with a variety of digital devices, including desktop computers, laptops, tablets, smartphones, and other devices (some likely not yet invented!). Although digital technology relies on computer chips, digital literacy is distinct from computer literacy. Computer literacy centers on practical skills associated with using traditional desktop and personal computers and software. As I discuss later in more detail, digital literacy has gone beyond computer literacy in that a digital literate person has a wide array of digital abilities—for example, how to digitally interact with online communities and through social networking, create and maintain a blog, as well as how to use an array of software to complete a project, such as a personal photostory with photographs, music, and video.

Digital literacy can be categorized into sub-literacies. First, there is computer literacy, which includes being able to connect hardware devices, install software, and use application packages. Second, there is network literacy, which includes being able to use a global network of interlinked computing devices. Although at first network literacy seems somewhat simplistic, it isn't. It includes being able to navigate the internet and within different networks, locating information, people, and communities, evaluating the trustworthiness of different sites, allowing others to find you online, joining online networks to become a part of conversations, understanding how to set up accounts with different networks, knowing how to protect your privacy and identity, understanding appropriate network etiquette, managing your reputation, listing, posting, commenting, and more.

Third, there is information literacy, which is also complex. While searching online (and offline) information literacy includes our ability to identify what information we need, understand how the information is organized, identify the most relevant sources of information for our given need, find those sources, evaluate the integrity of the information (e.g., is it current, biased or misleading?), evaluate the source of the information (e.g., is the author an expert in the field or someone pretending to be? is the source credible?) and possibly share that information. In other words, as the word *literacy* implies, people who are literate can read, write, and think critically. When a person is **digitally literate,** they can do these things through a multitude of devices, including how to locate, summarize, evaluate, and communicate information while using digital technologies, and through a variety of hardware platforms (computer hardware, cell phones, and other mobile devices) and with the use of software or applications.

Further, there are different forms of online digital literacy. One form is Web 1.0, which can be described as "a set of techniques characterized by static and non-interactive webpages and proprietary software design."[2] Web 1.0 digital literacies include the use of webpage design, email, and bulletin boards. One main characteristic of Web 1.0 technology is that it is an *asynchronous* form of discourse, meaning that data is sent in one direction. For example, when someone sends an email or posts a message on an online bulletin board it is an asynchronous.

Although Web 1.0 digital technology and associated literacies are still useful and popular, the creation of Web 2.0 has further revolutionized the different technologies and the forms of literacy associated with them.[3] To begin, technology with Web 2.0 has become more *synchronous*, meaning discourse can occur simultaneously. Web 2.0 encourages participation in the creation of content, and this content can have a level of multimodality. It can include video, music, and remixing texts with images, and this content can be shared with a single or multiple classmates and throughout the world.

I do not want to give the impression that digital literacy is exclusively connected to the use of the internet. Although knowing how to use online digital technology is certainly a big part of being digitally literate, digital literacy includes the use of technology offline, too. For example, digital literacy includes such things as knowing how to remix and audiorecorded a story with images, video and music.

As I discuss in the next section on the kinds of digital technology available to EFL/ESL teachers and students, digital technology has given us a great variety of ways to create and share content, including, but not limited to, the use of blogs, wikis, video sites like YouTube, social networking sites like Facebook, and video chat conferences. Further, as discussed later, new technology has also made it possible for students creatively to change the way they learn English—for example, how to use digital video and audio technology, combined with other technology, such as PowerPoint. The processes of creating these projects can include using the internet to create and maintain blogs, the use of wikis to collaboratively create text, and more.

What Kinds of Digital Technology Are Available to EFL/ESL Teachers and Students?

A wide variety of digital technological tools are accessible to EFL/ESL teachers and students. Some of these are services on the internet, such as email and Twitter® and are connected to websites. Other tools are computer programs that allow teachers and students to create their own materials. Here I consider some of these tools and how teachers and students might use them.

As we already know, one technology, *email,* has been around for a long time, and it is a popular for several reasons. Since email is asynchronous, it allows students, teachers, and colleagues to communicate over a period of time, and we can connect at our own convenience and schedule. Email also has the advantage of being able to involve people from different time zones, if the teaching-learning context calls for this, as well as in capturing the history of the interactions, allowing for collective knowledge to be more easily shared and dispersed.

Text messaging and **instant messaging (IMing)** have become a popular way to communicate as well, enabling us to create a private chat room with another person in order to communicate in real time. Although some users call both text messaging and instant messaging *texting*, there is a difference. Text messaging is a phone feature, and the mobile phone carrier bills the user separately. IM is a computer feature and uses a data plan but is free with some applications, such as Facebook. IM allows instant messaging over the internet as opposed to a phone network service but can be accessed from a portable device, such as smartphone. The main advantage of instant messaging is that it allows for seamless video, photo and text chatting with individuals or groups.

The convenience of IM, along with the notifications whenever somebody on your private list is online, makes this form of communication attractive. It is popular because, unlike email, the text can be read right away. I've used instant messaging with students for many reasons. If a student is not in class, I send a text to ask if there is a problem. I have even sent a short video clip with the class shouting out simultaneously, "We miss you!" I have also used it to follow up on conversations I have had with students in class, such as, "You didn't hand in your essay today. See you on Tuesday with your essay! Hand it in no later than Tuesday. Okay?"

I use Standard English while texting with students, and I ask EFL/ESL students to do the same with me. However, one issue is that texting has its own abbreviated English. For example, I could have written: "U didn't hand in UR essay today. CU Tues w/ UR essay! Hand in no L8R! K?" The issue is that students need to learn how to text in English to socialize on line using SMS language, but they also need to learn Standard English. So, I encourage them to use some common abbreviations like B4, AFAIK, LOL, U, BFN, BTW, BRB, GTG, PLZ, L8R, PPL (and often lower-cased), and other abbreviations while texting with others, but to use Standard English with me. In addition to using two forms of English, this provides a way for them to consider how the use of English is contextually based.

Most readers will know how to use the social network Twitter,® so, I will only briefly discuss it here. Through Twitter® students can use English to communicate with each through short messages, as well as images. I encourage students to use Twitter® because they can follow topics they like, such as sports or fashion, as well as contribute to an ongoing discussion. As an out-of-class assignment, I have asked students to follow a topic and then to write about what they learn either as an essay or in a blog.

One of the most useful technologies for EFL/ESL teaching and learning is **blogging.** For those of you who already blog, you know that it is used to describe websites that maintain an ongoing history of information on an array of topics. We can log onto public blogs to read and comment on entries written by the owner of the blog or others. Some blogs have links to articles on other websites and range from personal to retail to political to educational topics and can focus on one narrow subject or a whole assortment of subjects. Many blogs focus on a particular topic, such as sports, home improvement, mobile technology, web design, and most relevant to this book, teaching and learning EFL/ESL. Some blogs, though, are more like personal journals in which the writer discusses her or his daily life and thoughts.

Blogs tend to have a few things in common.[4] First, a main content area with posts is listed chronologically, newest on top. Often, they are organized into categories. Second, there is an accessible archive of older posts. This is often done in chronological order by date, but it could be organized alphabetically or in creative ways. Third, there is a way for people to leave comments about the posts. As I will discuss later, this is a feature that can be very useful to ESL/EFL students and teachers. Fourth, there is often a list of links to other related sites, sometimes called a *blogroll*. These are also very useful to students, especially if they are researching a topic. Fifth, blogs can have single or multiple authors. Being able to have multiple authors provides students with opportunities to make a blog a part of a collective classroom group project. This is the case of a collaborative photostory project done by students in Taiwan, discussed later in this chapter.

As with the teacher in Taiwan, EFL/ESL teachers have asked students to create their own blogs as a part of their English language learning experience. Some have used a free WordPress blogging tool (<u>wordpress.com</u>), as well as the blogging tool on <u>Blog.com</u> and <u>blooger.com</u>. They provide easy steps to set up the blog of space.

A **wiki** is another Web 2.0 technology that can be useful to teachers and students. A wiki is a server program that allows users to collaborate in forming the content of a website that allows users to add, delete, or revise content by using a web browser. One of the fun things about wikis is that a document can be created by a collaborative effort of the site visitors. An example of a well-known wikis is the Wikipedia, a free encyclopedia in many languages that visitors can edit or make additions or corrections simply by clicking on the Edit This Page button. However, most pages are regulated so that only invited guests can contribute. Most wikis are more open to collaborators but requests to join the wikis are required. This is protection for the organizer who wants to have some control over the content. It's fun to add that the term *wiki* comes from the Hawaiian phrase *wiki wiki*, which means, "really really fast," a name appropriate to the speed through the site can grow!

In support of educators, there are several (wiki) hosts that allow teachers to have classroom wiki that are advertisement-free. One of these is <u>wikispaces.com</u>.

A multimodal digital literacy that has become popular is **digital storytelling,** an easy form of digital media production that lets ordinary people produce facets of their lives, play with creative imagining, and more. This technology provides the means for users to create video with sound, animation, photos, and other electronic media. This form of storytelling arose with the start of accessible media production techniques, hardware and software, including but not limited to digital cameras, digital voice recorders, iMovie (Apple), and Windows Movie Maker. To learn more about how to create a digital story, I encourage you to log onto the Center of Digital Storytelling (http://storycenter.org). Those new to making audio and videos recordings with digital technology will likely appreciate DIVIS (www.popullar.eu), a website for teachers in Europe that encourages students to produce their own music with video. Another use of technology that can ease us into telling stories through electronic mediums is Fotobabble (www.fotobabble.com). This website allows you to upload photos and add an audio commentary and then post the photos on Facebook and other social websites.

These technologies allow individuals to share their stories over the internet on YouTube, Vimeo, and other electronic sharing systems. However, EFL teachers and students can also use this same technology as a way to learn English and gain digital literacy. They can work individually or collaboratively and have their own showings. I provide examples of how teachers have used MyBrainShark and Digital Storytelling in the next section and in Part III of this book.

What Are Examples of How EFL/ESL Teachers and Students Have Used Digital Technology?

My objective in answering this question is to show a variety of different ways teachers have used digital technology in their classrooms. I begin with how cell phone technology has been used as an attempt to enhance students' learning. Although this first example is not about learning English, it is included because this activity could easily be used in an EFL/ESL course. In this activity, teacher-researchers in Cyprus integrated cellphone use into an undergraduate course studying local environmental issues.[5] The students took photos of local places that they thought contributed to pollution and sent the teacher-researchers the photos, which the teachers then organized on the project website. The students could access the site to view and comment on the photos submitted by their classmates and themselves. I like this activity because of its simplicity and collaborative efforts that are taken by the class members. I also like way the students could comment on each other's photos. Personally, I would take this activity one step further by asking groups of students to select a local environmental issue, ask each group to create a wiki, and then create a collaborative document that could be shared with classmates and even posted online.

Another activity is having students produce a cellphone video diary. One teacher-researcher at a Japanese university asked her students to use their cellphones to video record their thoughts and opinions on topics they thought were relevant to them.[6] They stored their video recordings on a video storage website where they could tell stories and give comments in English about why each video was important to them. Their topics varied from a dinner with a student's family to a daily bicycle commute to the university. Students produced and commented on one video each week. They also uploaded some video files and posted them online, and they were able to share their videos and comments and stories with their classmates. The comments were used as the authentic content for class discussion, which encouraged them to become more inquisitive.

The next example in the use of technology took place in a course taught in Taiwan at a private college.[7] All first-year students are required to take a course titled Internet English; the objectives of this course are to further develop students' listening, speaking, reading, and writing as well as internet skills by doing a variety of activities using internet resources. The classroom setup made it possible to create a blended learning environment in which online technology was integrated into all the learning activities. The class met in a computer lab so that students would have access to the internet. Although students met in a classroom, they also used a *Yahoo Group* to maintain online communication. The syllabus and course materials were archived on this Yahoo Group site, and it linked students to websites that could be useful to students. A class wiki was also created and used to exhibit student-produced projects. The course also included the use of blogs (www.blogger.com). Students learned to create blogs at the beginning of the year, and their blogs served as learning portfolios that included everything they had accomplished in the course.

One of the activities in the course was a photostory project, which included the use of PowerPoint and Windows Movie Maker. Students worked in small groups of five and were asked to create one five-minute audio-visual resource about an artist of their choice. The teacher also asked them to add music that reflected the mood of the art. The teacher defined a photostory as "the arrangement of songs (English) and photographs or digital images of illustrations, drawings, sketches, or any visual artwork in a creative manner to tell a compelling story."[8]

One of my favorite activities is a digital identity project done with 18 middle school English language students in Toronto. The goal of the project was to provide chances for students to reflect on their identities, a complex undertaking for adolescents who are assimilating into a new culture while still maintaining aspects of their ancestral culture. Most of the students had been in Canada for less than one year and came from Asia.[9] These students were asked to create digital stories or poems in which they were asked to describe themselves with video to show their dynamic, multifaceted, and relational identities. Students searched for images, music, and video clips online and kept these items in a digital folder. As some of the students had had minimum computer experience, they were also given lessons on how to do internet searches, create folders on a shared network drive, download music and videos, save images, use Windows Movie Maker, use Photo Story software, and more.

What Is the Future of Digital Technology and Teaching EFL/ESL?

I include this question because technology is changing quickly. Not many years ago Web 2.0 technology and consequent use of blogs, wikis, video sites like YouTube, and social networking sites like Facebook and LinkedIn were not yet conceivable. I believe the same holds true for the future of technology. Perhaps Web 3.0 technology is already on the horizon or perhaps something non-digital will outdate digital technology, much like DVDs made VCR tapes obsolete and digital downloading is making CDs and DVDs obsolete.

Mark Warschauer, a long-time student and teacher of educational technology, may have the most insight into the future of technology and teaching English.[10] He believes that the emergence of a new platform of global capitalism, which is termed **informationalism,** will have consequences on the way that English is taught. He believes that new information technologies will transform the way we understand literacy. English users will need to gain digital literacy that allows them to navigate and do research on the internet, as well as be skilled at interpreting and authoring hypermedia (mixed use of graphics, audio, video, plain text, and hyperlinks). As this chapter has discussed, Warschauer emphasizes that digital literacy will become the norm. Due to economic and employment developments, non-native speakers will use English on a daily basis by presenting complex ideas and collaborating and negotiating with others from different cultural backgrounds through the use of technology.

In addition, technology will further enhance globalization, and this will expedite the spread of English as an International Language (EIL), as opposed to distinguishing between only EFL and ESL. This change will place more focus on teaching and learning English as an international language where English is spoken between more people when it is not the first language, and will change our notions of language, culture, and contextual use of English. EIL gives authority to the English used by non-native speakers, so the norm will shift from trying to teach and master native varieties of English (U.S., Canadian, British, or Australian). Warschauer highlights that curricula used in many English classrooms today, which are often based on grammar and functional elements of narrowly defined activities, will be ineffective. Rather, project-based learning, such as the ones I discussed on pages 63 and 117–120, will be essential if students are to master the complex English literacy and interactive skills required to function in a future global society.

However, although Warschauer is basing his ideas on current trends, we should not forget that the future holds surprises. World events could shift emphasis away from English. China, for example, has been deemphasizing the importance of teaching English in schools and placing more emphasis on Chinese language and culture. Is this a sign of changes to come? New technologies could also have an unpredictable consequence on the importance of English and how it is used.

What Problems Are Associated with the Use of Digital Technology?

Some of the problems EFL/ ESL teachers face with the use of digital technology include:

- the "digital native student and digital immigrant teacher" problem
- the "digital divide" problem
- the "phones in the classroom" problem

THE "DIGITAL NATIVE STUDENT AND DIGITAL IMMIGRANT TEACHER" PROBLEM

A **digital native**[11] is a person who was born into the digital age, and many of the today's students studying English are digital natives. They have been using digital technology their entire lives, although simply being a digital native does not make the student or teacher digitally literate. More likely, like with traditional literacy, some students are highly literate and others are less so.

A **digital immigrant** is a person who was born before the digital age and who has adapted to digital technology. Digital immigrants grew up, for the most part, with pre-digital technology. Older teachers like myself, as well as older EFL and ESL students, for example, grew up using a typewriter, audio cassette player, reel-to-reel tape players, VHS recorders, and dial telephones. I can remember being very creative with the newest technology. I still have reel-to-reel recordings of my grandfather singing southern folksongs from the late 1800s and early 1900s (now digitally mastered.) Many others were born into a world using desktop computers, CD players, and DVD players.

However, no matter when a digital immigrant teacher was born, many of us have adapted to the newest technology, and some (like me) embraced technological change. I enjoyed learning to use Microsoft products, and I learned to use every generation of software. I also learned to use Apple software and have kept up with technological advances with each. During the past few years I have enjoyed discovering new uses of Web 2.0 technology and am an active user of Facebook, Google, and other websites and use modern technology to create digital stories, interesting PowerPoint presentations, language learning activities, and more.

I have explained my brief history with the use of technology because I want to emphasize that some digital immigrants have adapted to the digital culture, partly out of necessity and partly out of interest. Nonetheless, we likely do have *digital accents*.[12] However, other language teachers have not kept up with technological change, and this is where the problem is. Technology has changed the way many students read, and process information. When faced with a teacher who has not adapted to technological advances, some students can become bored and misunderstood and, might be tempted to cheat (for example, by locating an essay online to turn in to a teacher who the student knows cannot use technology to spot plagiarism.); others might become distant from classmates and the teacher because the course does not have a class blog and other technology that makes the students feel part of a learning community.

THE "DIGITAL DIVIDE" PROBLEM

The **digital divide** is about those who have access to digital technology and the development of digital literacy and those who do not. Many of us are privileged to have access to portable digital technology—the latest smartphones, laptops, and other hardware—as well as access to people around us who support our use of the latest digital literacies. However, not everyone has such access. Although most people in the world today, including in some of the most remote areas within third world countries, have cellphones, there is still a very big divide between those who can fully make use of digital technology and those who can not.

This divide can affect teachers who have been born into the digital age and want to make use of digital technology while teaching but are faced with teaching students who are not digitally literate. Such classrooms might include adult education, immigrant, refugee, and EFL teaching in third world countries. However, although there are restraints, such as teaching English in places where students grow up in poverty or are constrained by the educational and social system, it does not mean that modern technology cannot be used.

Some immigrants to Canada, the United States, Britain, Australia, and other countries where modern technology has become important are faced with becoming digitally literate. If the teacher is lucky, the digitally challenged will have classmates who have already gained digital literacy, and they can become teachers. Such students might need to learn how to create, open, and save files; categorize and download files; conduct internet searches; open and negotiate webpages; and complete other very basic computer tasks before they can turn their attention to creating a blog, working on a wiki project, remixing a video with audio, or work on a storytelling project.

THE "PHONES IN THE CLASSROOM" PROBLEM

What do you think of students who bring phones into the classroom? Some teachers in some contexts complain that students are texting friends or looking up answers, checking email, during class. Most of these teachers think this is disrespectful and have a "no phone" rule in their classrooms. Some teachers even collect the phones at the start of class or ask students to turn off their phones and put them in a box at the door or in front of the class. However, other teachers find that phones can be a useful tool and encourage students to use their phones in a way that complements their language learning.

My own opinion is to allow students to use their phones in class if they are using it for a purpose that supports the classroom learning experience. For example, students might want to use an online dictionary, Google, or a blog that is related the lesson. They might also use their phones to practice making phone calls in English while doing role-play activities. Here are some examples:

- In a high-beginning class, one student could play the role of a pizza shop owner and another student could order a pizza. Students would have a chance to practice asking for and giving an address, name, kind of pizza, and phone number.

- Students could practice telling time while speaking aloud in groups and as a whole class by telling time in different time zones around the world. For example, "It's twelve thirty five PM here. Japan is thirteen hours ahead of us. So, it is one thirty five AM in Japan."

- The teacher might ask students to use the phone calculator to practice listening to and saying numbers. For instance, "What is 12 times 301 divided by 6?"

- The teacher might ask students to use their phone to look up synonyms to words during a reading lesson.

- The teacher could ask the students to use their phones to videorecord skits they put on in front of the class and to then make short transcriptions of the actual language used, asking students to analyze the transcripts, spot errors, and study non-verbal behavior.

In short, the phone can be a valuable tool when used for a purpose in the classroom, and although some students might check email or send text messages, if it is not disruptive and the student is still paying attention, why not? Isn't this something we do on a daily basis anyway with discretion?

TEACHER SELF-DEVELOPMENT TASKS

Talk Tasks

1. What is digital literacy?

2. What are creative ways to use Web 1.0 technology as a teaching tool with EFL/ESL students? There is no right or wrong answer to this question. Use your inventiveness!

3. What experience do you have with using Web 2.0 technology? Talk about your experience with others. Ask them about their experience.

4. What are creative ways to use Web 2.0 technology as a teaching tool with EFL/ESL students? There is no right or wrong answer to this question. Use your imagination!

5. Talk with two or three people who have been learning English as a foreign, second, or international language. Ask them if they use SMS language (e.g., B4, LOL, BTW…) when they text. Ask them if they compose texts in abbreviated English or try to use Standard English. What have you learned?

6. If a student does not know how to use SMS language to text, as a teacher, would you teach the student how to text with it? Why or why not?

7. What do you think the future use of technology will be in teaching EFL/ESL? Think creatively.

Observation and Talk Tasks

1. Find a public place where you can observe what people are doing with cellphones. How are they using their phones? If possible, meet with others who have done the same observation. Compare what you have observed.

2. If possible, observe a class in which the teacher and students are using current technology. Ask the teacher or a student how you could see the course syllabus? (Is it posted on a course blog?) Try to find out what the goals of the course are and the kinds of activities that students are doing to reach these goals. Then, observe the class. What are they doing? How are they doing it? Are the students immersed in the activity? If possible, talk to a student after the class. How do they like the course? Could you see yourself using similar technology to teach an EFL or ESL course?

Journal Writing Tasks

1. Write about your experience using Web 2.0 technology. For example, have you ever kept a blog? Worked on a wiki project with someone?

2. Write about one of the problems associated with digital technology and teaching ESL/EFL I discussed earlier in this chapter.

3. How interested are you in using video as a teaching tool? What teaching ideas do you have?

4. Go to some of the websites included in this chapter. Write about what you have learned.

RECOMMENDED TEACHER RESOURCES

Bloch, J. *Technologies in the Second Language Composition Classroom.* Ann Arbor: University of Michigan Press, 2008.

Bloch, J. and M.J Wilkinson. *Teaching Digital Literacies.* Alexandria, VA: TESOL, 2014.

Li, H., N. Gromik, and N. Edwards, eds. *ESL and Digital Video Integration: Case Studies.* Alexandria, VA: TESOL, 2012.

Lotherington, H. and J. Jenson. "Teaching Multimodal and Digital Literacy in L2 Settings." *Annual Review of Applied Linguistics,* 31 (2011): 226–46.

Rose, G. *Perspectives on Teaching Adults English in the Digital World.* Alexandria, VA: TESOL, 2015.

Sokolik, M. "Digital Technology in Language Teaching." In *Teaching English as a Second or Foreign Language, 4th ed.,* eds. M. Celce-Murcia, D.M. Brinton, and M.A. Snow. Boston: Heinle Cengage, 2014.

ENDNOTES

1 This definition stems my experience, as well as from reading Bloch (2008), Bloch and Wilkinson (2014), Li, Gromik and Edwards (2012), Lotherington and Jenson (2011), Rose (2015), and Sokolik (2014). I also consulted https://en.wikipedia.org/wiki/Digital_literacy.

2 Bloch and Wilkinson (2014, p. 8).

3 Bloch (2007), Bloch and Wilkinson (2014) and Zukerman (2003) have broadened my understanding of Web 2.0 technologies and literacies.

4 I found these common blog items on www.codex.wordpress.org.

5 See Uzunboylu, Cavus, and Ercag (2009).

6 See Gromik (2012).

7 Yeh (2012) describes this course in more detail.

8 Yeh (2012:66).

9 See Eamer and Hughes (2012).

10 See Warschauer (2012).

11 Marc Prensky (2013) coined the terms *digital native* and *digital immigrant.*

12 I discovered *digital accent* in Prensky (2013).

Culture is the shared assumptions, values, and beliefs of a group of people which results in characteristic behaviors.

—Storti 1997, 5

Culture and the Language Teacher

I *What is a reasonable working definition of* culture?

I *What cultural adjustment process do many expatriates experience?*

I *What are the benefits of adjusting to another culture?*

I *What cultural concepts can EFL/ESL teachers teach students?*

I *What problems do some EFL/ESL teachers have related to culture and language teaching and learning?*

What Is a Reasonable Working Definition of *Culture*?

Although there are many ways to define *culture,* here it refers to the common values and beliefs of a people and the behaviors that reflect them. At the risk of overgeneralizing, it is possible to talk about common beliefs and values and about how they can differ from culture to culture, as well as the behaviors associated with them.

To illustrate how values and beliefs can vary, let's look at the way people make use of time in two different cultures: mainstream North America and

Saudi Arabia. Time, for the average American, is very important. Americans are constantly setting deadlines based on time and will end conversations before they may be finished by looking at their watches and saying, "Oh! Excuse me! I have to go or I'll be late." American English is filled with references to time. Time is something to be on, spent, gained, kept, filled, killed, saved, used, wasted, lost, and planned.

In contrast, Arabs see time as flowing through time.[1] Social events and appointments do not always have fixed beginnings or endings. If a time for an appointment has been set, under many circumstances, it is acceptable to be late, especially if the person is engaged in a conversation. It would be rude to leave in the middle of it, since maintaining friendships and engaging in human interaction are more highly valued than being on time.

Another example of how values and behaviors across cultures can differ concerns the value associated with avoiding conflict and maintaining harmony. While some Americans value direct confrontation to solve conflicts, people from Asian countries generally value avoiding confrontations. They have developed subtle, indirect ways to resolve conflict. For example, if a person in Japanese society is upset with someone, he or she will likely not confront the other person directly but will behave in a particular way, such as being unusually silent or ignoring the person, providing the other person with clues that there is a problem.[2] Likewise, many Thais will avoid direct confrontation by being indirect. For example, if a Thai is angry at her friend, she will be indirect, perhaps by talking with another friend about the problem within earshot of the offending friend. Or she might invite everyone except the offending friend to eat lunch with her. For some Americans, especially males, being indirect would seem dishonest and insincere. Distrust can result. For many Asians, blatant, blunt, direct confrontation would disrupt the highly valued harmony among people.

Quite often, values and beliefs of a group of people have a deep philosophical foundation. For example, traditional Islamic Arab values can be traced in almost every respect to the Koran. The belief that God alone, not humans, can control all events derives from the teachings in this holy book, as does the belief that each person's fate is in the hands of God. Likewise, Theravada Buddhism is at the heart of traditional Thai beliefs. For example, the belief that emotional extremes should be avoided stems from Buddhist teachings.

What Cultural Adjustment Process Do Many Expatriates Experience?

Most of us have mixed emotions about moving to another country. This is true for those of us who have relocated to teach EFL, as well as students going abroad to study. We are excited about the prospect of a new way of life. We are delighted about discovering obvious differences: the shape of buildings, the products in stores, and the way people dress. However, as we find places to live, begin our jobs or begin to study, and use the transportation system, we feel the impact of the culture on our lives. We discover that we have to think about, even prepare for, the simplest daily activities, such as paying bills, buying food, doing laundry, taking a bus, and using a telephone. These activities soon weigh on us, resulting in culture shock. As one Peace Corps volunteer said: "In a very real sense, all the convenient cultural cushions we have become accustomed to having around are totally dislodged. You're left with only that within you for support."[3]

Some of us exhibit symptoms of culture shock. We may become depressed or nervous and may complain about the food, the weather, housing, and the host people's behavior. We might become physically ill, make irrational comments, have fits of anger over minor incidents, or become very homesick, spending endless hours online with friends and family back home.

Some of us react to culture shock by withdrawing. We stay home, sleep, and generally avoid contact with people in the host culture. Some of us temporarily withdraw to the expatriate community to ease the symptoms, seeking refuge from everyday problems by avoiding participation in the host culture. Some end up staying in this safe harbor, since it is familiar and comfortable. However, by surrendering to the seemingly more pleasant world of people like ourselves, we sacrifice dreams; our visions of making friends, learning the language, and living among the people of the host culture becomes blurred. For some of us, what was a pleasant refuge becomes a void in which life can become vaguely unsatisfying.

Although some of us seek refuge in the expatriate community to escape culture shock, others of us continue to endure, despite the discomfort. Instead of withdrawing, we reach out into the larger community, making friends and working out problems as they arise. We reflect on and learn from our experiences, and as we do this, we start to realize that we are adjusting. Everyday life becomes routine. We can get on a crowded bus like a native, give exact change for a purchase, have fun at a party, visit a friend in the hospital, play games that were once foreign to us.

Such adjustments are typified by an understanding that cultural behaviors and values are simply different. We still have cultural stress and problems to contend with, but we become more empathetic, understanding that people in the host culture have been raised in a culture different from our own. Likewise, we "develop a greater ability to tolerate and cope with the external cultural patterns. . . . We acquire alternative ways of behaving, feeling, and responding to others."[4] As we adjust, self-confidence increases, and as we interact freely, a new self-image emerges, a new identity as a participant in the host culture. Quite often, when it is time to return home, some of us are sad to leave, and there are those in the host culture who are sad that we are leaving.

What Are the Benefits of Adjusting to Another Culture?

Although adjusting to another culture can be an arduous experience, there are benefits that make the effort worthwhile. The benefits of successful cultural adjustment include:

- a fuller sense of security
- the possibility of greater success in the workplace
- the possibility of establishing meaningful relationships with people from the culture
- the possibility of gaining fluency in the language of the host country
- a deeper understanding of one's own culture
- a deeper understanding of oneself.

Storti points out that when living in another culture, "ignorance is the breeding ground for anxiety."[5] When we attempt to interact with people in the culture without knowing what is expected of us or what to expect, we become apprehensive. However, the more we learn about the culture through our experience, the easier it is to make predictions, and this can reduce apprehension. Another benefit for some EFL teachers and international students is that friendships with local people can develop over the course of living and working in the culture, and indeed, these friendships can become life-long. As we gain confidence through practice (and study) and control over the language and use of and culturally appropriate behavior, and as the local people get to know us, friendships develop. Although previously isolated, we are now invited to weddings and local religious events, to homes for dinner, and to participate in sports events.

Those of us who have successfully adjusted to the host culture also discover that we have a better understanding of our own culture. When in our own countries, most of us do not necessarily have opportunities to reflect deeply on our cultural selves as profoundly as we do during the cultural adjustment process. Having to face living in a place where values and behaviors are different from our own provides a way to reflect on our own values and behaviors. In short, after encountering another frame of reference, we can see what we never could before.

What Cultural Concepts Can EFL/ESL Teachers Teach Students?

Teachers can teach concepts that not only can bring about appreciation for people and culture, but also can be useful for students when placed in cross-cultural communication situations. In this section I address four of these concepts, and I include activities that aim at teaching these concepts to EFL students. The four concepts are:

- Cross-cultural communication includes adapting behavior.
- Cross-cultural communication involves problem-solving.
- To understand a culture, get to know individuals.
- To understand another culture, study your own.

CROSS-CULTURAL COMMUNICATION INCLUDES ADAPTING BEHAVIOR

A part of learning to communicate with people from other cultures is knowing how to adapt one's behaviors, including nonverbal and socio-cultural behaviors.

Non-Verbal Behaviors across Cultures

Non-verbal behavior includes kinesics, haptics, and proxemics. **Kinesics** includes body posture, gestures, stance, and movement. **Haptics** includes people's use of touch, while **proxemics** includes the use of space. In this section I point out and illustrate how these types of non-verbal behaviors differ across cultures, ways in which they can be problematic during interaction, and activities teachers can use to teach students about these differences.[6]

To introduce non-verbal differences across cultures, I often begin by teaching students that people in different cultures walk differently. To illustrate how people walk in different cultures, I ask volunteer students to let me follow them around the room, and I match their way of walking. Then, we reverse roles. I walk; they imitate. After doing this, I ask students how important they think it is, while living in another country, to change their way of walking. Some students think I am being silly (or even crazy!). But as the discussion goes on, they hear stories about how foreigners bump into people in crowded streets, trip people, even stop traffic because they are not walking like the people from the culture.

I also give lessons on how people shake hands differently in different cultures. For example, I show students that some Germans use a firm grip, pump the arm, and maintain strong eye contact while stepping closer during the handshake. Some Japanese use a weak grip, no arm pump, and no eye contact. I have students practice these different culturally adapted handshakes, and we talk about why it is important to be able to change the way we shake hands. We talk about the international acceptance of the handshake as a form of greeting between people from different cultural backgrounds, and we discuss how adapting our way of shaking hands when visiting a country shows respect to those we meet. Further, we discuss how misinterpretations can result if we do not adapt our ways. For example, based on a handshake, Americans sometimes misinterpret Germans as too aggressive and the Japanese as shy or passive.

Gestures can also be considered a part of **kinesic** behavior. Some gestures are emblematic, which means they represent meaning without using words. Some examples include a thumbs-up gesture, a two-finger peace sign, a hand movement to beckon another person to come to you, waving goodbye, and a head nod to say no. Although the meaning of some of these gestures is the same across cultures, such as the peace sign and a wave goodbye, other gestures can be quite different depending on how they are done, and even can be insulting in another culture.

For example, in the United States most people will beckon you to come to them by extending their hand, palm toward their face, and moving their fingers toward themselves. However, this gesture can annoy some Thais who are not fully aware of what the gesture means to Americans because this hand gesture is how they call animals to come to them, and it is important (at least at a subconscious level) within Thai society to differentiate between living beings at different status levels. The King is the highest; Buddhist monks are especially respected; and successful people and teachers come next, followed by workers, and so on. Beggars, prisoners, and animals are very low within the status system. In this regard, Thais will only beckon beings lower than themselves, such as animals, using the U.S. gesture. Instead, they beckon people at equal or higher status to come to them by extending their arm, keeping the palm down, then moving their wrist and fingers up and down and toward themselves.

Another area of non-verbal behavior that varies from culture to culture is touch. For example, American males touch each other more often and on more body parts than do Japanese males.[7] However, when compared to Arabs, Latin Americans, and Southern Europeans, these same Americans do not touch much at all. Since touch is a very personal behavior, it is well worth making students aware that differences in touching behavior exist. For example, most Thais do not like to be touched on the head by people they do not know very well, and some mothers will become annoyed if someone touches their children's heads. As such, an American might get into trouble if she or he playfully rubs a child's head.[8] Another example is greetings within some Latino cultures. Quite often a greeting can include touching the upper part of the left arm while shaking hands, but when this form of touch is used with a North American, it might be considered too familiar and result in a subtle misunderstanding of intentions.

Related to touch is **proxemics** or the use of space and distance, and this can also vary greatly across cultures. According to Edward T. Hall,[9] middle-class white Americans tend to keep a personal space of 1½ to 4 feet during informal contact with friends. However, people raised in other cultures adhere to different rules. For instance, for many Arabs the space used for ordinary social conversation is close to that used by North Americans in intimate conversation.[10] Arabs tend to stand and sit very close. Latin Americans, Greeks, and Turks are also from high-contact cultures and will also stand and sit much closer during everyday social interaction than those from low-contact cultures, such as North Americans, Northern Europeans, and Asians. People from low-contact cultures, when interacting with people who like contact, will back away, feeling very uncomfortable and perceiving the people who like high contact as invading their private space. Those from high-contact cultures might interpret this behavior as being distant and unfriendly.

As teachers, we can provide students with chances to gain awareness of the differences. Showing students clips from films and videotapes that record natural interaction of people from different culture—using intimate, personal, and social space in different cultural contexts—can sometimes bring about awareness. We can also have students from the same cultural backgrounds measure the distance they sit from one another while doing pair work, then compare this with the distance between members of other cultures. Choreographed role plays and dramas can offer another way for students to experience the distance they would encounter in a culture opposite from their own.

Sociocultural Behaviors across Cultures

In addition to nonverbal aspects of culture, EFL students can benefit from exposure to socio-cultural behaviors that follow the rules of speaking. These include the appropriate ways people interact in social settings, such as how to greet, make promises, approve, disapprove, show regret, apologize, request, complain, give gifts, compliment, invite, refuse an invitation, offer, and thank. The ways people in different cultures do these things are often quite different, although there is some similarity across some cultures.

To illustrate how these behaviors can be different across cultures, let's look at gift giving. In many countries, a person visiting a friend on a special occasion will take a gift. In America, the hostess will open the gift and thank the person. However, in China and Thailand the receiver of a gift will quite often set it aside, not opening it in front of the guest. When I asked a number of Thais why they wait to open the gift, they all responded that they are afraid that they might hurt the guest's feelings if they don't like the gift and this is obvious to the guest. When I asked those with Chinese cultural background why they wait, I consistently got the response that opening the gift would make the guest feel that the host is more interested in the gift than in the friend or friendship.

The way people compliment each other can also differ from culture to culture. North Americans tend to compliment each other often. They compliment a person's new hair cut, clothing, work, home, children, cooking, garden, choice of wine, grades in school—almost anything. In other cultures, people do not compliment each other as often, and the way the compliment is given is often different. In Japan, for example, a compliment will be slightly indirect, such as the one I recently heard, "Your house is very big! It must be expensive!"

The way people react to compliments can also be different. Most North Americans will accept a compliment at face value, while Japanese and Chinese will often react with modesty. For example, an American hostess's typical reaction to the compliment, "This food is delicious!" would be, "Thank you! I'm happy you like it." However, a Japanese hostess would likely react with something like, "Sono hoto nai desu" [That's really not so].

As EFL/ESL teachers, we can teach students that knowledge about ways people interact with each other in culturally defined settings can be useful. We can provide readings and lectures on the topic. We can also have students do role plays and other activities. However, this is not enough. I believe we also need to teach them the value of problem solving.

SUCCESSFUL CROSS-CULTURAL COMMUNICATION INVOLVES PROBLEM-SOLVING

Imagine the scenario in Figure 8.1. Three people are going to meet in Paris to discuss a business idea. One is a Canadian who has lived in France for 15 years and speaks fairly fluent French. A second is Indonesian and can speak fluent English, but only a little French. A third is French and can speak fluent English. Since all three share English as their common language, much of the interaction will be done in English. But there is still a problem. Which nonverbal behaviors—such as gestures, touch, and use of space—will they use? Which discourse behaviors—such as complimenting, apologizing, complaining, offering, and requesting—will they use? Whose cultural rules are followed? If all act in ways appropriate to their native cultures, how can they avoid misinterpretation of each person's behavior?

I pose these questions to introduce the idea that interacting with people from other cultures can be complex. Simply informing students that there

FIGURE 8.1: A Cross-Cultural Problem: U.S. University Dorm Life

Siriporn, a 22-year-old from suburban Bangkok, arrived at a U.S. university full of enthusiasm. She wanted to be an excellent student. Studying was the first thing on her mind. She attended all her classes and did her required readings before each lecture. She would study at the library until it closed and then go to her dormitory room to study some more.

But she had a problem. Her U.S.-born roommate had many friends, and they all liked to meet in her room to talk and eat. They would simply walk into her room, sit down on her bed, and start to talk, eat potato chips, and play music. Sometimes they would stay up very late, and after they left, she had to clean potato chip crumbs, off her bed.

Siriporn thought they were inconsiderate, and she attempted many times to get them to leave so she could study. Twice she walked out of the room in a hurry and without speaking. Another time, while walking with a friend from Japan, she said within earshot of her roommate, "I wish my roommate would not have parties every night." But, nothing Siriporn said or did seemed to make a difference. Her roommate's friends kept coming into her room. She became more and more frustrated, sometimes feeling helpless and angry.

What is the problem? What conflict between the two behaviors and values created this problem? Is it related to the U.S.-born roommate's personality, or is the conflict cultural? Why do you think Siriporn's ways to solve the problem did not work? How could Siriporn solve this problem?

can be differences in culturally based nonverbal and socio-cultural behaviors (and the values associated with them) is not enough. If our goal is to teach students *how* to interact in English in a variety of contexts with other non-native speakers of English, as well as with native speakers, then, in addition to informing students about culturally defined behaviors, we can introduce them to the value of problem solving. It is through problem solving that our students can go beyond simply collecting interesting knowledge about cultures. They can have a way to assess a situation and identify behaviors that they predict will be appropriate to use within this situation.

One way to teach this process is to have students introduce real cross-cultural problems they face. In ESL settings, this is easy to do. Students interact with people from the host culture and with ESL speakers from a variety of cultures. However, in EFL settings this approach is problematic. With the exception of some students, who, for example, work in the tourist industry or in international business, most students do not have daily contact with people from other cultures. An alternative to using real cross-cultural problems is to use case history scenarios. For example, "A Cross-Cultural Problem: U.S. Dorm Life" is an activity I wrote for U.S.-bound Thai students in which they read and talk about a situation involving an unhappy Thai, work at identifying the problem and the reasons it exists, and generate a list of suggestions that aim at solving the problem.

I suggest teachers write their own problem sets. Problems can be based on knowledge about the students and the types of culturally based situations they might someday face, or they can simply be based on the students' interests. One classic book that has given me ideas for developing problem sets is *Intercultural Interactions*.[11] It presents a host of situations and problems to solve. Another book, specifically on problem-solving activities based on critical incidents between Chinese and Americans is *Turning Bricks into Jade*.[12] My own book, *What Do International Students Think and Feel?* also includes many problems that students have.[13]

TO UNDERSTAND A CULTURE, GET TO KNOW INDIVIDUALS

It is possible, as I have done in this chapter, to generalize about the cultural values and behaviors of a large group of people. Such generalizations can be useful, for example, to gain a general idea of the differences (and similarities) between people from different cultural backgrounds. However, there is a danger in categorizing a group of people into one single set of values and behaviors since this can lead to stereotyping. Not all British, for example, are reserved. Not all Japanese are indirect. Not all Americans are competitive.

As such, in addition to making generalizations, I teach students the importance of getting to know one person at a time, treating each as a distinct and unique individual. This includes how each individual behaves in different social situations, as well as the values each has. With this in mind, the question is, how can we teach students this concept? One way is to discuss it with them as a whole class; for some students, especially those who already like to personalize their experiences, this can make a difference in the way they perceive learning about people from different cultural backgrounds.

Another way to focus on the individual is to draw the students' attention to the differences among individuals in their own culture and have them relate this knowledge to other cultures. For example, I sometimes do a values clarification activity I call "Who gets to test the drug?" in which students read statements about the lives of seven people, all quite different from each other. One is a homeless drug addict, another is a bright college student, another a middle-aged scientist, another an elderly person who has worked all his life to solve societal problems, and so on. Each person has the same life-threatening disease, and the students are asked to select one of these people to participate in testing a new miracle drug that has the potential of reversing the disease. Students make their own individual choices and then meet in small groups to come to an agreement on their selection of one person to test the new drug.

One reason to do this activity is that it meets criteria, as discussed in Chapter 4, for promoting communication among students. It decreases the centrality of the teacher, provides students with chances to negotiate meaning, and allows them to decide for themselves what they want to say and how they want to say it. However, I also use this activity to show the students how individuals in a culture can vary in their beliefs and values. After the students negotiate who should be given the chance to test the drug, I ask them individually why they selected a particular person. For example, one student might select the scientist because she is doing important medical research, another the student because he is young and has a bright future, another the elderly person because he has contributed so much to society and deserves to be rewarded. I also emphasize that some agree on what they value, while others differ in what they believe is important. I then make the point that it is important to get to know what each person values, rather than making a generalization that all people in a culture believe in or value the same things.

TO UNDERSTAND ANOTHER CULTURE, STUDY YOUR OWN

A fourth concept worth teaching is that much can be gained from studying one's own cultural behaviors and values. Since acquiring the rules of one's own culture is a fairly unconscious process, students are most likely not aware of many aspects of their own culture. Even everyday behaviors—such as how change is given at a store, or how people greet each other and bid farewell, complain, apologize, compliment each other, and enter and leave a classroom—are usually not apparent to most EFL students. By providing students with opportunities to consider how people interact in their own culture, as well as their own individual values and ways of behaving, they can gain the insight useful to them when encountering people from other cultures. I base this assumption on the idea that by knowing one's own values and behaviors, it is easier to recognize those of others, as well as make necessary changes in behavior when needed. In short, contrasts help.

To teach students about their own cultures, the teacher can design questions that provide students with chances to explain their own culture to the teacher and classmates. For example, a friend who is teaching EFL in Japan sometimes uses an old but useful textbook, *Explain Yourself: An English Conversation Book for Japan*.[14] The entire book consists of different topics, sketches that illustrate the topic, and lists of questions. Topics include the Japanese New Year, sumo wrestling, baseball, funerals, weddings, public baths, university life, temples, and different festivals. Here's a sample of the questions on weddings:

Who pays for the weddings?

Who is usually invited to weddings?

Who sits where? What is the order of the speeches?

What is an *o-miai* (arranged marriage)?

What factors do the two families consider important when arranging an *o-miai*?

What is a bridal school?

My friend pointed out that students not only gain practice in talking about their own culture in English but also raise questions about his culture: "When is a popular time for Americans to get married?" and "Who is usually invited to the wedding?"

Another way to teach students about their own culture is to use photos and pictures. For example, by showing Thai students pictures that illustrate the ways Thais sit, it is possible to highlight that in their culture it is impolite to point one's foot at another person (unless they are close friends). By showing pictures of how people in other cultures sit, they can easily recognize the differences, especially noting that people in some cultures sit cross-legged, the foot pointing outward. The students could even practice sitting in other ways, providing a cross-cultural experience for them.

The teacher can go beyond simple behavior by also introducing readings or talking about the values associated with certain behaviors. For example, in the lesson on sitting in Thailand, the teacher could lead a discussion on reasons Thais sit the way they do, making the point that Thais do not point their foot at others because it will disturb the other person's *kwaan* or spirit essence. Many Thais believe that they have many parts to their *kwaan* and any part can escape the body if disturbed, leaving the person less than whole.[15] Thus, Thais do not point the foot (where the worst kwaan are) at someone's head (where the best are) because this could be disturbing. Such knowledge can spark students' interest in values across cultures and deeper cultural knowledge.

What Problems Do Some EFL/ESL Teachers Have Related to Culture and Language Teaching and Learning?

Problems some EFL/ESL teachers face include:

- The "I can't seem to adjust" problem
- The "learning the language of the host country" problem

THE "I CAN'T SEEM TO ADJUST" PROBLEM

As discussed earlier in this chapter, EFL teachers, as well as ESL students and non-native EFL teachers studying abroad, go through a process of cultural adjustment that includes experiencing the loss of the familiar. Things taken for granted at home suddenly require close attention. Taking a bus, buying soap, doing laundry, paying bills, or looking up a telephone number can all require far more effort than was expected. For some, these everyday problems create an emphatic emotional disruption, and it feels like cultural adjustment will never take place. But there are things we can do in a new culture to make the adjustment process easier:

- Give yourself time.
- Identify, accept, and treat symptoms of culture shock.
- Talk with others who have successfully adjusted.
- Learn as much as possible about the host culture.
- Identify adjustment issues and work through them.
- Study the language of the host culture.

First, recognize that cultural adjustment takes time. Adjustment is a gradual process. It will not happen overnight.

Next, it is important to identify, accept, and treat the symptoms of culture shock. To identify the symptoms, it is necessary to step back and reflect on personal feelings and behavior. As I discussed earlier, symptoms include feeling emotionally distressed (homesick, easily angered, depressed, nervous, etc.), complaining about things that affect our lives (housing, food, weather etc.), and withdrawing (sleeping a lot, avoiding people from the host culture, spending all free time with other sojourners). Recognizing the symptoms of culture shock can in itself be therapeutic. But it is also important to accept the symptoms. For example, if I am depressed, I recognize that I am depressed. I simply remind myself that it will not last long.

Third, talking with others who have successfully adapted to the culture can also be useful. It lets others know that our uneasiness, lack of confidence, and everyday problems in getting around and doing simple things is temporary. It is also possible to learn about what others have done to adjust. People usually like talking about their experiences, and most sojourners are more than happy to act as mentors, especially if they have created a happy life for themselves in their second country.

Fourth, it helps to learn as much as possible about the host culture. While some want to know about geography, others are interested in history, art, education, politics, psychology, and religion. I personally like to read translated short stories and novels since they give me a window, as reinvented as it is, into understanding much about the host culture.

Finally, it helps to identify adjustment issues and change, as some issues can hamper efforts to adjust to the new cultural surroundings. Issues can vary according to the culture and circumstances, and it is not always easy to realize what the issue is, but time and effort can have a positive outcome.

Allow me to illustrate this with my own experience. When I was younger and living in Thailand, I *went native*, meaning I wanted to become Thai, and this goal led to an identity crisis. I studied and used Thai with everyone, lived with a Thai family, made friends with Buddhist monks, and practiced Buddhism in my daily life. I ate nothing but Thai food, wore Buddhist amulets, and more. However, even though I was trying hard, I started to realize that Thais were not fully treating me as being Thai, and I felt hurt and confused. However, through this pain, I came to the realization that my effort to be Thai was an identity issue. I was raised as an American middle-class individual who was trying to be like people who were born and raised in rural Thailand. Thais there were not going to treat me as they would treat a Thai, but I realized that they would treat me like an American who loved Thailand, behaved in culturally appropriate ways, spoke Thai, and showed respect for Thai culture. In short, when I was able to understand my identity issue, I could relax and be myself, and it was easy to enjoy life in Thailand.

A student in the U.S. from Grenada told me about an identity issue she had during the early months of her stay in the U.S. In Grenada, stout people are often admired because it is a sign of happiness and well-being. As the student from Grenada put it, "When someone gains weight, people will say, 'She looking good!' which really means she's added some weight."[16] This student started to have an identity issue when she discovered that in the U.S., heavy-set people are sometimes criticized, made fun of, and even shunned, which made her feel terrible. She wanted to be accepted and started to diet to drop weight, but this simply made her unhappy. She changed from being a happy, successful, and beautiful young woman to feeling like an unattractive overweight person who did not fit in. Luckily, she worked through this issue, discovered that not all people in the U.S. dislike heavier people, and that she could be happy simply being herself.

The point I am making here is that when we adapt to another culture, there are going to be issues, and we need to face these issues, understand what they are, and work through them. Not all issues are solvable, but many are, and by working through them we will adapt.

Sixth, when we learn the language of the host culture, it is possible to gain an even deeper understanding of the culture and its people, making adjustment not only possible but, at least to me, interesting and even fun.

THE "LEARNING THE LANGUAGE OF THE HOST COUNTRY" PROBLEM

The problem of learning the language of the host country is specific to both ESL students and EFL teachers living abroad who want to learn the language of the host country. However, the problem here is discussed with the EFL teacher in mind. Most of us start out with great enthusiasm. However, many give up. It is not because we do not want to become fluent in the language. Most of us dream of gaining great proficiency. Rather, we give up because we get too busy to study the language or find we lack opportunities to actually use the language. We speak English to our students, the office staff, and administrators. We make friends with other EFL teachers and with fluent English-speaking acquaintances from the host culture, and we end up speaking English with them outside the workplace. When we venture out into the country, we meet people who jump at the chance to use English with a native speaker, and we oblige. As it turns out, opportunities to use the language of the host culture become limited. However, some of us are determined, and it helps to have a plan.

Suggestions for learning the language of the host country include:

- Continue studying the language. Don't stop.
- Take on the responsibility for your own learning.
- Create and implement a learning plan.
- Build relationships with people in the community based on appropriate use of the language.

If we want to become fluent in the host country language, we have to devote considerable energy and time to studying it. We start out with wonderful intentions. We join a language class, do our homework, and attend classes regularly. But obligations get in the way. Eventually, we stop going, put the book on a shelf, and tell ourselves we will start again when we have more time. However, studying a language is an ongoing process, and it requires consistent discipline and interest and a willingness to concentrate on studying. Basically, if our goal is to become very fluent and literate in the language, we have to be willing to devote years to this endeavor.

We also have to take responsibility for our own learning, which includes creating a plan to learn the language that might include attending classes and collecting and studying language texts. Perhaps more important is our need to have a plan designed to make use of all the resources available to us, including people in the community. For example, to gain spoken fluency, Terry Marshall[17] suggests we (1) decide on what to learn for the day (e.g., how to buy train tickets); (2) prepare an imagined conversation in the target language with the help of a native-speaking mentor/tutor; (3) practice the conversation; (4) communicate the studied language to native speakers by going into the community, finding people, and speaking to them (e.g., at the train station); (5) evaluate our progress.

Having a plan is a start. Implementing it is another matter. Going into the community to find people to use the language with is not always easy. However, it can be done. For example, when I moved to Japan, I purposefully lived in a place where no other foreigners lived, and when approaching the study of Japanese, I used the community. I talked with people at the public bath, the local stores, and the laundry. Being single at the time, I went on dates with women who I knew would be willing to speak Japanese with me. I also joined a yoga club where I could use Japanese, went on weekend hiking trips with a non-English speaking Japanese, and drank a few beers each week at a place where few were interested in speaking English with me. During my lunch hour, I spent ten minutes chatting with a friend in Japanese on the phone, and I used Japanese with a group of American and Australian friends, all interested in mastering the language. I learned a lot from these friends, which is why I support teachers having students speak English with each other in class.

My efforts to find contexts to use Japanese did something unexpected for me. I established a network, becoming a member of several groups within the community—for example, the yoga club, a local restaurant, and the community center. I discovered that as my Japanese got better, my relationships with people in the community became more complex, and that as these relationships became more complex, I needed to learn more Japanese.

TEACHER SELF-DEVELOPMENT TASKS

Talk Tasks

1. *Culture* can be defined in many ways. For example, I define *culture* as the shared values and beliefs of a group of people and the behaviors that reflect them.

   a. What merit do you think this definition has?

   b. What are other ways to define culture?

2. Review and discuss my points on teaching cultural concepts to students.

   a. What are the concepts I discuss? Explain each.

   b. Why do I recommend that EFL teachers teach students cultural concepts? What are the benefits? Do you teach cultural concepts to students? If so, how?

   c. Select one of the cultural concepts. Design a lesson that aims at teaching this concept.

3. Here are three brief research tasks for you. Feel free to do one or more of them.

    a. If you are living abroad, here is a task for you. The way names are listed in telephone books sometimes differs from culture to culture. Locate a phone book. How are the names listed? Are they listed the same or differently from how they are listed in phone books in your native culture? What other differences do you notice?

    b. Each culture has its own special holidays. Go online. Look at holidays in different cultures. See how many different types of holidays you can come up with.

    c. Pick two different cultures. Find out how people in these cultures generally offer guests a drink, such as a cup of tea. Find out how people accept or refuse the offer.

4. Storti provides this following graphic model (Figure 8.2) of the process of adjustment.[18]

FIGURE 8.2: **Storti's Model of the Process of Cultural Adjustment**

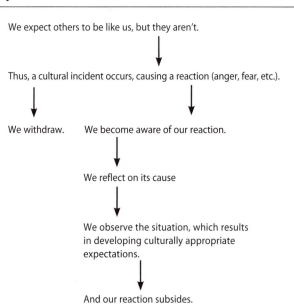

We expect others to be like us, but they aren't.

Thus, a cultural incident occurs, causing a reaction (anger, fear, etc.).

We withdraw.   We become aware of our reaction.

We reflect on its cause

We observe the situation, which results in developing culturally appropriate expectations.

And our reaction subsides.

Study this model. Notice that there are two possible ways for us to react to a cultural incident. We can withdraw, for example, by moving into the expatriate community, or we can work at adjustment through reflection.

a. Explain what Storti's model means.

b. Talk about the benefits of taking the "reflective" path. You might want to refer to the section on the benefits of cultural adjustment in this chapter.

c. Tell stories about your own and others' cultural adjustment.

5. How are people in different cultures polite?

Observation and Talk Tasks

1. Videotape one of your classes. Analyze the interaction by studying how you and the students:

a. Use eye contact while listening

b. Touch (or don't touch)

c. Keep space or distance while standing or sitting

How do your behaviors reflect your native culture? How are students' behaviors different or similar to yours? Meet with other teachers to talk about what you discovered.

2. Try these matching techniques. Then talk to someone who also has tried them. What did you learn from the experience? Consider how matching behaviors can be used as a way for you to learn a language, as well as the value it has for EFL/ESL students.

a. Sit next to someone who speaks a different language. Match this person's posture, gestures, facial expressions, and breathing. Do this for a few minutes.

b. Sit in the middle of a movie theater. Do whatever the audience does. Laugh when they laugh. Sigh when they sigh. Sit the way they sit.

c. Watch people doing things, such as paying for an item at a store, getting a waiter's attention, eating a dish of ice cream, and counting with their fingers. Imitate them. Try to match their behaviors as they did these things.

Journal Writing Tasks

1. Write your ideas about teaching students cultural concepts. If you try out any of the ideas, reflect on how you thought the lesson went.

2. If you now live in a foreign country, or have lived in one, write about your own cultural adjustment process and problems.

3. Write what you have learned from matching people's behaviors. Make a list of possible behaviors you could match.

RECOMMENDED TEACHER RESOURCES

Readings on Cultural Concepts

Bennett, M. J., ed. *Basic Concepts of Intercultural Communication, 2nd ed.* Boston: Intercultural Press, 2013.

Hinkel, E. "Culture and Pragmatics in Language Teaching and Learning." In *Teaching English as a Second or Foreign Language, 4th ed.*, eds. M. Celce-Murcia, D. M. Brinton, and M. A. Snow, 394–408. Boston: Heinle Cengage, 2014.

Hall, E. T. *Beyond Culture.* Garden City, NY: Anchor Books, 1981.

Samovar, L. A., R. E. Porter, E. R. Daniel, and C. S. Roy, eds. *Intercultural Communication: A Reader, 14th ed.* Independence, KY: Cengage Learning, 2015.

Readings on Cultural Adjustment

Begley, P.A. "Sojourner Adaptation." In *Intercultural Communication, 12th ed.* eds. L. Samovar, R.E. Porter, and E.R. McDaniel, 387–93. Belmont, CA: Thomson Wadsworth, 2006.

Gebhard, J. G. *What Do International Students Think and Feel? Adapting to U.S. College Life and Culture.* Ann Arbor: University of Michigan Press, 2010.

Kohls, L. R. *Survival Kit for Overseas Living, 5th ed.* Boston: Intercultural Press, 2011.

Kim, Y. Y. "Adapting to a New Culture." In *Intercultural Communication, 14th ed.* eds. L. Samovar, R.E. Porter, E.R. McDaniel, and C. S. Roy, 385–97. Independence, KY: Cengage Learning, 2015.

Nunan, D. and J. Choi. *Language and Culture: Reflective Narratives and the Emergence of Identity.* New York: Routledge, 2010.

Storti, C. *The Art of Crossing Cultures, 2nd ed.* Boston: Intercultural Press, 2007.

Weaver, G. "Understanding and Coping with Cross-Cultural Adjustment Stress." In *Culture, Communication and Conflict,* ed. G.R. Weaver, 177–93. New York: Pearson Publishing, 2000.

Readings on Teaching Culture

Berardo, K. and D. K. Deardorff. *Building Cultural Competence: Innovative Activities and Models.* Sterling, VA: Stylus Publishing, 2012.

DeCapua, A. and A. C. Wintergerst. *Crossing Cultures in the Language Classroom, 2nd ed.* Ann Arbor: University of Michigan Press, 2016.

Fantini, A. E., ed. *New Ways in Teaching Culture.* Alexandria, VA: TESOL, 1997.

Hall, J. K. *Teaching and Researching Language and Culture.* New York: Pearson, 2002.

Moran, P. R. *Teaching Culture: Perspectives in Practice.* Boston: Heinle & Heinle, 2001.

Storti, C. *Cross-Cultural Dialogues: 74 Brief Encounters with Cultural Differences, 2nd ed.* Boston: Intercultural Press, 2017.

Wintergerst, A. C. and J. McVeigh. *Tips for Teaching Culture: Practical Approaches to Intercultural Communication.* New York: Pearson, 2010.

ENDNOTES

1 See Nydell (2002).

2 Doi (1973) discusses the psychological makeup of Japanese.

3 From Wallender (1977, 7).

4 See From Lewis and Jungman (1986, xxi). Others who discuss the process of cultural adjustment include Adler (1987), Begley (2006), Kim (2015), and Storti (2007). Also, see my research on international students studying at U.S. universities (Gebhard 2010, 2013).

5 From Storti (1989, 94).

6 Anderson (2015), Hall (1966), McDaniel (2015), DeCapua and Wintergerst (2016) offer detailed discussions on non-verbal behavior across cultures.

7 See Barnlund (1975) for a discussion of touch in Japanese and American cultures.

8 By rubbing a Thai child's head we could disturb the *Khwan* (spirit essence) of the child. Some Thais believe that we have 23 Khwan throughout the body, and the most sensitive is in the head. If rubbed, this part of the Khwan can escape. See Klausner (1983) and Heinze (1982).

9 See Hall (1966, 15).

10 From Nydell (2002).

11 See Brislin et al. (1986).

12 See Wang et al. (2000).

13 See Gebhard (2010).

13 See Nicholson and Sakuno (1982).

14 See Heinze (1982).

15 This quote is from a narrative in Gebhard (2010).

16 See Marshall (1989) who provides guidelines based on his Peace Corps experience.

17 See Storti (2007).

Part 3
Teaching Language Skills

9

Listening is not just hearing. It is an active process that may begin even before the first speech signal is recognized, and it may go on long after the input or spoken information has stopped.

—Goh 2014, 73

Teaching Students to Listen and Comprehend Spoken English

▌ *What does listening include?*
▌ *What kinds of listening activities do EFL/ESL teachers use?*
▌ *How do EFL/ESL teachers use the media to teach listening?*
▌ *What problems do some EFL/ESL teachers have teaching students to comprehend spoken English?*

What Does Listening Include?

I guide my discussion by focusing on aspects of listening, including active listening, the processing of what we hear to make sense out of it, and two purposes for listening.

ACTIVE LISTENING

Listening is not a passive activity. Rather, listening places many demands on us. When we participate in face-to-face or telephone exchanges, we need to be receptive to others, which includes paying attention to explanations, questions, and opinions. Even when we listen during one-way exchanges—for example, while listening to lectures, radio dramas, films, television news, and musicals—we are active. Consider, for example, how many times you shouted at, laughed at, or agreed with (either out loud or inside your head) a person giving a television commentary.[1]

PROCESSING WHAT WE HEAR

Another aspect of listening is the way we process what we hear. There are two distinct processes involved in comprehending spoken English: **bottom-up processing** and **top-down processing.** Bottom-up processing refers to decoding a message that the listener hears through the analysis of sounds, words, and grammar, while top-down processing refers to using background knowledge to comprehend a message.[2] For example, imagine that Joe is a tourist in a foreign country. He is staying at the Federal Hotel, and he wanders away to see some local sites, only to discover he is lost. Joe then decides to approach someone, whom he asks, "Excuse me, couldja tell me howta getto to the Federal?" From a bottom-up point of view, the person listening to Joe arrives at meaning by identifying the specific words relevant to the message (such as recognizing that the "Federal" is a hotel), recognizing strings of sounds and being able to segment them (e.g., recognizing that *couldja* is two words, *could you,* and that *howta getto* is *how to get to),* and identifying grammatical and functional clues pertinent to the message (e.g., recognizing that *could you* indicates that a request is about to be made and that *how to get to* indicates asking for directions).

While successful bottom-up processing relies on recognition of sounds, words, and grammar, successful top-down processing hinges on having the kind of background knowledge needed to comprehend the meaning of a message. This can be in the form of previous knowledge about the topic—for example, knowing the hotels in the tourist area. It can also be in the form of **situational knowledge**—for example, knowing there are lost tourists in the area who frequently ask for directions. Finally, background knowledge can be in the form of **schemata** or plans about the overall structure of events and the relationship between them."[3] For example, when someone who looks lost approaches you in a tourist area and says, "Excuse me," you can predict this person is about to ask for directions, location, or something related to being a tourist.

This last kind of background knowledge or schemata relates especially to our real-world experiences and the expectations we have, based on our experiences, about how people behave. The schemata we draw from includes our experience in assigning specific kinds of interaction to an event—for example, knowing how to listen to jokes, stories, and requests. Likewise, it includes the way we categorize knowledge. For example, if we frequently walk through a tourist area, we will know the names of hotels and can group people as tourists and non-tourists. Schemata also includes being able to predict a topic in discourse and infer a sequence of events—for example, expecting that a lost tourist will initiate and move through a conversational routine, including getting our attention, asking for directions, and possibly checking understanding by paraphrasing the directions.

The importance of background knowledge is especially obvious when we consider the language processing problems of foreign students who come to the United States. Many students are considered to be highly talented at bottom-up processing of English, and within their EFL settings they are considered to be very fluent speakers of English. Nonetheless, upon arrival in the United States, some soon discover that they cannot communicate as easily as they had hoped. Here is an example of a student who came from Somalia.[4] This student went to McDonald's® to get something to eat, and when he placed his order at the counter, he was asked, *Would you like this forhereortogo?* He looked at her inquisitively and said nothing, since he could not understand her question. She repeated her question louder, *Forhereortogo?* which did not help. The person behind him then helped him with his bottom-up processing, telling him that the string of words consisted of *For here or to go,* but he still had no idea what the speaker meant. Finally, the person behind him said, *Would you like to take this order out, or would you like to eat it here?* and the student finally understood, having gained the necessary background knowledge to process the culturally based question.

THE PURPOSES OF LISTENING

In addition to bottom-up and top-down processing, we can consider **interactional** and **transactional functions** of language.[5] When language is used to fulfill an interactional communicative function, the focus is on creating harmonious interaction among individuals. As a social phenomenon, interactional use of language centers on such safe topics as the weather, food, and beautiful things. These topics are neutral, or non-controversial, and shift quickly. Because these topics are non-controversial, they promote agreement between speakers and listeners, which in turn creates a harmonious relationship.

Unlike interactional use of language, transactional use focuses attention on the content of the message. Emphasis is on transferring information, and unlike interactional uses of language, it is important for the listener to comprehend the content of the speaker's message. Topics vary from context to context and can include almost any content. Examples of interactional use of language include a doctor advising a patient on how to take a prescription drug or a student listening to a lecture on marriage in the Philippines.

What Kinds of Listening Activities Do EFL/ESL Teachers Use?

An understanding of top-down and bottom-up processes of listening and of the transactional and interactional functions of language provides an awareness of what listeners do as they listen, and this knowledge is useful when we consider the listening activities we have students do in our classrooms. In this section I focus on activities we can use to provide EFL/ESL students with a variety of listening experiences.

IDENTIFYING LINGUISTIC FEATURES

The aim of activities that focus on identifying linguistic features is to make students more aware of the linguistic features of spoken English. As such, they center on bottom-up processing. Since the aim is to provide chances for students to develop their perceptual abilities, little attention is given to transactional or interactional purposes. One activity is to give students practice in listening to the way sounds blend in spoken English. The teacher (or a recorded voice) says a phrase, such as *didja,* followed by a sentence, such as *Didja go to the store?* The student then identifies the written version from a list.

The idea of the activity in Figure 9.1 is to show students what sentence stress is and how it influences the rhythm of spoken English. For example, after listening to and marking *He's a terrific actor,* students can see that major words (nouns, main verbs, adverbs, adjectives) receive stress while minor words (pronouns, determiners, articles, prepositions) do not, and that when words have more than one syllable, only one syllable—for instance, *if* in *terrific*—receives primary stress.

To do the activity in Figure 9.2, the teacher can use any minimal pair (two words that differ only in one sound), making the selection based on sounds that are new or problematic for students. Of course, the teacher can also select pairs that students can easily distinguish so they feel successful. To do this activity, the teacher says the string of words, for example, *Liver. River. River.* Each students puts up one finger each time he or she hears *Liver* and two fingers for *River.* The teacher can challenge the students by increasing the number of words in the string and saying them faster.

FIGURE 9.1: A Stress and Rhythm Listening Activity

Listen to the conversation. Put a mark over each stressed syllable.

A: That was a really good movie!

B: Yeah, Michael Cane. He's a terrific actor. Very funny.

A: What are your favorite Michael Cane movies?

FIGURE 9.2: A Minimal Pair Listening Activity

Listen to each word. Each time you hear *river*, put up one finger. Each time you hear *liver* put up two fingers.

1. river

2. liver, river

3. liver, liver, liver

RESPONDING TO REQUESTS AND COMMANDS

Listen-and-respond activities highlight bottom-up processing because the listener listens to identify specific words and grammatical command structures. One type of activity is **Total Physical Response (TPR)**.[6] An example of a TPR lesson is shown in Figure 9.3. While doing TPR with EFL/ESL students, I have found Berty Segal's advice quite useful.[7] Segal suggests that teachers begin by demonstrating the commands, doing them with the students. The teacher can also reduce anxiety by giving commands to the whole class, then to small groups of students, and finally, after the students have lots of practice, to individual volunteers.

There are many possible commands that students can practice. To create commands, we simply need to select "action" verbs, such as *stand up, sit down, walk, skip, hop, turn, stop, pick up, put down, sing, touch, point, smile, frown, laugh, throw,* and *catch*. These verbs can be combined with nouns and other words to make up commands, each activity emphasizing listening for a purpose. For example, students can listen to the same verb said many times with different nouns, such as *Touch your nose. Touch your chin. Touch your mouth.* or *Point at the clock. Point at the door.* Or students can listen to different combinations of verbs, for instance, *Open your book to page 32. Close your book. Stand up. Point to the door. . . .* Some students appreciate humor, too. For example, I observed a third grade ESL teacher once say, *Jose, put your nose in Maria's armpit.*[8]

Another way to provide ways for students, especially children, to listen and respond is by playing Simon Says. Like TPR, the teacher gives a command. But the listener is only supposed to follow the command if it is

FIGURE 9.3: **TPR**

Teacher Command:	Stand up.
Student Response:	(Students stand up.)
Teacher Command:	Go to the blackboard.
Student Response:	(Students walk to the blackboard.)
Teacher Command:	Write your name on the board.
Student Response:	(Students write their names.)

preceded by the phrase *Simon says*. Most children love this game. Anxiety levels go down. Attention levels go up.

Another activity liked by both children and adults who are young at heart is the Hokey Pokey. The students and teacher form a large circle, listen to the Hokey Pokey song, and follow the commands: "You put your right foot in. You take your right foot out. You put your right foot in and shake it all about. You do the Hokey Pokey and turn yourself around. That's what it's all about!"[9]

INTERACTING AS A LISTENER

The goal of interactive listening activities is to focus students' attention on how they can maintain social interactive relations. Both bottom-up and top-down processes can be a part of these activities, depending on the design. One such activity is called Chat. Students view short videotaped segments of interaction in different settings—for example, at the dinner table, the fitness center, a grocery store, the checkout counter. The idea is for students not only to work at comprehending the interaction, but also to consider what a "safe" topic is and how the interaction is maintained. To accomplish this, as students view the video, they can:

- check off those topics that were discussed from a list of possible topics.

- follow along with a written script, highlighting the things listeners do to keep the conversation going (e.g., using head nods and encouraging remarks, such as *uh-huh, What else?* and *No kidding!*).

- complete a set of multiple choice and true/false questions about the interaction (e.g., True or False? Josh likes to chuckle to show he is listening).

Eavesdropping is another way to focus students' attention on the function of listening during conversations. The goal is to teach students the value of listening in on conversations and a few strategies for doing so. The activity in Figure 9.4 is an eavesdropping activity from Porter and Roberts.[10] The

FIGURE 9.4: **Eavesdropping**

You are at a party given by the Director of Studies at your school. A lot of teachers and students are there. You can hear pieces of conversation. Try to guess what the people are talking about. You hear four different conversations. Would you like to join any of them?

	Topic	Are you interested?
1.	_____	
2.	_____	
3.	_____	
4.	_____	

students are told that they are guests at a party and that they can eavesdrop on conversations. They then listen to short segments of party conversation and complete a worksheet.

After students complete such eavesdropping activities in class or in the listening lab, I ask them if they would like to try their eavesdropping skills outside the classroom. If they agree, I send them out in teams of two or three. Their task is to observe and capture pieces of conversation, including short dialogues, and to write up their eavesdropping experience and prepare to tell classmates something they learned. Of course, this is much easier in ESL settings, where there are plenty of English language conversations going on (e.g., in college dorms, grocery stores, and restaurants), but it is also possible for EFL students to listen in on English conversations, especially in big cities (e.g., at fast-food restaurants, tourist areas, and department stores). It is worth mentioning that not all students like to eavesdrop. Some consider it an invasion of privacy, and when students object, I respect their wishes not to practice this activity. However, some students have told me how much they like to eavesdrop since they can capture authentic use of English that they can practice in their minds.

Another interactive listening activity is called Matching.[11] Although this activity is a little too outlandish for some, students can be asked to match others' nonverbal behaviors, including head nods, gestures, and facial expressions. The goal is to show the value of observing the behaviors others use as they listen, as well as to focus students' attention on their own use of nonverbal behavior during a conversation. To introduce the concept of matching, I demonstrate by having one student talk on a familiar topic while another listens. At the end of their demonstration, I show a few selected aspects of the listener's behavior, such as quick Japanese head nods. I then have students practice matching other students' behaviors in the same way. Although students sometimes need lots of coaching and coaxing and have to work through fits of laughter, some students soon discover that to be a good listener in another language requires not only knowledge of topics and vocabulary and grammar, but also adapting the nonverbal behaviors we exhibit as we listen.

COMPREHENDING EXTENDED SPEECH

Transactional in nature, comprehension activities center on comprehending stories, extended speech, and lectures. As with all the activity types in this chapter, there are many possible comprehension activities. One that can be used with beginners and more advanced students is a picture-ordering activity that includes listening to a story and then putting pictures in the order of the events in the story. Students can also draw their own pictures. For example, students can view or listen to a weather forecast and, under the relevant days of the week, draw pictures that represent the forecast as shown in Figure 9.5.

FIGURE 9.5: **Picture-Ordering Activity**

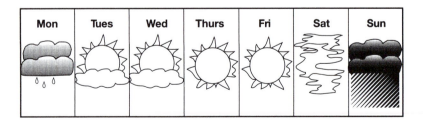

Cloze listening tasks can also be used as comprehension activities. The activity shown in Figure 9.6 is an example.

Taking notes can also engage students in listening to extended speech, as in Figure 9.7.

FIGURE 9.6: **Holidays**

Listen to the short lecture. As you listen, read the text. Listen a few times. Then complete each blank with one of the vocabulary words. Keep in mind, there are more words than blanks!

Vocabulary:

restaurants	Hungarians	person's	includes	year
holidays	celebrate	name	birthday	treat

Text:

There are some very interesting _____ in different countries.

_____, for example, have a Name Day. Each day of the

_____ has a person's name. If it is a _____

Name Day, then he or she has to _____ friends. This

_____ taking friends out to _____ for meals.

FIGURE 9.7: **The Joy of Traveling**

Listen to the travel story three times.

The first time:
What countries did the young woman visit?
What types of transportation did she use?

The second time:
Which country did she like the most?
What are three things the woman says she likes about the country?

The third time:
Listen to the woman's descriptions of the places she visited.
Which place would you like to visit? Why?

PROBLEM-SOLVING

Problem-solving listening activities are transactional because they provide ways for students to comprehend content to solve problems through their use of both bottom-up and top-down processes. There are, of course, a variety of possible activities. In one of my favorite activities,[12] the students are detectives listening to a recorded report about a murder; and as they listen, they complete a grid on the alibis of the suspects. Based on what they hear, their task is to narrow down the suspects to select the prankster. Here is my version of the report students listen to.

> Yesterday, on Halloween, Jerry Gebhard, an ESL teacher, had his car and house windows soaped between 8:00 PM and midnight at his home near campus. The suspects, his students, described their activities on the night of the event. Yoko said she had dinner alone from 8:00 to 9:00, and then practiced her flute. Several people heard her playing. She then watched TV for an hour with other students in the dormitory lounge. At 11:00 she was studying in her room. Several students saw her there. Andre said that he was watching TV from 8:00 to 9:00 and was studying alone in his room from 9:00 to 11:00, and then he went to bed. However, a classmate said he saw Andre and Lilia walking away from campus at 9:30. Bahlal said he was at the library from 8:00 until 10:00, then he took a walk with his friend until around 11:00, when he went to his room to study. Several people saw Bahlal at the library. Mohammad said he was talking with Lilia in the dorm hallway from 8:00 to about 9:15, and he was with another friend until 10:00, watched TV until 11:00, and then went to bed. Lilia claimed she talked with Mohammad from 8:00 to around 9:00 or so, then went to her room to study and sleep.

To add a touch of humor, teachers can use the names of students in their class. See the example in Figure 9.8 of what the grid looks like when it is completed by the students.

FIGURE 9.8: **Sample Grid**

Name	8:00–9:00	9:00–10:00	10:00–11:00	11:00–12:00
Yoko	eating dinner alone	playing flute	tv in lounge	studying in room
Andre	tv in lounge	alone in room	alone in room	in bed sleeping
Bahlal	at library	at library	walking with friend	studying in room
Mohammad	with Lilia	with friend	tv in lounge	in bed sleeping
Lilia	with Mohammad	studying in room	studying in room	in bed sleeping

How Do EFL/ESL Teachers Use Media to Teach Listening?

There are many ways in which EFL/ESL teachers can make use of media in our listening classes. Radio, for example, offers songs, advertisements, talk shows, and drama. Television offers an abundance of materials: quiz shows, comedies, reality shows, soaps, cartoons, documentaries, educational programs, news, weather forecasts, movies, award shows, and commercials.

Folk, rock, and popular songs offer students exposure to one form of authentic English through the media, and many students, young and old, enjoy listening to (and singing) songs. EFL/ESL teachers use a variety of different songs, including everything from "The ABC Song" to "Yesterday" by the Beatles. However, most agree that students benefit from the listening experience when the songs are taught so that the lyrics are comprehensible. One way to do this is to provide short lessons on vocabulary and grammar, followed with different listening activities.

Singing lines in the song and participating in other ways can also help make the lyrics comprehensible. For example, as children listen to "Old

MacDonald,"[13] they can point at pictures of animals, as well as sing animal sounds and the "e-I, e-I, oh."

OLD MACDONALD

Old MacDonald had a farm
E-i, e-i oh
And on this farm he had a cow
E-i, e-i oh
With a *moo moo* here
And a *moo moo* there
Here a *moo,* there a *moo*
Everywhere a *moo moo. . . .*

As the list of techniques in Figure 9.9 shows, there are also creative things we can do in our classrooms with video clips from TV programs, films, commercials, and teacher-made videotapes of interactions.[14]

To illustrate how teachers can process authentic video materials, here is an example from my own teaching in Hungary of an episode of an old U.S. situation comedy called *The Wonder Years.* I began by writing a set of questions on the board: How many people are talking? How old do you

---

FIGURE 9.9: Techniques: Processing Authentic Video Materials

Silent Viewing: Students view video material without sound to consider what is going on and guess what speakers are doing and saying.

Soundtrack Only: Students hear the soundtrack without the picture and speculate on what speakers look like, the setting, and the location.

Beginning Only: Students view the beginning of a sequence, then predict what will happen next.

Ending Only: Students view the ending and consider what happened earlier.

Split Viewing (One): Some students view the material without sound. Others listen without viewing. Groups come together to create a fuller understanding of context and content.

Split Viewing (Two): Half the class sits with back to screen. Half can see the screen. Both can hear. Pairs then build a fuller understanding of context and content.

---

think they are? What is their relationship? What are they talking about? We then listened to two minutes of the show without a picture and answered the questions written on the board, after which I gave them a new set of questions: What approximate year is it? What are the people doing? What do you think the story is going to be about? I then played the sound and picture of the first five minutes of the show, including the two minutes they had already listened to. After answering the questions, we viewed the show until just before the climax. I then had students meet in groups to write down and announce their predictions about how the show would end. We then viewed the ending to see if any of the predictions were correct and to compare the students' creative endings with the original.

Before ending this section, it is important to add that modern technology provides listening teachers with opportunities to bring a wide variety of media into the classroom or language lab. Chapter 7 provides a glimpse into how technology can broaden the possibilities.

What Problems Do Some EFL/ESL Teachers Have Teaching Students to Comprehend Spoken English?

Problems some EFL/ESL teachers face include:

- The "teaching students how to take control of their own listening" problem
- The "How can I judge the authenticity of commercial EFL/ESL listening materials?" problem

THE "TEACHING STUDENTS TO TAKE CONTROL OF THEIR OWN LISTENING" PROBLEM

Teachers sometimes want students to take more control of their own listening, but they are not sure how to do this. One approach to this problem is to teach students strategies they can use independently to manage their listening, and there are a number of textbooks and professional publications that address how to do this.[15]

One strategy we can teach students is how to predict and guess words from the context. For example, if someone simply said, "I didn't like that movie. It was too surreal" and you did not know what *surreal* means, you would not be able to comprehend it. However, if the speaker went on to say, "It was eerie, almost like I was watching a dream," and you understood these words, you could deduce that *surreal* means strange or weird. Another strategy we can teach students is to ask for confirmation. For example, using the movie example, the listener could ask, "I'm not sure I got what you said. You didn't like the movie because it was kind of strange, like you were in a dream? Is my understanding correct?"

Further, as teachers, we can also teach students to monitor their own listening by having them paraphrase their understanding back to the speaker. For example, "So you said you don't like the movie we just watched. You said it was strange, surreal as you put it, because it made you feel like you were dreaming." The difference between confirming and paraphrasing is that, when confirming, the listener is not sure he or she understands, so the confirmation request is more like a question. On the other hand, paraphrasing can be done anytime. In fact, I encourage everyone to paraphrase no matter what first or second language they are speaking because it helps comprehension.

Finally, second and foreign language listeners can benefit from reflecting on their own processes of listening. They can do this by considering questions such as, What do I do when I don't fully comprehend? How often do I pretend to understand and hope I will comprehend as the conversation goes along? What strategies can I use to improve my listening? Do I ask questions to clarify? Do I paraphrase to check my comprehension? How much risk am I willing to take during a conversation to expand my listening comprehension? Am I willing to feel foolish? Will audio recording conversations and reviewing them help me? Will writing down new words I hear help my listening?

THE "HOW CAN I JUDGE THE AUTHENTICITY OF COMMERCIAL EFL/ESL LISTENING MATERIALS?" PROBLEM

Truly authentic listening experiences focus on varieties of pronunciation and intonation. For example, pronunciation includes simulation of sounds, such as blending two or more words into a single sound, as in *Didja (Did you)*. Pitch and emphatic stress are used to represent a nuance in meaning, and the rhythm of English is set through the use of sentence stress. Major words (e.g., nouns, verbs, adjectives, adverbs) receive sentence stress, while minor words (e.g., articles, prepositions, auxiliary verbs) do not, as in *You'll* <u>*find*</u> *the book on the* <u>*table.*</u>"

Authentic listening also includes hearing a variety of grammatical structures, not just one or two said over and over again—the use of fragments or sequences of loosely connected words and clauses, rather than well-formed sentences. It also includes interruptions and two or more people speaking at once (rather than each person taking a distinct turn), as well as one speaker dominating the interaction, lots of attention signals (such as *Mmmmm* and *Uh-huh*), and different examples of background noise.

Another way to determine whether commercial video and audio materials are based on authenticity is to study whether or not the materials are corpus-informed. Simply put, are the materials based on a linguistic analysis of a multitude of data on what people actually listen to? (See Chapter 6 for more on corpus-informed materials.)

TEACHER SELF-DEVELOPMENT TASKS

Talk Tasks

1. Have you ever been in a conversation in English in which you lacked the appropriate background knowledge to completely comprehend what you were listening to? Describe your experience. What was the content? What background knowledge did you lack? Why did this lack of knowledge make it difficult for you fully to comprehend the content?

2. What kinds of listening activities have you experienced either as a teacher or as a student? Which activity types in this chapter haven't you experienced? Which would you like to try out in your EFL/ESL classes?

3. Meet with another teacher. Together, select authentic listening material from a published text or the media (e.g., a song, film, TV situation comedy, cartoon, news show, or TV or radio advertisement). Based on the ideas in this chapter on using the media, and on your own ideas, create a step-by-step lesson plan that aims at making this authentic material comprehensible to a group of students with whom you are familiar.

4. Do you think that the use of non-authentic listening materials (e.g., exaggerated enunciation) can help beginning-level students to develop their listening abilities?

Observation and Talk Tasks

1. Record a conversation between friends. (Make sure you get their permission first.) Select three minutes from this conversation. With other teacher/friends, analyze what goes on in the conversation. What gives the conversation its authenticity?

2. This task has multiple parts.

   a. Study the criteria for authenticity (Figure 9.10) and the worksheet (Figure 9.11). What do these words mean: *intonation, pitch, pronunciation, enunciation, assimilation, clause, pace*? Are there any other words or ideas you want to know more about? If possible, look up the words in a specialized dictionary, such as the *Longman Dictionary of Language Teaching and Applied Linguistics*.

   b. If possible, discuss the meanings of the words you studied with other teachers.

   c. Locate published listening materials that focus on person-to-person interaction in social contexts (rather than, for example, on teaching students to listen to the news). Using the criteria for authenticity and the worksheet (Figure 9.11) evaluate the authenticity of these materials. How authentic is the language in the materials?

   d. Based on your experience of analyzing the authenticity of the published listening material, consider the appropriateness of the material for different levels of students. Do you think the material is too difficult? Appropriate? Too easy? Why or why not? If possible, share your opinions with other teachers.

   e. Listen to the material one more time. This time consider the vocabulary used in the listening material. How difficult is the vocabulary as it relates to the designated level of the student? Appropriate? Too difficult? If too difficult, how might the vocabulary in a listening selection limit students' abilities to process meaning?

FIGURE 9.10: Evaluating the Authenticity of Listening Materials

These criteria provide a way to judge the authenticity of language used in commercial listening materials, by people as they interact in social contexts.[16]

Intonation: Criteria	Intonation: Questions
Intonation is not authentic when marked by exaggerated and frequent pitch movement and when each word receives equal stress.	Does the intonation amuse you? Remind you of an indulgent mother talking to a baby? Is the pitch exaggerated or natural?
Pronunciation: Criteria	Pronunciation: Questions
Pronunciation is not authentic when each word is clearly enunciated. Rather, blending of sounds is normal.	Does the pronunciation seem artificial? Do speakers enunciate each word? Or do they blend sounds?
Speaker Domination: Criteria	Speaker Domination: Questions
In normal conversations one speaker will dominate the conversation.	Are all speakers saying an equal amount or does one person say more?
Complete Sentences: Criteria	Complete Sentences: Questions
Informal speech is characterized by fragmentation. In short, people talk in clauses and single-word utterances.	Do speakers use all complete sentences? Or do they use short loosely connected clauses and words?
False Start: Criteria	False Start: Questions
In authentic situations a speaker might begin to say something and then change his or her mind and begin again.	Do speakers begin with a single idea and continue to express that idea? Or, do some speakers begin, stop, and restart?
Hesitation and Filler: Criteria	Hesitation: Questions
In authentic speech, speakers will sometimes use hesitation words or sounds to process their thoughts.	Does the speaker begin to talk by using sounds such as *Ahh* or *Hmmm*? Does the speaker use them in the middle of talking?
Distinct Turns: Criteria	Distinct Turns: Questions
People do not wait for others to stop talking. They interrupt.	Do speakers wait for others to finish or do they interrupt?
Pace: Criteria	Pace: Questions
Authentic speech is characterized by rapidity and variability of pace.	Are all the speakers speaking at the same pace? Are they talking too slowly?
Background Noise: Criteria	Background Noise: Questions
Normal listening situations include background noise.	Is there normal background noise?

FIGURE 9.11: Worksheet for Evaluating the Authenticity of Listening Materials

Title: _____ Author: _____

Publisher: _____ Level: _____

Video: _____ / audio: _____

Lecture: _____ / List. scenario: _____

Corpus-informed: yes _____ no _____

Overall Evaluation of Authenticity: _____

1————————2————————3————————4————————5
Not authentic   Very authentic

Evaluation of Authenticity of Particular Components

Intonation	1____	2____	3____	4____	5____
Pronunciation	1____	2____	3____	4____	5____
Speaker domination	1____	2____	3____	4____	5____
Complete sentences	1____	2____	3____	4____	5____
Distinct turns	1____	2____	3____	4____	5____
False starts	1____	2____	3____	4____	5____
Pace	1____	2____	3____	4____	5____
Filler	1____	2____	3____	4____	5____
Background noise	1____	2____	3____	4____	5____
Other	1____	2____	3____	4____	5____

Journal Writing Tasks

1. Write what you learned from doing the observation tasks.

2. Consider your own experience in learning to listen in a foreign/ second language. Based on your reflections, what listening experiences do you believe helped you to gain in your abilities to comprehend the language? What experiences do you believe did not help you? Do you believe this is the same for other language learners?

3. Write freely on your ideas for teaching students to comprehend spoken English.

RECOMMENDED TEACHER RESOURCES

Select Listening Textbooks with Audio Components

Brown, S. and D. Smith. *Active Listening (Books 1–3)*. New York: Cambridge University Press, 2006.

Dunkel, P.A., P.L. Lim, W. Smatzer, and E. Pialorsi. *Listening and Notetaking, 4th ed.* Boston: Heinle Cengage, 2014.

Chase, B. T., K.L. Johannsen, P. MacIntyre, K. Najafi, and C. Fettig. *Pathways: Listening, Speaking & Critical Thinking*. Boston: National Geographic Cengage, 2012.

Gilbert, T.L. *Listening Power 3, 11th ed.* New York: Pearson Education, 2011.

Hartman, P., N. Douglas, and A. Boon. *Inspire*. Boston: National Geographic Cengage, 2014. (listening & speaking).

Salehzadeh, J. *Academic Listening Strategies: A Guide to Understanding Lectures*. Ann Arbor: University of Michigan Press, 2005.

Readings on Teaching Listening: Concepts and Activities

Brown, S. *Listening Myths: Applying Second Language Research to Classroom Teaching*. Ann Arbor: University of Michigan Press, 2011.

Flowerdew, J. and L. Miller. *Second Language Listening: Theory and Practice*. New York: Cambridge University Press, 2005.

Goh, C.C.M. "Second Language Listening Comprehension: Process and Pedagogy." In *Teaching English as a Second or Foreign Language, 4th ed.* eds. M. Celce-Murcia, D.M. Brinton, and M.A. Snow, 72–89. Boston: Heinle Cengage, 2014.

Lynch, T. *Teaching Second Language Listening*. Oxford, U.K.: Oxford University Press, 2009.

Nemtchinova, E. *Teaching Listening*. Alexandria, VA: TESOL, 2013.

Richards, J. "Listening comprehension: Approach, Design, Procedure." *TESOL Quarterly* 17, no. 2 (1983): 219–40.

Richards, J. and A. Burns. *Tips for Teaching Listening: A Practical Approach.* White Plains, NY: Pearson Education, 2012.

Rost, M. *Teaching and Researching Listening, 2ⁿᵈ ed.* Harlow, U.K.: Longman, 2011.

Vandergrift, L. and C.C.M. Goh. *Teaching and Learning Second Language Listening: Metacognition in Action.* New York: Routledge, 2012.

ENDNOTES

1   See Brown (2011), Goh (2014), and Vandergrift and Goh (2012) for more on active listening.

2   Listening processes are also discussed in Flowerdew and Miller (2005), Goh (2014), Vandergrift and Goh (2012), and Richards and Burns (2011). Pèregoy and Boyle (2012) provide a rich discussion on listening processes in ESL K–12 settings, focusing on integration of listening, speaking, reading, and writing.

3   See Richards (1990, 51).

4   See *Cold Water,* a videotape produced by Ogami (1988), to view the Somali student telling this story.

5   Brown and Yule (1983) and Richards (1990) discuss the functions of language as they relate to listening.

6   Total Physical Response (TPR) was developed by James Asher. His 1982 book, *Learning Another Language through Actions,* outlines his beliefs and teaching practices. Larsen-Freeman and Anderson (2011) and Richards and Rodgers (2011) also discuss TPR theory and practice. TPR is discussed in many other places as well.

7   See Segal (1983).

8   This a line from Segal and Sloan's video, *TPR and the Natural Approach* (1984).

9   The "Hokey Pokey" can be found on *It's Toddler Time,* produced by Bueffel and Hammett (1982).

10   This listening activity is from Porter and Roberts (1987).

11   I learned about matching behaviors to gain rapport by studying the work of Bandler and Grinder (1979), Lankton (1980), and Rosen (1982).

12   The idea for this activity comes from Ur (1984).

13   The "Old MacDonald" song can be found in many places, including *Action Songs for Indoor Days* produced by David White (1978).

14   The techniques discussed here on how to have students process authentic video materials come from Lonergan (1981), Sherman (2003), and Stempleski (1992).

15   Nemtchinova (2013) briefly discusses listening strategies. Flowerdew and Miller (2005), Mendelsohn (1994) and Vandergrift and Goh (2012) provide more extensive discussion. My own approach is fairly close to that of Rost (2011).

16   See Porter and Roberts (1987). My ideas on judging the authenticity of listening materials are directly influenced by the work of Porter and Roberts.

10

It is through talk that people construe their cultural worlds, display and recreate their social orders, plan and critique their activities, and praise and condemn their fellows.

—Frake 1980, 334

Teaching Students to Speak in Class

I *What does it mean to converse in a second language?*
I *How do EFL/ESL teachers teach speaking to beginners?*
I *What kinds of activities do EFL/ESL speaking teachers use with post-beginners?*
I *How do EFL/ESL teachers teach pronunciation?*
I *What problems do some EFL/ESL teachers have teaching students to speak in English?*

What Does It Mean to Converse in a Second Language?

Conversing in a second language means knowing how to maintain interaction and focus on meaning; use conversational grammar; introduce, develop, and change topics; take turns; apply conversational routines; and adapt style to match the setting/context.[1]

MAINTAINING INTERACTION AND MEANING

Conversations have both transactional and interactional purposes. When speaking and when the purpose is transactional, the focus is primarily on the meaning of the message. Is your message getting to the listener? For example, imagine explaining how to find your home to a new friend or describing your aches and pains to a doctor. When the speaking purpose is interactional, the focus is on maintaining social relations—greeting, complimenting, and chatting with friends. Are you able to keep the conversation going? Many conversations include both interactional and transactional purposes.

USING CONVERSATIONAL GRAMMAR

To truly communicate, you must also be able to use conversational grammar, which is different from standard grammar because it is based on how people actually talk. It features small chunks, mostly clauses and single words, as opposed to complete sentences. (This is true for both interactional and transactional turns.) Here is an example.

Jack: Hi, what's up?

Jane: Not much.

Jack: Headed to the bookstore?

Jane: Yeah. Have to buy my art course supplies.

Jack: Oh, good! Glad I ran into you! What do we have to buy?

Jane: Colored chalk, ah, sketch pad. Hmmm, charcoal sticks.

INTRODUCING, DEVELOPING, AND CHANGING TOPICS

Carrying on a conversation also requires speakers to introduce, develop, and change topics. This aspect of conversational management can be complex, the selection and development of a topic done through a process of negotiation. This includes opening a conversation with a formulaic expression such as *What's up?* To get past this initial greeting and before going onto another topic, other conversational cues or "formulas" are needed; for example, you may ask the person (or guess from the context) if he or she is busy or free to talk, how much time he or she has, and what topic should be talked about.

In our own language it is natural to select topics to talk about with people we know and people we don't know. But in another language, it is not easy to know how to do this—that is, what is safe to talk about and what isn't. For example, many students who come to the United States to study English are hesitant to talk about a variety of different topics that as Americans we are comfortable talking with strangers about—values or social standards (in certain circumstances), personal or financial needs (in certain circumstances), or the health of our family or self. In many other countries, these topics are not generally discussed with strangers or acquaintances.[2]

TAKING TURNS

To take part in a conversation also means to take turns, and there are both short and long turns. A short turn includes just one or two utterances, such as in the *What's up?* conversation. A long turn takes place when it is necessary for a speaker to explain or justify something, to provide an anecdote, or to tell a story. Many EFL/ESL students have difficulty taking long turns in a conversation because to do so requires them to take on responsibility for generating a sequence of utterances that gives the listener a good understanding of what they are saying, something that is not always easy to do in a first language, much less a second.[3] Some students have trouble taking both long and short turns, which could be a result of previous language-learning experiences, but possibly also because they lack the strategies in English for taking a turn, such as using interjections like *Mmhmm* to signal a request to speak, and quickly adding something to what a speaker just said. In conversations with multiple participants, EFL/ESL students might wait for a pause in order to contribute; if they are talking to Americans, that pause may not come, which makes knowing how to interrupt with expression like *Excuse me, may I jump in here.* another useful strategy.

CARRYING OUT CONVERSATIONAL ROUTINES

Conversing also means participating in conversational routines, many of which require a sequence of short turns. These routines are used regularly in our daily interactions—for example, paying for a newspaper, greeting a friend in the street, leaving a party, apologizing to a teacher, complimenting a friend, and offering something to a guest. Although all these interactions aren't scripted to a person, there are consistent patterns and rules. For example, consider the following interaction at a dinner party in the U.S.

> *Mrs. Jones:* Ann, would you like some more chicken?
>
> *Ann:* Oh, no thanks! Delicious! I can't eat another bite.
>
> *Mrs. Jones:* Well, there's plenty. Help yourself!

Now, the same interaction at a dinner party in Beijing.

> *Mrs. Liu:* Ann, some more? (Mrs. Liu reaches for the plate.)
>
> *Ann:* No, thank you!
>
> *Mrs. Liu:* I insist. Have some more. Have some more.
>
> *Ann:* No, thank you.
>
> *Mrs. Liu:* Oh, come on. Have some more.
>
> *Ann:* (Silent)
>
> *Mrs. Liu:* (Puts the chicken on Ann's plate)

While the routine in the U.S. is to offer something to a guest one or two times, often indicating to the guest to help herself, the pattern in China is often for the guest to refuse the offer several times, waiting for the host to insist. Since there are a wide variety of other such routines associated with daily functions, and these can vary from culture to culture, problems quite often arise for EFL/ESL students, especially when they try to directly transfer a routine from their native cultural experience into their English.

ADAPTING STYLE

Conversing also includes the selection of conversational style to match the formality of the situation. Jack Richards provides a good example of how native speakers of English adapt their style when asking someone the time.[4] From informal to formal, language is adapted in social settings in the following ways: *Got the time? What's the time? Do you have the time? Would you know what time it is? Could I trouble you for the time?*

EFL/ESL students have trouble adapting style, sometimes being too formal in an informal setting, in part as a result of applying the style rules from their first language. For example, in the United States some Asian students will use last names in situations that call for first name use, such as Mr. Brown, rather than John. Furthermore, ESL students who are not accustomed to calling older people or those with a higher status by their first names will often avoid addressing them by any name.

On the other hand, in an effort to sound more informal in their use of English, students can really miss the mark. This is what happened to the rural Thai adult I was tutoring some years ago. I was invited to a reception at a hotel in a northeast Thai town, mostly for Americans. I thought this would be a perfect time to expose this young man to conversations beyond ours. So, I invited him to go along. At the reception, he was doing fine, when suddenly, while in the middle of a conversation about Thai food, he smiled, looked at the elderly husband and wife, and said in an eloquent manner, "Please excuse me. I have to take a piss." Of course, no one took offense and even found it amusing, knowing he was learning English. But, it does show the need for us to teach students how to adapt style to different contexts.

How Do EFL/ESL Teachers Teach Speaking to Beginners?

With beginners, especially those students at the survival level, teachers usually limit the scope of the conversations so that these conversations are manageable and the students are successful. One way teachers do this is to control the kinds of questions they ask, using yes-no, either-or, and identity questions. As these question types only require students to give single-word answers, they can focus attention on comprehending the meaning in the questions. See Figure 10.1.

Teachers also limit the scope of a conversation through the use of simple charts, schedules, and advertisements. To create such an activity, some teachers use charts like that in Figure 10.2 which simply requires students to identify words and give short responses to questions.

FIGURE 10.1: **Questions for Beginners**

Yes-No Questions	Do Nigerians like to play soccer? Did you get up early? Can you speak French?
Either-Or Questions	Do Nigerians like to play or watch soccer? Did you get up early or late? Which can you speak better, French or English?
Identity Questions	Which sport do Nigerians like to play most? What time did you get up? What languages can you speak?

FIGURE 10.2: **Sample Chart**

New York	Pittsburgh	Flight
lv 10:15 AM	ar 11:05 AM	121
lv 12:45 PM	ar 1:35 PM	232
lv 4:40 PM	ar 5:30 PM	330

The schedule offers possibilities to ask a variety of questions: *What time does flight 121 arrive from New York?* (11:05 AM). *Does the flight leaving New York at 4:40 PM arrive in Pittsburgh at 5:35 PM?* (No). *How long does it take to fly from New York to Pittsburgh?* (50 minutes).

Another beginning activity is dialogue practice. Most EFL/ESL texts include dialogues. Some teachers, who are using corpus-informed grammar and vocabulary words related to speaking, write their own short dialogues so they can control the content. At a beginning level, such dialogues can include useful conversational routines. Here is a short example:

Person A: Could I borrow your pen?

Person B: Sure. No problem.

Person A: Thanks.

As beginners gain vocabulary and routines, the task can be made more complex. In this dialogue, students select from the available choices. Notice that Person B can either accept (+) or turn down (–) the request; Person A then reacts appropriately.

Person A:	Person B:
Could I borrow your pen?	Sure, No problem. (+)
May I use your book?	Yeah. Here you go. (+)
Got a pencil?	I'm sorry! I need it right now. (–)

As students become more proficient, teachers also create open-ended dialogues such as this one, allowing students to draw from their memory:

Person A: Could I borrow five dollars?

Person B: _____

Person A: _____

What Kinds of Activities Do EFL/ESL Speaking Teachers Use with Post-Beginners?

Quasi-communicative activities, like the ones in the previous section, also work well with students beyond the beginning level to warm up, review, or teach a new concept. However, with students at this level, it's important to go beyond quasi-communication exercises to give students opportunities to interact freely in English. The sample activities provide students with the kind of language practice that will enable them to express themselves in spoken English, although they also include some reading and writing.

DIALOGUE WRITING, SKITS, ROLE PLAYS, AND IMPROVISATIONS

One activity many students like because they can consider their own interactive needs is to write their own dialogues. When students act out their dialogues, they become skits, the idea being for students to practice and then perform in front of the class. Role-play activities are similar to skits in that students are expected to act. However, unlike skits, students are not provided with lines but are given a situation and roles to play. It's important to note that while some students are natural performers (actors), others are not and are uncomfortable with these types of activities.

Video drama is similar to role play. However, each role play is videorecorded so students can reflect on their use of language. This can lead to improvisation. One teacher, Tracy Forest, has students work in groups to specify the framework. She includes specifying when and where the scene takes place (in a cafeteria at noon on a Friday), who is participating in the scene (two close friends), and a recent event shared by the participants (Student B had borrowed $10.00 from Student A and promised to pay it back last week). She also has students describe how they feel about the other person and what is taking place (Student A sees that Student B has money and feels Student B should pay him or her back. Student B only has $12.00 and wants to go to a movie with friends that evening). She also has students define what they are doing when the scene begins (standing outside the cafeteria) and decide on an opening line (Student A: "Do you have the $10 you borrowed from me?").

Forest points out that the goal of preparation is for the students to create a basic set of facts that will build a conversation, using a wide range of linguistic options. She also points out that although the actual improvisation takes only about five minutes, its success depends on the longer 30 minutes or so of preparation time. Also, the videorecording of the performance can provide rich materials for follow-up lessons.[5]

BUZZ GROUPS[6]

This activity got its name because students sound like a group of busy bees while working on a task. To create a buzz group, the teacher selects a topic that will likely interest students and have some purpose; it's useful to try authentic tasks such as planning an actual trip to a museum or planning a party or picnic. Other topics might be based on questions like How can the police protect the public against crime? and How can we keep the ocean clean? An example of a buzz group I have used with a variety of EFL/ESL students appears in Figure 10.3.

Although some buzz group activities can be done with almost any group of students, some can be contextually designed for a specific group. To illustrate this point here is a buzz group activity on Who Will Be the Next Student Director of the American Language Institute (ALI)? After dividing students into small groups, I gave them this handout (see Figure 10.4).

GAMES AND RELATED ACTIVITIES

EFL/ESL teachers often use games in the conversation class. A variety of games exist—games to teach grammar, vocabulary, spelling, and pronunciation; there are all kinds of games—picture, psychology, memory, guessing, card and board games, to name a few.[7]

FIGURE 10.3: **Who's a Good Language Learner?**

In your group, make a list of the kinds of things a good language learner does. You will be asked to list these things on the board. To stimulate your thinking before you make your list, answer these questions.

- What do good language learners do in class? At home?
- What do you do that helps you to learn English?

FIGURE 10.4: **Who Will Be the Next Student Director of the ALI?**

We are going to elect a student director of the ALI. This person will attend some meetings with the director and staff and will be your representative in the director's office. We are going to divide you into groups.

So, here's your chance to change the ALI. In your group, talk about what you want at the ALI. What do you want to keep? What do you want to change?

A student lounge?	Smaller classes?	More chances to write?
More electives?	More trips?	More homework?
Less homework?	More time on computers?	A pop machine?
Guest speakers?	A more active ALI club?	An ALI softball team?

Consider other ideas, too! What kind of language program would you really like to have at ALI? After discussing what you want at the ALI, select a member of your group to run for student director. As a group, write a speech for this person to deliver. Help this person to practice the speech. After each of the group's candidates gives his or her speech in front of the student body, we will vote, by secret ballot, for the next ALI student director.

One game many people are familiar with is 20 Questions, in which students use English to narrow down possibilities through the use of yes-no questions. To play this game, two students identify something in the room—for instance, the teacher's pen, the fan, or the calendar—and their classmates have 20 chances to guess what that object is.

In the Strip Story,[8] students are put into small groups and given one or two lines of a short story. They are told not to show their lines to other students. Instead, they have to negotiate who has the first line, second line, and so on. Slowly, they put the story together. An alternative way to play is to take the strips away after they've read them and have them put the story together from memory. A cartoon version also exists in which students put a cartoon sequence together, each describing his or her strip to others without showing it to them.

Teachers sometimes make up their own strip stories while some others discover stories used by other teachers, passed down through the years. Here is an example of one strip story I discovered while teaching at a Thai University.[9]

WHO'S THE LAZIEST BOY?

An old man was walking along the road.

Suddenly he saw three boys lying on the grass under a tree.

He said, "I'll give a gold coin to the laziest boy. Who's the laziest boy?'

The first boy jumped up, ran over to the old man, and said, "I'm the laziest boy. Give me the coin."

The old man shook his head and said, "No, you aren't. Lie down again."

The second boy held out his hand. "I'm the laziest boy. Give me the coin."

The old man shook his head again. "No, you aren't. Lie down again."

The third boy said, "Please come over and put the coin in my pocket."

"Yes," said the old man, "You're the laziest boy!"

And he put the coin into the boy's pocket.

Another activity is a matching game called Same or Different? Students are divided into pairs and given a set of pictures, Sets A and B. Some of the pictures in the set are the same and some are different. Without showing the pictures, and within a limited amount of time, the two students must decide which pictures are the same and which are different.

PRESENTATIONS

Presentations provide students with opportunities to develop their speaking abilities by speaking in front of their classmates. Some students get very nervous about having to give a presentation, and the teacher might need to help such students to lower their anxieties. I believe, however, that some anxiety is facilitative as it motivates students to prepare and to put forth their best efforts.

A set of books I appreciate are called *Present Yourself 1 & 2*.[10] I like this *set* because it is visually pleasing, introduces themes along with useful grammar and vocabulary, and provides chances for intermediate level students to systematically work through and practice how to give a presentation from note cards on topics that build from fairly easy topics (e.g., a good friend, a favorite place, I'll show you how) in Book 1 to more complex topics (e.g., a person to admire, a good vacation, in my opinion) in Book 2. I used these books in Korea with first-year college students and could see the confidence and improvement students gained through the use of them.

However, although the books can certainly make the teacher's job easier, there are some student behaviors that the teacher needs to give attention to. Some students will feel overly anxious about presenting in front of classmates, and others will try to memorize their presentation because they are really good at memorizing, have memorized presentations for past teachers and had been praised for it, or have never really had to speak in front of classmates on a topic without extensive notes. As the goal of giving presentations, at least in my mind (and the *Express Yourself* author's mind), is to learn to present from PowerPoint slides, some students will still memorize, and it might take time and patience to teach these students how to develop their own presentation style and voice. Sometimes all it takes is lots of practice.

Another concern is the use of PowerPoint slides. If the teacher wants to make the presentation a little more formal, students can use slides. In Korea my students wanted to experience both informal casual presentations and more formal ones, and I agreed. However, I tried to teach them that although using slides can be useful in a formal presentation, the slides should not be the presentation. Presentation slides should simply emphasize what the topic is. The words, photos, video or chart on the screen are simply there to support what the speaker is talking about. The eyes of the audience should be on the speaker most of the time, not the screen. However, one common challenge is that some student-presenters want to show off their PowerPoint skills so they create content-full slides so that the audience's eyes are not on them.

I think students gain a lot simply from preparing for, practicing, and giving a presentation. Students want feedback on their presentations, so I like to get the students involved in creating a feedback form as it gives them a voice and some ownership of what goes on in the class, as well as builds awareness about expectations. See the example of the oral presentation feedback form (Figure 10.5).

Some teachers videorecord presentations, which allows the evaluators (speaker, classmates, teacher) to review them with the purpose of doing a more in-depth critique.[11] I have found that looking more deeply into the presentation provides some students with more awareness about their presentation content and behavior. If time permits, I favor having students study their recorded presentations outside class, sometimes in small groups or pairs, and then write up what they have learned. I also like to meet with students in small groups outside class to join in the critiquing process.

DIGITAL TECHNOLOGY AND SPEAKING ACTIVITIES

As discussed in Chapter 7, digital technology has broadened the way students can learn English, and learning to speak English is no exception. To begin, videoconferencing tools[12] offer a way for teachers to open face-to-face communications across distance, such connecting a class of Japanese students with students in the U.S. through the use of Skype and FaceTime.

There are a lot of creative ways to use video tools. Simply surfing the web can offer a great variety of ideas. One site that attracted me was Niki's Learning Technology Blog,[13] where a teacher posted 20 webcam activities

FIGURE 10.5: Sample Oral Presentation Feedback Form

Content	Comments
Content presented is believable	
Key points are obvious.	
Organization/Structure	
Presentation is organized & structured	
Introduction gains the audience's attention	
Introduction explains the purpose of the presentation	
Style	
The presenter did not read the speech, but talked from notes or PPT slides	
Content knowledge is evident	
Speaker showed confidence	
Time was used well/not rushed	
The presenter did not stand in one spot, but moved around.	
The presenter purposefully used gestures, pauses, & other nonverbal cues	
Use of PowerPoint	
Slides supported the presentation, not the presentation itself	
Slides are easy to see/read. Not too much information on the screen.	
Media (video clips, photos, charts, etc.) supported the point the presenter was making.	

for EFL and ESL students. One of his ideas is called Favorite Poems or Haiku. She asks students to videorecord themselves reading their favorite poem/haiku. She then adds them to a class webpage (or blog) as a class poetry collection. Another version of this is to ask students to write their own poetry or haiku and then ask them to read it. In an activity called Create a Collaborative Story she emails students a video with the first line of a story and asks them to listen to it and record their own, and then to pass it on to another student. This way, the class builds a story over a period of time, which is later played in class. In an activity called Guess the Object, students record a description of an object without showing it, and viewers have to listen to and guess what the object is. She points out that getting students to generate these video clips will help them to be concise and really pinpoint the key concepts behind describing objects.

Another activity that is on Niki's blog is to use video as a way for students to create an interactive learning diary. She asks students to send her a video summary of what they think they have been learning and she responds by pointing out that the recordings form a learning record through which students can review and perhaps see how they have improved. Given time, he points out that they can literally see and hear the improvements in their speaking ability.

Another way to use digital technology to help students gain speaking skills is to ask them to keep a *digital oral dialogue journal.* I did this with my intermediate-level speaking class in Korea, and most of the 15 students said they liked it. I started the dialogue by giving a topic: When did you begin to learn English? What kinds of experiences have you had as a language learner? Can you tell stories about your language learning experience? Have you had any English teachers who you really liked? Why do you like them? I encourage them to be extemporaneous. However, I also know that some students need notes—words they are learning and want to use—as well as grammatical structure. As long as they wean themselves away from a dependency on these notes and do not read from a script, I fully accept their use of notes when they begin their oral journals. I try to make my replies conversational, and I offer encouraging feedback, while at the same time letting them know when I do not fully grasp what they are trying to say. I also ask questions that help them clarify meaning, as well as tell my own related stories. As the main goal is to help develop fluency and spontaneous speech, I do not correct their grammar or pronunciation unless they ask, and as I write about next, students will ask! I also learned (the hard way!) to limit entry time to less than five minutes.

Although the spoken dialogue journal in my class was meant to promote fluency, it can also focus on specific aspects of speaking. For example, Kathy Brenner[14] explored the use of *digital dialogue journals* to help students with pronunciation. As she points out, pronunciation problems can overwhelm some students and impede their ability to communicate and be understood. She recommends the use of oral journals to provide chances for students to improve problematic enunciations, intonation, stress placement, and expansion of students' listening skills, as well as develop fluency. Important to her, getting teacher feedback can create a strong incentive for students to listen at their own pace without worrying about embarrassment in the classroom.

How Do EFL/ESL Teachers Teach Pronunciation?

Some teachers prefer to have students use a pronunciation text.[15] Many pronunciation texts provide explanations, drawings that illustrate how sounds are made, work on minimal pairs, and lots of practice activities for students in pronunciation of consonant and vowel sounds. More advanced texts focus on intonation patterns, sentence stress placement, emphatic stress placement, and more. While texts are quite useful in teaching pronunciation, it is often necessary to teach beyond the text or develop activities for students. Each class of students has its own pronunciation issues.

TEACHING PRONUNCIATION: CREATIVE ACTIVITIES

Presented here are a few activities to teach pronunciation.[16] One activity makes use of minimal pairs (two words pronounced exactly the same except for one difference—e.g., *lice* and *rice, lap* and *lab)*. The teacher selects pairs that are problematic for students and lists them on the board. For example, students from Spain might benefit from grappling with these minimal pairs:

List A:	seat	eat	each	sheep
List B:	sit	it	itch	ship

The teacher begins by calling out a word and then students tell the teacher whether it is from list A or B. Once the students understand the rules, they take turns selecting and pronouncing words, while classmates and the teacher tell the speaker the correct answer.

Another activity uses a kazoo to focus on patterns of intonation.[17] With a kazoo, the teacher can avoid words and grammar and focus only on intonation patterns. A number of intonation patterns can be taught— for instance, patterns for declarative sentences, yes-no questions, and tag questions. It is possible for the teacher to demonstrate the pattern by humming into the kazoo, as well as to have students practice the patterns without the words. In addition to intonation patterns, a kazoo can be used to show students correct accent placement on words (e.g., ÌNteresting rather than interestÌNG), as well as how sentence stress works (major words, like nouns, main verbs, adjectives, and adverbs receive stress while minor words like prepositions, pronouns, and articles do not receive stress).

To prepare another activity is the pronunciation computer where the teacher needs to collect samples of students' English during classroom activities.[18] The teacher writes these samples (words, phrases, sentences) on the board and numbers each item. The students, who are sitting in a semicircle facing the board, are then told to study the list of language items and to raise their hands if they would like to practice an item. They are also told that the teacher is now a computer and that the students have to turn the computer on and off by saying *start* and *stop*. The point is for students to pick an item from the board and say it before the computer will model the English pronunciation. The job of the pronunciation computer is to stand behind the students and to continue to give the pronunciation of the line given by the student each time the student says it; the computer says it into the student's ear until the student tells the computer to stop.

A number of teachers have discovered that using Carolyn Graham's Jazz Chants is a constructive and fun way to give students practice using natural stress and intonation patterns of conversational American English. Graham has published a number of Jazz Chant books for children and adults over the past 25 plus years.[19] I like Jazz Chants because most students enjoy following the audiotaped chants, appreciate the humor, recognize and use the natural intonation, and are willing to try out new things. For example, I have had no problem getting adults to practice whispering and talking loudly in English when chanting to Graham's jazz chant, *Sh! Sh! Baby's Sleeping!*[20]

TEACHING STUDENTS STRATEGIES FOR SELF-IMPROVEMENT

We can also teach students how to take on responsibility for improvement of their own pronunciation. Figure 10.6, adapted from Joan Morley, provides self-improvement strategies teachers can teach students to use.[21]

FIGURE 10.6: **Strategies to Improve Pronunciation**

Strong, Vigorous Practice: Use vigorous practice with strong muscular movements. Use slightly exaggerated mouth movements, overly articulating words. Don't hurry. Take time to articulate as clearly as possible.

Self-Monitored Practice: Listen closely to and monitor yourself on both the sounds and the rate, rhythm, and vocal qualities. Pay attention to stress points, pitch rises and falls, and rhythmic patterns.

Slow-Motion Practice: Half-Speed Practice. Try slow motion, or half-speed, practice for a strong sense of kinesthetic touch-and-movement feedback and for the feeling of articulation.

Loop Practice ("Broken Record" Practice): Use an endless-loop practice of 20 or more strong and vigorous repetitions of a phrase or word with focus on kinesthetic feedback.

Whisper Practice (Silent Practice): Use whispered or silent practice to focus on articulation and the feeling of articulation.

Mirror Practice (Video Practice): Use mirrors to view the articulation of specific sounds. If possible, zoom in on a close-up of your face as you articulate words.

What Problems Do Some EFL/ESL Teachers Have Teaching Students to Speak in English?

Problems some EFL/ESL teachers face include:

- The "fluency" problem
- The "students won't talk" problem
- The "error treatment" problem
- The "any native speaker can teach conversation" problem

THE "FLUENCY" PROBLEM

Definitions of **fluency** back many years, and partly because there is no agreement about what fluency is.[22] I personally favor a simple definition: The ability of the speaker to use the language creatively, coherently, accurately, and without awkward pauses for long periods of time.

In my experience as both an EFL and ESL teacher, I have interacted with students who have been studying and using English for years. Some are very fluent, including being accurate. That's quite an accomplishment.

Others are fluent in that they are creative and do not have awkward pauses, but they have never fully developed grammatical accuracy. Further, some students are very accurate but struggle to express themselves and often pause. I often ask myself why there is a difference, and I think part of the reason is personality. Students simply have different learning styles, attitudes, and aptitudes. However, some of the reason could be their language learning experience. A tentative conclusion, based solely on my observations through the years, is that students who have learning experiences in which the teachers have emphasized accuracy and do not provide many opportunities for them to express themselves are not especially fluent when speaking. On the other hand, I have also seen students who learned English in settings where accuracy was not considered important. These students interacted a lot in English, perhaps doing communicative activities without any emphasis on grammatical form, and many can express themselves fairly coherently without awkward pausing, but some have become fossilized, repeating the same grammatical error over and over.

So, the questions is: How can we provide opportunities for students to speak both coherently and accurately without awkward pausing? Some teachers favor teaching grammatical structures after which they then closely tie them to communication activities through which students can apply what they are learning.[23] Other teachers like to provide communicative activities, such as information gap activities, board and other games, role-plays, and other such activities discussed in Chapter 4. They allow the students to deduce the grammatical rules or teach them the rule after the activity. I have done both because they allow students to express themselves and comprehend what others are communicating, as well as generate necessary input for them to acquire more of the language. Further, some teachers believe that feedback is important for students to develop accuracy, and they offer it on word choice, grammar errors, pronunciation, and more. (This topic is discussed as a separate problem later in this chapter.)

THE "STUDENTS WON'T TALK" PROBLEM

Some students will not talk in class because they are too shy or anxious. This is not only true for beginners, but also for some students who are fairly advanced in their listening, reading, and writing abilities. Perhaps they are anxious because they have not had many chances to speak or because teachers in the past have been critical of their English. Whatever the reason, when faced with quiet, anxious students, the problem for the conversation teacher is, how can we get these students to talk? Before anything else, we need to gain their trust. The students need to know that we are on their side, that we do not expect them to speak perfect English, and that we realize it takes time and effort for them to learn to converse in English.

As teachers, we also need to provide opportunities for students to feel at ease in the classroom. One way to do this is through warm-up activities. In fact, the objective of using warm-up (or icebreaker) activities is to relax students and help get them over their apprehensions. There are, of course, a great number of possible ways to warm up students for a conversation class. One way is through the use of techniques drama teachers use to get anxious students to relax and to provide an inviting atmosphere.[23] A few examples are given in Figure 10.7.

The use of quasi-communication activities, such as dialogue practice, can also engage "quiet" students in speaking. As students are able to rely on context and print, they are sometimes more willing to speak. As students

---

FIGURE 10.7: **Drama Techniques**

A Breathing Warm-Up Exercise: The students and the teacher close their eyes, breathe slowly in through their noses for three seconds, hold that breath for nine seconds, then slowly release it through their mouths for six seconds. This is repeated several times.

Walking Warm-Up Exercise: The teacher and students clear away furniture from the center of the room. While standing, they form a circle. They then begin to walk in a circle in their usual way. After a turn or two around the circle, the teacher then calls out commands, such as "Walk like you are chest high in water," "Walk on clouds," "Walk like you were a marionette," and "Walk like you are on hot sand."

A Voice Warm-Up Exercise: While sitting or standing in a circle, the teacher begins by whispering a word or phrase, for example, "Hello!" The next person says the word a little louder, but still in a whisper, the next a little louder, and so on, until the word comes back to the teacher, perhaps even as a shout. A variation is to slow down or speed up the way the word or phrase is said.

---

become more and more comfortable with these pre-communication activities, we can coax them to participate in the fluency-type activities, such as problem-solving, skits, and buzz groups. And, success builds success. From my experience, as students feel the success they have at negotiating meaning, the more risks they are willing to take in expressing their ideas in English.

THE "ERROR TREATMENT" PROBLEM

As EFL/ESL teachers, we have choices in regard to treating students' language errors. We can decide not to treat language errors, or we can decide to treat them. If we decide to treat them, there are other decisions that need to be made. *When* should errors be treated? *Which* errors should be treated? *Who* should treat them? *How* can they be treated?

As for **when** to treat errors, they can be treated at the moment the error is made or treatment can be delayed. A problem with instant treatment is that it can disrupt communication. A problem with delaying treatment is the possibility that students who made the errors will not recognize the errors as being their own.

Making decisions about **which** errors to treat is not an easy task for the teacher. Some teachers base their decision on their estimate of the stage of acquisition of the student—for example, treating irregular past tense verb errors such as "He eated it" (an early stage error) while ignoring regular past tense verb errors (a later stage error). As Allwright and Bailey have said, "The dilemma . . . to English teachers is the question of whether or not treatment of learners' errors . . . will help speed the acquisition of correct form, or simply be futile until the learners reach a stage of development where they can make use of such feedback."[24] Faced with such a dilemma, some teachers take a different approach. Instead of considering the acquisition stage of the student, they base their treatment on whether or not the error interferes with meaning during communication. For example, if there is some confusion over the meaning of "I am very enjoy," the teacher might treat the error: "Do you mean, 'I enjoyed the movie'?"

The teacher also has a choice about **who** treats the error. Of course, the teacher can treat the error, but so can the student who made the error or even the whole class. One problem in asking students to treat each other's errors is the very real possibility that they will not cooperate.

Even more problematic is **how** to treat the errors. Returning to an example given in Chapter 2, some teachers will treat the error in ways that are not obvious to the student.[25]

> *Anna:* I have no brother.
>
> *Teacher:* Two sisters? (using rising intonation)
>
> *Anna:* Because my mother she dead when I was three years old.
>
> *Teacher:* She *died* when you were three?
>
> *Anna:* Yes. She dead when I was three years old.

It is possible to make it clear to the student that errors are being treated, as well as offer an activity that draws the student's attention to the error and the correction.

> *Maria:* I have 30 years.
>
> *Teacher:* Which is correct: "I have 30 years" or "I am 30 years old"?
>
> *Maria:* I am 30 years old.

Another error treatment activity involves classification. For example, when a student makes an error such as, "I sleep late" (meaning "I slept late"), the teacher can write the error and the correction on the board for the student to see.

Correct	Incorrect
I slept late.	I sleep late.
I am 30 years old.	I have 30 years old.
I'm going to study.	I going to study.

The teacher can also do a mini-lesson or conversation to let the student practice the correct form.

> *Teacher:* José, did you get up early this morning?
>
> *José:* No, I slept late.
>
> *Teacher:* Do you sleep late everyday?
>
> *José:* No, I usually get up early. Today I slept late.

THE "ANY NATIVE SPEAKER CAN TEACH CONVERSATION" PROBLEM

Native speakers of English are frequently asked to teach conversation simply because they are native speakers. This idea is based on two assumptions. First, the native speaker is most qualified to expose learners to authentic use of English. Second, those who teach the speaking course do not need special qualifications as teachers (unlike teachers of reading and writing). The idea is that if you are a native speaker of a language, you can teach others to speak it simply by using the language with them.

The first assumption is partially true. Native speakers of English likely expose students to the teacher's culture and fine nuances of English simply by interacting with them. Of course, this depends on how they interact with students. For example, I have observed native speakers who have lived in a country for several years interact with students by using behaviors of the students' culture, as well as pronounce words and use intonation that resembles the way their students speak. However, the fact they are native speakers does not make them more qualified to teach speaking than a teacher who learned English as a foreign or second language. In fact, many such learners have incredible experience and talent with speaking English in a variety of cultural contexts. In addition, the fact that they have had to go through the process of mastering speaking skills gives them insights into the kinds of problems students face, as well as speaking practice and feedback they need. The only possible problem is that some of their students (and some administrators) have negative perceptions and attitudes toward them. The teacher sometimes has to convince them that her or his experience and abilities are beneficial to the students.

The second assumption is false. As shown in this chapter, teaching students to converse in another language is quite challenging. It requires those who teach it to develop an understanding of what learning to converse in a second or foreign language entails, as well as the ability to make use of activities that provide opportunities for students to speak. In addition, teachers need a great variety of skills in classroom management, as well as in interpersonal and cross-cultural communication.

TEACHER SELF-DEVELOPMENT TASKS

Talk Tasks

1. Have you learned to converse in a foreign or second language? What was the experience like? What problems did you have? Can you relate your experience to the learning experiences of EFL/ESL students?

2. Using the pictures of the four seasons in Figure 10.8, create a lesson for beginners. Imagine that you will show the pictures on the board, and that you, the teacher, will have a conversation with the class about the seasons. To prepare for your conversation, write down a series of yes-no questions, either-or questions,

FIGURE 10.8: **The Four Seasons**

and identify questions. See how many possible questions you can list. Consider both display and referential questions, as well as the content you include in your questions. After listing your questions, meet with another teacher who has also made a list. Compare your lists. Combine your list of questions.

3. Review the activity types in this chapter. Meet with other teachers to answer these questions. Which activities do you like the most? Why? Which have you used as a teacher or experienced as a learner?

Observation and Talk Tasks

1. Listen to a conversation between two EFL/ESL learners. Quickly note examples of the errors the students make. Do you believe that these students will someday speak without making these same errors if given many opportunities to speak English?

2. Record a class you teach or a friend's class. As you listen to the recording, note examples of your error treatment behaviors. Do you or the teacher treat their errors? If so, how? When? What types of errors? Look for a pattern to treat errors. Then, talk with other teachers who have also analyzed how they treat language errors. Do you treat errors in similar ways? Together, generate an alternative plan for treating students' errors. Implement it to see what happens.

3. Observe a friend's conversation class. What kinds of speaking activities does the teacher use? What do you see this teacher doing in the class that you would like to use in your teaching?

Journal Writing Tasks

1. List your ideas to teach beginners through the use of yes-no, either-or, and fact-type questions and quasi-communication activities. Feel free to draw sketches and list procedures you would use in your teaching.

2. Write about your own experiences in learning to converse in a foreign or second language.

3. What do you think makes students anxious about speaking a foreign or second language? What ideas do you have about reducing students' anxieties?

RECOMMENDED TEACHER RESOURCES

Select Textbooks for Speaking Classes

Feak, C.B., S.M. Reinhart, and T.N. Rohlck. *Academic Interactions: Communicating on Campus* (Book + DVD). Ann Arbor: University of Michigan Press, 2009.

Folse, K. and J. Ivone. *First Discussion Starters: Speaking Fluency Activities for Lower-Level ESL/EFL Students.* Ann Arbor: University of Michigan Press, 2002.

Folse, K.S. and R. B. Lockwood. *4 Point: Speaking for Academic Purposes.* Ann Arbor: University of Michigan Press, 2017.

Gershon, S. *Present Yourself 1: Experiences, 2nd ed.* (Student's Book with Audio CD). New York: Cambridge University Press, 2014.

Graham, C. *Jazz Chants: Old and New.* Oxford, U.K.: Oxford University Press, 2000.

Grant, L. and E.E. Yu. *Well Said: Pronunciation for Clear Communication* (adult through beginner). Boston: National Geographic Cengage, 2017.

Helgesen, M., S. Brown, and J. Witshier. *English Firsthand, 4th ed.* (book series). New York: Pearson Education, 2010.

Jensen. B.S. *The Michigan Guide to the TOEIC(R) Speaking Test* (with audio CD). Ann Arbor: University of Michigan Press, 2011.

Professional and Other Readings on Teaching Speaking

Bohlke, D. "Fluency-Oriented Second Language Teaching." In *Teaching English as a Second or Foreign Language, 4th ed.*, eds. M. Celce-Murcia, D.M. Brinton, and M.A. Snow, 121–35. Boston: Heinle Cengage, 2014.

Bolen, J. *39 No-Prep/Low-Prep ESL Activities for Teenagers and Adults.* Amazon.com, 2015.

Folse, K.S. The *Art of Teaching Speaking: Research and Pedagogy for the ESL/ EFL Classroom.* Ann Arbor: University of Michigan Press, 2006.

Goodwin, J. "Teaching Pronunciation" In *Teaching English as a Second or Foreign Language, 4th ed.*, ed. M. Celce-Murcia, D.M. Brinton, and M.A. Snow, 136–51. Boston: Heinle Cengage, 2014.

Grant, L. *Pronunciation Myths: Applying Second Language Research to Classroom Teaching.* Ann Arbor: University of Michigan Press, 2014.

Jones, T. *Pronunciation in the Classroom: The Overlooked Essential.* Alexandria, VA: TESOL, 2016.

Klippel, F. *Keep Talking: Communicative Fluency Activities for Language Teaching.* New York: Cambridge University Press, 1985.

Lazaraton, A. "Second Language Speaking." In *Teaching English as a Second or Foreign Language, 4th ed.*, ed. M. Celce-Murcia, D.M. Brinton, and M.A. Snow, 106–20. Boston: Heinle Cengage, 2014.

Murphy, J. *Teaching Pronunciation.* Alexandria, VA: TESOL, 2013.

Nation, S.S.P. "Second Language Speaking." In *Handbook of Research in Second Language Teaching and Learning, Vol* II., ed. E. Hinkel, 444–54. New York: Routledge, 2011.

ENDNOTES

1   My ideas here are influenced by the work of Brown and Yule (1983), Bygate (1987), Nation (2011), and Nation and Newton (2009).

2   Barnlund (1975) discusses conversation topics in Japan. The complexity of spoken discourse is evident by reading Wong and Waring (2010).

3   The complexity of turn-taking is evident through reading the collection of articles in Atkinson and Heritage (1984) and Schenkein (1978).

4   See Richards (1990, 73).

5   See Forest (1992, 81). Also see Pitts (2016).

6   Bleisten, Smith, and Lewis (2013) discuss similar activities. They call them "Getting Lost in Communication" Activities (pp. 29–30).

7   Several sources describe and illustrate games used in conversational classrooms. Classic books that are still in print include Wright, Betteridge, and Buckby's *Games for Language Learning* (1994) and Rinvolucri's *Grammar Games* (1984). Newer books include *ESL Games: 176 English Language Games for Children* by Vernon (2015) and *Language Games: Innovative Activities for Teaching English* by Andrade (2009).

8   The Strip Story was created by Robert Gibson (1975).

9   To the best of my knowledge, a materials writer at The Language Center, Chalalongorn University, Bangkok, created this strip story.

10 See Gershon (2015a, 2015b).

11 See Lazaraton (2014) for a discussion on the use of video recording and critiquing presentations, as well as useful suggestions on facilitating individual, group, and impromptu presentations.

12 There are a variety of apps that can be used. One is MailVu, a simple to use app that runs in the browser and enables students to record a short message that can be sent by email. Another is Skype, the most well known video chatting app. Oovoo is a Skype competitor.

13 Nikpeachey.blogspot.com

14 See Brenner (2008). Also see Aoki (2014) for a review of literature on the use of digital dialogue journals.

15 See Henrichsen et al. (1999), and Gilbert (2014).

16 A great variety of pronunciation activity ideas can be found in the pronunciation section of Bailey and Savage (1994, 199–262), and Goodwin (2014).

17 Gilbert (n.d.) discusses the use of the kazoo to teach intonation.

18 "The Pronunciation Computer" was originally designed by Charles Curran (1976).

19 Graham's original 1978 book is simply titled *Jazz Chants*. Two of her other books include *Holiday Jazz Chants* (1999) and *Jazz Chants Old and New* (2003).

20 This chant is from Graham (1978).

21 See Morley (1987, 86).

22 Bohlke (2014) provides a review of literature on how fluency has been defined throughout the years.

23 See Larsen-Freeman (2014) and McCarthy and O'Keeffe (2014).

23 The warm-up activities I give are from Via (1987) and my own experience.

24 See Allwright and Bailey (1991, 102). Also see Ellis (2008).

25 This example is from Gebhard, Gaitan, and Oprandy (1987, 228).

11

Comprehension may be regarded as relating what we attend to in the world around us—the visual information of print in the case of reading—to what we already have in our heads. And learning can be considered as modifying what we already have in our heads as a consequence of attending to the world around us.

—Smith 1994, 53

Teaching Students to Read for Meaning

- ▌ *What does it mean to be an engaged reader?*
- ▌ *How do EFL/ESL teachers teach beginners to read?*
- ▌ *What kinds of reading activities do EFL/ESL teachers use with post-beginners?*
- ▌ *How can teachers teach vocabulary in a reading class?*
- ▌ *How can teachers use grammar in a reading class?*
- ▌ *How can teachers help students to improve their metacognitive reading strategies?*
- ▌ *What problems do some EFL/ESL teachers have as reading teachers?*

What Does It Mean to Be an Engaged Reader?

Engaged readers read for different purposes while processing text into meaning and using a wide variety of skills and strategies.

THE PURPOSE OF READING

We read a lot of things and for different purposes! We read some of these alone—for example, the news over morning coffee or tea. We also read things and talk about them with others. For example, we might

201

read the movie listings to select a film to see or we might read a menu item at a restaurant to the waiter to ask if he or she recommends it. We read some things while sitting, others while walking, and still others while driving. We also read a short story or novel for pleasure, an email or text response to a question we asked a friend, and a blog about food simply to learn something new. In short, we usually have a reason to read.

PROCESSING WHAT WE READ

Engaged readers also process their reading through bottom-up, or low-level, processing and top-down, or high-level, processing. I discussed these same processes in Chapter 9 on listening comprehension. With reading, these processes are the same but in a visual sense.[1] To comprehend written language, we rely on our ability to recognize words, phrases, and sentences (bottom-up, text-driven processing), as well as on our background knowledge related to the content of what we are reading (top-down or conceptually-driven processing). These two processes interact as we read, resulting in a degree of comprehension.

However, bottom-up reading processing is different from listening in that readers need visual strategies, rather than auditory strategies, to process written syntax (for example, word order) and lexicon (words and the meaning of words). In addition, they need to be able to process orthography (letters), decode words, as well as have an ability to process reading phonology (for example, the intonation used in reading when we read aloud inside our heads or to an audience).

Certainly, the reading process is much more complex than what I introduce here. However, I can provide one very important idea, backed by research findings, about how EFL/ESL students learn to process what they read that can be quite useful to EFL/ESL teachers: Students learn to process what they read by reading. In other words, the more they read, the better they become at processing what they read. This is because as they process text, they build a wider vocabulary, knowledge of the second language, the world, and text types.[2] The implications are that EFL/ESL teachers need to have students read a variety of texts and to read as extensively as possible.

STRATEGIES USED BY READERS TO COMPREHEND TEXT

Engaged readers also use a wide variety of reading strategies. One definition of **strategies** that I like is N.J. Anderson's. He says that strategies are "the conscious actions that learners take to improve their language learning . . . . Because strategies are conscious, there is active involvement of the L2 learner in their selection and use."[3] As these strategies are active, they are **metacognitive**, which means the reader (in the case of reading strategies) is aware of the strategies he or she is using while reading. However, not all readers, even those who are highly engaged, are aware of the strategies that they use to comprehend text. Further, readers who are not fully engaged and have trouble comprehending text can benefit from learning how to use strategies that help them to read efficiently.

Five metacognitive strategies that engaged readers tend to use are **questioning, predicting, visualizing, summarizing**, and **making connections**. Later in this chapter I discuss how they can be taught, including a process of awareness-building and a variety of activities that help students to become more engaged readers.

SKILLS USED TO READ

In addition to the strategies readers use to make sense of print, successful readers also learn basic reading skills.[4] They can **skim** a text to get the general idea of a passage. For example, engaged readers can read a newspaper headline and the first paragraph or two to determine what the story is about and whether they want to read the article. Successful readers can **scan** things they read to locate facts or specific information—for example, to locate a number in the phone book or a file from a list on a computer screen.

Successful readers can also **read for thorough comprehension.** This means they read to understand the total meaning of a passage. This kind of reading is often done in academic and other settings where complete comprehension is necessary. In addition, successful readers can **read critically.** Critical reading requires that readers evaluate what they read and consider whether or not they share the author's point of view or are convinced by the author's argument or position. Finally, successful readers **read extensively.** This means they read broadly in areas of interest, such as mystery novels, or in a field of study, such as history or cooking.

How Do EFL/ESL Teachers Teach Beginners to Read?[5]

Before being able to skim, scan, read for thorough comprehension, read critically, and read extensively in English, students need opportunities to build their bottom-up processing abilities in the language. In other words, they need time and practice building knowledge of sentence structure and vocabulary, as well as experiencing reading within meaningful contexts.

This can be done in several ways. One way, of course, is to use texts, and there are a number of beginning-level grammar and vocabulary texts on the market. Most of these books include lots of exercises, charts, graphs, illustrations, and photos. Reading texts written for beginners also offer students tightly controlled grammatical structures and vocabulary while providing stories relevant to a particular reading audience (e.g., young adults). (See the Recommended Teacher Resource section.)

EFL/ESL students at the beginning level can also benefit from teacher-created vocabulary-building activities, especially if these activities are based on the students' immediate, or at least felt, needs.

Teachers also create activities that provide contexualized reading experiences. One way is with pen or email pals. Students in one class can write to students in another, or the teacher can link students across schools, even countries. These letters can be handwritten, or, email offers speed and often a fun way for students to communicate. The letters from students become the reading text; when students truly connect, the letters offer students a valuable reading and learning experience. If students' oral skills are more developed than their reading skills, they can generate their own reading texts by recording their life stories, which the teacher and a digital program can transcribe and edit. These stories then become reading material for the students.

What Kinds of Reading Activities Do EFL/ESL Teachers Use with Post-Beginners?

As students improve their processing abilities, teachers can have them do activities to develop their skills to skim, scan, read for thorough comprehension, read critically, and read extensively and develop their metacognitive reading strategies.

SKIMMING ACTIVITIES

Readers skim to gain a general impression of a book, story, essay, or article and to determine whether to read it more carefully. The activities[5] illustrate ways that students can practice this. The first example (Figure 11.1) asks the reader to skim a passage and then identify the best title.[6]

A second example of a skimming activity is more extended; students are given a topic and expected to select relevant books, websites articles, and other reading materials. To prepare, the teacher collects reading materials on a variety of narrowed topics, such as sports of Chinese origin, Italian fashion, computer games, and travel in Eastern Europe. The teacher also adds readings (comprising about half the total readings) on closely related topics, such as sports in Latin America, New York fashion, computer programs used in business, and travel in Western Europe. The teacher sets up the class library, asks each student to select a specific topic from a list, and has students locate and skim readings from the class library, searching for readings on their topic. The idea is to see how many of the topic-specific readings the student can discover.

SCANNING ACTIVITIES

While skimming is quick reading to find the general idea, scanning is quick reading to locate specific information.[7] For example, we scan catalogs, dictionaries, event calendars, book indexes, menus, a wide variety of print on the internet—basically any source in which we need to locate specific information.

FIGURE 11.1: **The Best Title**

Read the passage quickly. Then select the best title.

Mary Ashworth couldn't believe it! She had purchased a lottery ticket six months ago, put it in her wallet, and forgot about it. One day while at the store, she found the ticket and decided to see if she had won. To her amazement, she had won the top prize of two million dollars! She remarked enthusiastically, "I really couldn't believe it! I almost threw the ticket away without checking to see if I won anything!"

Which title is best?

a. The Good Shopper

b. The Lucky Lottery Winner

c. Six Months Ago

d. The Lost Wallet

Another way to give students practice with scanning is to have a contest. Students form teams, and each student receives a handout that includes facts. I sometimes use fact sheets on different countries—for example, on China's 14 coastal port cities. Equipped with a long list of questions and answers, the teacher throws a question out to the class. The first team to answer the question correctly gets two points. If a team gets the answer wrong, it loses a point. The team with the most points wins.

Another scanning activity is an internet scavenger hunt.[8] The teacher prepares a list of questions that the students are asked to answer using the internet. For example, the teacher could ask students to go to a website on world populations and to find out how many people live in different countries or major cities. Likewise, the teacher could send students to a website on dog breeds to find out what the most popular breed of dog is in different countries. Students then can use a search engine to look up each question and scan the website they have selected to find the answers to each of the questions. When I do this activity, I like to ask students to prepare scanning questions for classmates (and the website addresses and answers for me). I then use the student-generated questions during the scavenger hunt/contest.

READING FOR THOROUGH COMPREHENSION: ACTIVITIES

Unlike skimming and scanning, activities that aim at having students read for thorough comprehension require them to read meticulously. The goal is for the students to understand the total meaning of a reading selection, and there are a number of techniques teachers can use to get students to interact with the reading material:

- Students study the title and skim to capture the main idea.

- Students read two paragraphs and predict what will follow.

- Students do several different scanning tasks, such as underlining past tense verbs in red and adverbs indicating sequence (e.g., *first, second, next,* etc.) in blue, circling words they do not recognize, and putting stars next to words that seem important. After each task, they briefly discuss what they underlined, circled, or starred.

- After students have a sense of what the reading material is about, they read silently while answering true-false or multiple choice questions.
- Students meet in groups, consider the text, write down questions, and give them to another group to answer.
- Students draw pictures of the main characters in a story or draw pictures that illustrate the storyline.
- Students, working in groups, reconstruct material previously cut into pieces (also called a jigsaw task).
- Students read a story with the conclusion missing, then write their own endings.
- Students give the reading material a new title.
- Students put a set of pictures or photos in order to show the storyline or content.
- Students meet in groups to summarize an article and to separate main ideas from supporting ideas and examples.
- Students listen to the teacher discuss how the piece of writing is organized.

This list illustrates some of the activities teachers use in reading classes, and there are, of course, other ways to teach reading, as well as ways to creatively combine a number of reading activities into a single lesson. And it is through such a combination of activities that students have opportunities to read thoroughly. With this in mind, here is a reading lesson I designed for a lower-intermediate ESL class, including a story I wrote and a combination of activities. Through this example, I encourage you to write your own stories and activities for students in your classes.

> My wife, Yoko, and I got up very early on Saturday. We had a busy day ahead of us. Before leaving the house, we shut the windows. Then we noticed our cat, Kiku, sitting comfortably on a chair. "This won't do," Yoko said. "We better put Kiku outside for the day."
>
> Yoko said goodbye to Kiku just before she got into the car. The cat didn't look happy. He wanted to go back into the house to rest comfortably on the chair! But this was impossible. At least, this is what we thought!

We then drove to see my mother at a retirement home. But my mother wasn't home. So we walked in the garden. Yoko spent some time at the small white fountain in the middle of the garden.

After we walked in the garden, we drove to the countryside to join relatives at a family reunion. Yoko talked with Aunt Nita and my cousin Ann for a long time. She also talked with Uncle Gene, who always seems to be wearing white slacks and shoes.

We left the reunion early to go to a wedding party. Our friend Agnes is from Poland, and she married her childhood sweetheart, Wojtek. They had a wonderful time, although they missed their families in Poland on such an important day.

Finally, late at night, we went home. And guess what! We found Kiku in the hall of the house! How did that cat do that!?

Here are the activities students completed:

- Students answered questions before they read (e.g., *How many of you have ever had a cat as a pet? How many cats? What do cats like to do?*).
- Students studied a blown-up photo of Kiku the cat next to a drawing of a chrysanthemum while listening to an explanation about the meaning of Kiku's Japanese name, meaning chrysanthemum.
- Students looked at the reading while tracing some of the script with their finger, spelling out words. As a class, they wrote the same words in the air with their index fingers.
- Students looked for words they had studied the week before, such as *fountain, garden, and countryside.*
- Students underlined verbs in the past tense, and then counted the number of past tense verbs.
- Each student read the story silently and responded true or false to such statements as (1) Kiku is a dog, (2) Yoko and her husband visited three places, (3) Yoko and her husband visited his mother after going to a picnic.
- While in groups, students read each paragraph together and then had one person in each group summarize it.

- After students finished reading the summaries, they arranged seven drawings into the same order as the events in the story.

- As a group, students answered the following question: *How did Kiku get back in the house?* Then each group gave their answer to the whole class.

- As a class, students gave the story possible titles while the teacher wrote them on the board.

CRITICAL READING

There are at least three things to remember when asking students to do critical reading. First, students still need to do the kinds of activities that lead to full comprehension, as discussed earlier. Second, students need to make judgments about what they read: *Do I agree with the author's point of view? How is my view different? Does the author persuade me to change my view? Is the author's evidence strong?* Third, we need to be careful about what we ask students to make judgments on. In other words, we need to select content that is not only interesting to the students as readers, but also something they can relate to. For example, young adults from Japan, Mexico, and California will likely be more interested in reading and giving opinions about earthquake survival than will people in places not affected by earthquakes. Likewise, young students are apt to have better-informed opinions about popular rock stars and youth fashion than the average adult would.

EXTENSIVE READING

The goal of extensive reading is to improve reading skills by processing a quantity of materials that can be comprehended and pleasurable. Teachers who implement extensive reading set up an open library (in the classroom or school library) where students can select from an assortment of reading materials.[9] The teacher's job is to guide the reader to materials that are comprehensible, letting the students make their own choices.

As a part of the extensive reading experience, teachers often ask students to report on what they have read. One way to do this is to have students interview each other through the use of question prompts. For example, if a student reads a short story, the question prompts might include:[10]

- What is the story title?
- What kind of short story is it?
- Did you like the story?
- Why did you like it, or why not?
- Would you recommend the story?
- Who is the story's author?
- What is the main message in the story?

Another activity, which can be fun for students, is to ask them to write a letter to one of the characters in a story they read.[11] After selecting one of the characters, the students write a letter that focuses on agreeing or disagreeing with something the character did or said or lists questions that the readers would like to ask the character related to the book. Another creative idea is to engage students in thinking about what happens in a sequel to a story they read. The teacher can ask them to think about what might happen later to the main characters.[12]

How Can Teachers Teach Vocabulary in a Reading Class?

Vocabulary is important. Without it we cannot understand the intended meaning of the writer. With this in mind, reading teachers can provide ESL/EFL readers with opportunities to increase their active vocabulary by following basic guidelines along with corresponding activities.[13] First, teach beginners high-frequency words. They are not difficult to find. Simple Google searches of the 1,000 most frequently used words in American English conversations, the 2,000 most frequently used words in English academic journals, or the most frequently used adjectives in English will reap results. Many of the wordlists have been generated from the use of the Corpus of Contemporary American English (COCA) or another corpus research base (see Chapter 6). Further, if you want to do your own search, COCA is free.

Second, these frequently used words merit continuous attention. As such, I like to think of teaching vocabulary as a process of (1) introducing a word or set of words, (2) following up with a detailed study of the word or words, and (3) lots of contextual practice to reinforce and expand students' understanding of the word(s). The goal constantly on my mind is that students will be able to "call up the meaning of a word as it is recognized" when they read, something that reading theorists call **lexical access.**[14]

The brief introduction of words that I give is often before students read, but I sometimes have them read first and tell me what words they want to study. I do this when I think the class will understand much of the passage or I do this simply out of curiosity. I do not take much time to introduce new word. One reason is because students quite often simply forget a word the first time they are exposed to it (unless it is especially meaningful). Another reason is that long explanations about what words mean can bore the students. I have observed too many teachers take 20 minutes of a reading class to try to explain what the vocabulary words mean when all the students really needed was a quick translation or a picture or a few questions to get them started. Since I want students to spend much of the class reading, I save a more detailed study of the words for a time after they have read and comprehended the passage at some level.

The more detailed study of vocabulary includes asking students to analyze and expand their understanding of these words. Here are a few activities that can help the students expand their understanding of words.[15] The first asks students to analyze a new word by looking at the prefixes, roots or bases, and suffixes. For example, if the word is *redo*, we can ask them what *re* means, as well as create a list of things we sometimes do again, such as homework, an essay, or makeup, as well as think up other words with the prefix *re-*, such as *rethink, reorganize,* and *revise.* If the word is *preview*, we can ask them what *pre-* means, what the base is, and what it means. We can follow that up with listing things we can preview, such as movies, TV shows, a new computer commercial, as well as think up other words that have the same prefix, such as *precaution, precede,* or *preapprove.* Likewise, if the word is *endless*, we can ask what the root or base of the word is, as well as what the suffix means ("without"). If the students are ready, we could ask them to think of other words with same suffix, such as *effortless, ageless,* and *lawless.* If there are two words: *protector* and *announcer,* we can ask them to identify the suffixes (*or* and *er)* and tell them it means "one who," for example "one who protects." The students can also come up with example words with *–er* or *–or,* such as *swimmer, basketball player,* and *teacher,* as well as make up short sentences, such as *I am a swimmer* or *I swim everyday.*

Another activity is to ask students to identify synonyms. The choice and number of words depends on the level of the student and words they have already studied. The idea here is to give them practice with studying words they have already been introduced to in their reading passages, as well as strengthening their sight vocabulary (words they know as soon as they see them). Figure 11.2 shows an example activity.

The same kind of activity can be done with antonyms, as shown in Figure 11.3.

An activity I have used throughout my years of teaching in to are students to write their own dictionary.[16] Some authors and publishers call this a **vocabulary log.** I have found this is especially helpful for some beginning students. In the past I had them use index cards, a hole punch, and a metal rings. More recently students like to use an iPad or computer. The advantage of using index cards or an iPad is easy access. The idea behind asking students to write their own dictionaries is they will need to analyze and

FIGURE 11.2: Identifying Synonyms

The word is *strong.* Which words have the same meaning? Circle six words.

happy	robust	solid	poor	late	angry	beautiful	nutritious
tough	angry	tired	wealthy	weak	sturdy	durable	resilient

FIGURE 11.3: Identifying Antonyms

The word is *strong.* Which words have the opposite meaning? Circle six words.

sad	frail	solid	poor	fragile	angry	creative	tired
tough	hardy	tired	sturdy	weak	unsteady	durable	funny

FIGURE 11.4: An Example Dictionary Entry – Beginner

Happy – feel good.   adjective
Sad – feel unhappy.

I am happy. She is a happy person. Happy Birthday

think about the word, create a record of the words they are studying, and be able to review them. Besides building the students' reading vocabulary, an additional benefit is that they will sometimes refer to the words they want to use in a conversation or writing assignment both inside and outside of class.

I encourage students to be creative with their dictionaries (see Figure 11.4). During the first few weeks, I include dictionary time in class to teach them how to create their own personalized dictionary. Later, it becomes a homework assignment, and hopefully some of the students will continue to add words and phrases to their dictionaries on their own. Some of the things that I encourage students to include in their dictionaries are: a word they want to remember and use; an easy-to-understand definition; synonyms; the part of speech and different forms of the word (noun, verb, adverb, adjective, preposition...); whether the word or words is standard or colloquial/idiomatic English; drawings or photos; example sentences, and anything else that helps them understand the word and be able to recognize the word while reading.

How Can Teachers Use Grammar in a Reading Class?

Some teachers do not like to use grammar in a reading class because they believe it takes time away from reading. Other teachers are not confident with teaching grammar or have not had much experience studying it and

214 | Teaching English EFL/ESL, Third Ed.

explaining it. However, it may be worth the effort to help students comprehend the passages they read.

Although grammar can become complex, it also can be an interesting subject to study. Personally, I am happy that I took a few grammar classes, especially those that were taught as a tool for ESL/EFL teachers to use in the classroom. I ended up building on my basic courses and texts, and through the many student-questions I have answered and concepts I have taught throughout my career, I have expanded my grammatical knowledge and have found that an understanding of grammar when teaching reading, as well as other skill areas can be quite useful.

Grammar had been a very important part of teaching reading to ESL and EFL students in the past. For example, the **Grammar Translation method** was used, and is still used to some extent, in reading classrooms around the world. More recently grammar has become a smaller part of teaching reading as it has been replaced by reading activities discussed earlier in in this chapter.[17] However, teaching grammar can still be useful to students, especially with helping them to comprehend text. In this section I provide some examples of ways that grammar can be possibly beneficial to students who are working on their English reading comprehension.

The basic idea of using grammar in a reading class is to teach students how to analyze the sentences they read in a way to aid comprehension. Some teachers take the time to teach students to identify parts of speech, including nouns, pronouns, verbs, adjectives, adverbs, determiners, and prepositions. One reading activity I learned from Paul Nation[18] is for the teacher to select words from a passage that students are reading and to write them on the board along with the line number. The students then study the passage sentence, find each word, and say whether it is a noun, a verb, an adjective, or an adverb by writing *n., v., adj.,* or *adv.* after it. The words selected for this activity are usually words that can be different parts of speech in dissimilar contexts. Nation points out the value of being able to identify the part of speech of a word in a specified context.[19] First, when trying to guess the meaning of a word from the context, knowing the part of speech of the word will provide extra meaning, such as an adjective before a noun usually means the writer of the passage is modifying or describing the noun in some way, such as in the sentence *She has exceptional talent at playing the piano.* It also makes looking up the word in a dictionary much easier because the meanings of words are usually classified according to the part of speech of the word.

Another use of grammar is with teaching students to recognize **cohesive devices.** Cohesion means to "interconnect, unify, and interrelate ideas." When ideas are not cohesive, they are fragmented or disjointed. Grammatically, there are many ways that writers connect ideas, and one basic way is through the use of **coordinating conjunctions,** including *and*, *but*, *or*, *yet*, and *so*. These words connect two ideas or clauses in specific ways. The use of *and* is adding an idea, such as in *We went to the city on Sunday, <u>and</u> we had a good time.* The use of *but* shows that what follows will introduce something that is true despite being contrary to what was just written, as in *I hate the taste of kale, <u>but</u> I eat it anyway.* The use of *or* connects two (or more) alternatives, such as in *We could go to the movies or watch TV at home.* The use of *yet* is similar to the word *nevertheless*, as in *Some people know they should exercise, <u>yet</u> they don't exercise much at all.* The use of *so* indicates a reason for an action or situation, or its result, as in *They were late for class, <u>so</u> they walked faster.* It does not take long for beginners to recognize and make use of these conjunctions in their reading and other skills as they have them in their first language. However, being aware of such conjunctions and what they mean make students feel like they are making progress, and I believe helps them to read with more comprehension.

The same is true with **subordinating conjunctions,** which indicate time. These include words such as *when, before, after,* and *while,* as well as others including *if, as if, even if, as long as, whenever, although, as, because, rather than, in order that,* and more. When students learn to identify a subordinating conjunction, affiliate it with meaning, they have yet one more tool to process the meaning of the text (see Figure 11.5).[20]

Another cohesion lesson is to teach students to identify words that show comparison.[21] Such comparative words include *same, similar, identical, equal, different, other, additional, more, fewer, less, adjectives* or *adverbs + -er.*[22] Pointing out such words as they compare two or more things can help students understand a passage. Figure 11.6 shows an example of a reading passage and activity that helps students understand comparison. The teacher previously gave an example of a reading passage on a projected slide and circled and discussed words of comparison.

FIGURE 11.5: Identifying Subordinate Conjunctions

Instructions: Read each sentence. Circle the subordinate conjunction.

1. When he gets home from school, he checks his email.
2. He checks his email when he gets home from school.
3. Although the weather has been exceptionally warm, the woman has been wearing heavy sweaters.
4. The woman has been wearing heavy sweaters although the weather has been exceptionally warm.
5. If you had a chance to visit any city in the world, where would you go?
6. Where would you go if you had a chance to visit any city in the world?
7. Whenever I give you a lot of reading homework to do over the weekend, some of you groan.
8. Some of you groan whenever I give you a lot of reading homework to do over the weekend.

Discussion Questions: What did each subordinate conjunction tell you about time in each sentence? Can a subordinate conjunction go anywhere in the sentence? What punctuation mark do we usually use with the conjunction?

FIGURE 11.6: Understanding Comparisons

Instructions: Read the passage.[23] Circle the words that show comparison.

All the states in the U.S. have had some population growth since 2010. The fastest growing state is North Dakota. In 2010 there were 672,591 people. In 2015 there were 756,927. North Dakota grew more than 12%. The populations of Hawaii and North Carolina have almost identical growth. Hawaii grew by 5.24% and North Carolina by 5.32%. However, Hawaii is smaller than North Carolina and has fewer people. Hawaii grew from 1,360,301 to 1,431,603 people living in the state. North Carolina grew from 9,535,483 to 10,042,802 people. North Carolina is not increasing its population faster, but it does have many more people living there than Hawaii.

Discussion Questions: North Dakota is the fastest-growing state. Its growth is faster than what? Hawaii's growth is almost identical to what state? North Carolina has more people than what state?

Of course, there are additional ways to use grammar to help students comprehend what they are reading. My goal here is simply to show that grammar can be useful way to aid student comprehension of text.

How Can Teachers Help Students to Improve Their Metacognitive Reading Strategies?

As mentioned earlier, engaged readers use a wide variety of reading strategies to improve their reading comprehension. Because these strategies are active, they are **metacognitive,** which means the reader is aware of the strategies he or she is using while reading. Becoming aware of the strategies they use as they learn to read in English is not necessarily easy for all students, and teachers can help them to build their abilities to use metacognitive strategies.

A very systematic way to teach reading strategies is provided by Kelly and Clausen-Grace,[24] who teach students how to build metacognitive awareness. They have a cyclic model that includes four phases: **think-aloud, refining strategy use, letting strategy-use gel,** and **self-assessment** and **goal setting.** They also focus on five cognitive strategies as they can use as they go through this process, including **questioning, predicting, visualizing, summarizing,** and **making connections.** Each cognitive strategy is started during a think-aloud session. During this time the teacher models the strategy (e.g., predicting), and the students try to tell the teacher what he or she is doing while reading, For example, when teaching students how to predict, the teacher will say aloud, "I am studying the title. Now I am studying the subtitle to predict what I am going to read." The instructions teachers follow, as provided by Kelley and Clausen-Grace, are:

1. Introduce, explain, and define the strategy components for students.
2. Apply the strategy components while you read aloud.
3. Ask students to tell you which strategy component you're using.
4. Clarify the purpose of the strategy.

Gradually, in subsequent lessons, the students can take turns reading aloud. After the strategy use has begun to gel, the majority of the mental work changes to the students, while the teacher and classmates act as coaches during reading times. After several weeks, each student self-reflects and writes a plan centered on one part of the strategy that he or she would like to improve. During silent or group reading time, the teacher provides coaching and reading conferences. The goal is to monitor students' use of their metacognitive strategies as they read independently.

Other teachers are not as systematic, but they do work at helping students become more aware of the metacognitive reading strategies they use. Some of the activities that teachers use that offer students practice with the strategies of questioning, predicting, visualizing, summarizing, and making connections are shown. One such reading activity (Figure 11.7) helps students build their questioning strategy that uses the *think aloud* protocol.[25]

FIGURE 11.7: **Using Think-Aloud to Teach Students How to Ask Questions as They Read**

1. Select a appropriate text to model the questioning strategy.

2. Explain the strategy to the students. Use a handout or the computer and screen in front of the room to show how the strategy works. Include both the text and the reader's questions to illustrate the think-aloud protocol. Here is an example:

   Homelessness in Hawaii is a big problem. (*What kind of big problem?*) Entire families are living in tents in parks and along canals. (*Really? Children, too? Why doesn't the government help them? Can't they find jobs?*) People are homeless because the cost of living is very high in Hawaii, and they don't have enough money to pay for housing. Many homeless work at minimal wage jobs, but they don't make enough money to feed their families, send their children to school, and pay for other needs. Government agencies try to help them find housing, but there are so many restrictions that many families will not accept their help. (*Why not? What kind of restrictions?*)

3. Ask the students to finish reading the article and then to stop and list questions they have as they read.

4. Group students and ask them to read the text aloud along with their questions.

Another metacognitive reading activity, created by Suzanne Boon, provides students with practice making predictions. She asks students to consider internet news websites with which they are familiar. She then passes out pre-reading questions that students can apply to the news. These questions include: What do you already know about this topic? Looking at the news column heading, what do you believe the story might be about? Write at least three ideas. If there are pictures, what do they show? What do you think the story is about based on the pictures.[26] She then asks the students to read the article to see if their predictions match the content of the article and asks them to discuss whether their predictions were true, and if so, what parts of the text and pictures helped them to prove their predictions.

Another metacognitive reading strategy is to have students tap into their senses as they read[27] (see Figure 11.8). I have used this strategy for many years and find that some students have fun drawing the storyline

FIGURE 11.8: Using Our Senses as We Read

1. Select reading material that is easy for students to read. This could be a descriptive essay, short story, or poem.

2. Ask students what our senses are: seeing, hearing, smelling, tasting, touching.

3. Read the essay or story aloud. Ask students to close their eyes as you read. Also ask them to use their senses—to see, hear, smell, taste, and touch—as they listen to the story.

4. Ask the students to read the story silently, and as they do to draw what they see, as well as write down words that represent what they smell, taste, and hear. For example, if the reading is about camping in the wilderness, the reader might smell and taste smoke, hear insects and a river flowing, and hear the voice of the character or characters.

5. Give students a chance to recreate their drawing and words onto a separate piece of paper and to show it to classmates.

6. Ask students to read again silently, this time applying their senses to the content.

7. Ask students if they felt differently about reading while using their senses, and if so how it was different. For example, some students say they could see more and hear the narrator's voice and even smell things within the setting.

and creating voices for characters in a story or assigning a voice for the author in a descriptive essay, as well as using their other senses in creative ways. Many have said that by tapping into their senses they improve their comprehension, too.

Students can also learn to summarize what they read. This metacognitive strategy helps them to realize if they comprehend. It also helps them to further process what they have read to make sense out of it if they have not fully comprehended the passage. Sometimes I like to have students write a short summary of what they have read. If their classmates are also reading the same story or article, I ask them to read each other's summaries and write comments or add to the summary. When I do this, I ask students to create a pen name that only they know. I then have them put their summaries in a pile and ask them to randomly pick summaries to read. The pen names hide the identity of the student. If some students have a problem with comprehension and summarizing, then they won't be embarrassed, and classmates who do comprehend and can write detailed summaries sometimes feel freer to write productive comments and fill in gaps in the summary.

Richard Day offers another way for students to practice summarizing through jigsaw reading.[28] He selects an article that is fairly easy for the students to read. He then cuts some of the material into paragraphs or sections. He then divides the class into groups and gives each person in the group a different paragraph or section to read. After they read, he asks them to take turns summarizing their paragraph/section and then to put the paragraphs/sections into the correct order. He then asks each group to read the entire article and to create a verbal summary. A volunteer then summarizes the article aloud to the other students.

Another metacognitive reading comprehension strategy is being able to identify transition words in the text, and S. Kathleen Kitao offers an activity for students to practice identifying and giving meaning to words that connect ideas.[29] She begins by teaching transition words and their connected meaning. For example, she teaches students words to recognize when additional information is being added (*and, furthermore, moreover, in addition, also*), words that show consequence (*so, therefore, as a result, as such*), words that show cause and effect (*due to, because, on account of, as a result*), words that show contrast (*however, but, although*), words that provide order (*first, second, next*), and more. She shows these connecting words in a passage that students read and study. Following this she gives students a new passage. She then uses think-aloud (discussed on pages 217–218) to illustrate each of the connecting words and their meaning. Here is my own example of what this think aloud activity might be:

> Yoko grew up in a busy bright noisy city in Japan. *As such,* (consequence transition) she was both excited and scared when she visited a mountain resort. It was a dark wooded place. The dark woods disturbed her. She never experienced such darkness before. *Moreover,* (additional information) the sounds of the woods frightened her. Even the sound of squirrels running on the roof startled her, *and* (additional information) the sound of the wind in the trees worried her. *As a result,* (consequence) during the first night there, she turned on all the bedroom lights and hid under her bedcovers.

After doing the think aloud activity, Kitao gave students another reading passage and asked them to identify each connecting word and type of transition. She also gave students a handout with the transitions deleted from it and asked them to fill in the blanks and to identify the transition type.

What Problems Do Some EFL/ESL Teachers Have as Reading Teachers?

Problems some EFL/ESL teachers face include:

- The "intermediate-level slump" problem
- The "background knowledge" problem
- The "getting students to read" problem

THE "INTERMEDIATE-LEVEL SLUMP" PROBLEM

At an intermediate level of language proficiency, EFL/ESL readers quite often hit an **intermediate-level slump.**[30] This is because they have learned basic reading skills by reading dialogues in textbooks, short stories with limited introductory vocabulary, and directions in a text or a printout. Once these conventions of reading have been studied and become easier, readers start using information-based texts, which opens up learning to very large amount of language. Not only are students exposed to enormous amounts of new vocabulary but also more complicated rhetoric, expository style, and more. As N.J. Anderson puts this, learning to read is like an "inverted pyramid. As students achieve higher levels of language proficiency, there is an increase in the amount of material available to learn."[31]

This intermediate stage is frustrating for some students. As they began learning to read, progress was quick. They could complete basic tasks successfully and felt like they were learning. However, when faced with larger and larger amounts of reading material, the process slows down, and students feel like they have stopped learning.

When students experience intermediate-level slump, the teacher needs to encourage them, but more than this, teachers need to provide tasks that students can accomplish. For example, stuudents can learn to read personal emails, articles on familiar matters, and more advanced narratives. At this stage teachers can teach them ways to expand their reading vocabulary, involve them in identifying main ideas, scan, and differentiate between facts and opinions. Further, N.J. Anderson offers this advice: "Perhaps the greatest mistake that a teacher can make at this level is to expect too much from the readers. This is not to suggest that teachers should not have high expectations but that those expectations should be focused on moving the reader from learning to read to reading to learn."[32]

THE "BACKGROUND KNOWLEDGE" PROBLEM

Students' ability to comprehend the content of reading material depends in part on their knowledge about the topic of the reading selection. To increase students' potential comprehension, the teacher can lead a variety of pre-reading activities that build background knowledge.

One activity is to have a short discussion about the topic. For example, the teacher might lead off discussion with the following set of questions before asking students to read an article on the lifestyles of sumo wrestlers: *How many of you have ever watched sumo on TV? What happens during a match? What are some of the rules in sumo? What do you know about the lifestyles of sumo wrestlers?* If time is limited, written reading previews could be used. Similar to a movie preview, a reading preview introduces the student to the main idea of the reading. Pictures, sketches, or photographs can also be used to introduce the topic of a reading.

Another pre-reading activity is to take a field trip to a historical or cultural site or event or to watch a film or video clip about the topic of the future reading. For example, students could watch part of a videotaped sumo match and view a short documentary on the lives of famous contemporary sumo wrestlers.

THE "GETTING STUDENTS TO READ" PROBLEM

In some EFL/ESL teaching settings, students do not necessarily value reading. It is a constant struggle for teachers to get students to read in and out of class. When faced with such an attitudinal or motivational problem, teachers are often at a loss about what to do.

Although there is no single or simple way to change students' attitudes toward reading, there are things teachers can try.[33] First, we can begin with the following assumption: "People learn better when what they are studying has considerable meaning for them . . . when it really comes out of their own lives . . . when it is something that they can in some way commit themselves to or invest themselves in."[34] Second, we can work at discovering what brings meaning to the life of each student in our classes. We can do this by observing students: What do they talk about? Show interest in? Carry around with them? Some nonreaders will read if the reading matches their interest, such as learning to develop photos or learning to cook. When given the right conditions, problem readers will spend time reading because they have an invested interest in learning something they consider to be important or useful.

Third, we can do our best to introduce students to readings that match their interests, mostly through extensive reading activities. By putting together a collection that includes the readings and content in which students express interest, we can most easily guide students toward materials that interest them. Such a collection for adults might include mysteries, how-to books, old letters, grammar books, catalogs, sports magazines, poems, forms, menus, academic books, and adventure stories.

TEACHER SELF-DEVELOPMENT TASKS

Talk Tasks

1. Meet with a friend. Work through the following steps:

    a. Make a list of materials that students can use to practice scanning.

    b. Locate one of these materials.

    c. Create a scanning activity.

2. Meet with a friend. Work through these steps:

    a. Locate a reading passage. If you are now teaching a reading class, you might want to select material you plan to teach or are required to teach.

    b. Study the list (given earlier in this chapter) of techniques teachers can use to have students interact with reading materials.

    c. Based on the list of techniques to have students interact with reading materials, and on your own creative ideas, generate a reading lesson that contains at least five different reading activities to help students process the passage you selected.

    d. Find others who have done this same activity. Give each other copies of your lesson plans.

3. Study the discussion and activities on teaching students to use metacognative reading strategies. What does "metacognitive" mean? Which strategies do you use as a reader?

4. Study the example metacognative reading strategies discussed in this chapter. Select one, and with a partner, brainstorm ways to teach this strategy to EFL/ESL students.

5. Do you agree that teeaching students grammar can help students improve their reading skills? Explain.

Observation and Talk Task

1. Try one of the reading lessons created in Talk Task 1 or 2. Record the lesson. Then select three two-minute sections from the tape to listen to. As you listen, note alternative ways you could teach the same aspect of the lesson.

Journal Writing Tasks

1. Study the activity types discussed in this chapter. Which do you like the most? Why? Which types have you used as a teacher or experienced as a learner?

2. Write about your experiences in learning to read a second language.

3. Select one of the problems from the section What Problems Do Some EFL/ESL Teachers Have as Reading Teachers? Write about why this is a problem for some teachers, and perhaps for yourself as a teacher.

4. Write about teaching students to improve their metacognitive reading strategies.

RECOMMENDED TEACHER RESOURCES

Professional Readings on Teaching Reading

Anderson, N.J. "Developing Engaged Second Language Readers" In *Teaching English as a Second or Foreign Language, 4ᵗʰ ed.,* eds. M. Celce-Murcia. D.M. Brinton, and M.A. Snow, 170–87. Boston: Heinle Cengage, 2012.

Birch, B.M. *English L2 Reading: Getting to the Bottom.* Mahwah NJ: Lawrence Erlbaum, 2002.

Day, R.R., ed. *New Ways in Teaching Reading.* Alexandria, VA: TESOL, 2012.

Day, R.R. *Teaching Reading.* Alexandria, VA: TESOL, 2015.

Grabe, W. and F.L. Stoller. "Teaching Reading for Academic Purposes" In *Teaching English as a Second or Foreign Language, 4ᵗʰ ed.,* eds. M. Celce-Murcia, D.M. Brinton, and M.A Snow, 189–207. Boston: Heinle Cengage, 2012.

Mikulecky, B.S. *A Short Course in Teaching Reading: Practical Techniques for Building Reading Power.* White Plains, NY: Pearson, 2011.

Vaille, B. and J. Quinn Williams. *Creating Book Clubs in the English Language Classroom.* Ann Arbor: University of Michigan Press, 2005.

Professional Books on Teaching and Learning Vocabulary

Folse, K. *Vocabulary Myths: Applying Second Language Research to Classroom Teaching.* Ann Arbor: University of Michigan Press, 2004.

Lessard-Clouston, M. *Teaching Vocabulary,* Alexandria, VA: TESOL, 2015.

Nation, I.S.P. *Teaching Vocabulary: Strategies and Techniques.* Boston: Heinle Cengage Learning, 2008.

Nation, I.S.P. *Learning Vocabulary in Another Language, 2ⁿᵈ ed.* New York: Cambridge University Press, 2014.

Nation, I.S.P. and S. Webb. *Researching and Analyzing Vocabulary.* Boston: Heinle Cengage Learning, 2011.

Select Textbooks for Reading Classes

Lockwood, R.B. and K. Sippell. *4 Point: Reading for Academic Purposes*. Ann Arbor: University of Michigan Press, 2016.

Silberstein, S., B.K. Dobson, and M.A. Clarke. *Choice Readings*. Ann Arbor: University of Michigan Press, 1996.

Silberstein, S., B.K. Dobson, and M.A. Clarke. *Reader's Choice, 5th ed.* Ann Arbor: University of Michigan Press, 2008.

Smith-Palinkas, B. and K. Croghan-Ford. *Key Concepts: Reading and Writing Across the Disciplines*. Boston: National Geographic Learning, 2009.

Zemach, D. *Building Academic Reading Skills*, Book 1 (*2nd ed.*) & 2. Ann Arbor: University of Michigan Press, 2009, 2016.

Zwier, L.J. and M.S. Weltig. *Mastering Academic Reading*. Ann Arbor: University of Michigan Press, 2010.

Textbooks Series with Emphasis on Combining Reading with Other Skills

Boardman, C.A. and L. Barton. *Challenges: Reading and Vocabulary for Academic Success*, Books 1–3. Ann Arbor: University of Michigan Press, 2016.

Broukal, M. *Weaving it Together: Connecting Reading and Writing, 4th ed.*, Volumes 1–4. Boston: National Geographic Learning, 2016.

Browne, C., B. Culligan, and J. Phillips. *In Focus: A Vocabulary, Reading, and Critical Thinking Skills Course*, Books 1–3. New York: Cambridge University Press, 2014.

Folse, K., series ed. *Four Point: Reading and Writing: English for Academic Purposes* (3 levels). Ann Arbor: University of Michigan Press, 2011.

Smith, L. C., and N. M. Mare. *Reading for Today, Books 1–5*. Boston: National Geographic ELT, 2017.

Williams, J. D. Wiese, J. McEntire, J. Williams, K.J. Pakenhan, and P. Vittorio. *Making Connections: Skills and Strategies for Academic Success*. New York: Cambridge University Press, 2013.

ENDNOTES

1 Many sources address second language reading processes. Some include Birch (2002), Carrell, Devine, and Eskey (1988), Day (2015), Grabe (2009), and Peregoy and Boyle (2012).

2 See Day and Bamford (1998) and Krashen (1988, 1993).

3 N.J. Anderson (2005:757). Also see N.J. Anderson (2014:173).

4 The way I categorize reading skills is consistent with Day (2012c), Grellet (1981), Mikulecky (2011), and Silberstein, Dobson, and Clarke (2008).

5 In a book of this scope, I can only give a few example activities. Other activities can be found in Day (2012c), Grellet (1981), and in published EFL/ESL reading texts.

6 The idea for this activity came from Grellet (1981, 69–70). The passage and titles are my own.

7   Silberstein, Dobson, and Clarke (2008), Day (2012c), and Grellet (1981) provide an abundance of ideas on how to teach scanning skills.

8   This idea is from Parks (2012).

9   Graded readers (Beginner through Intermediate) for children and adults can be a part of the extensive library materials.

10 These prompts were designed by Kluge (1993), who also offers procedures for setting up and carrying out interviews. See Day (2012c, pages 3–46).

11 This activity was created by L.P. Day (2012).

12 This activity was created by R.R. Day (2012b).

13 The guidelines for teaching vocabulary in a reading class have been derived from reading Coxhead (2014), Folse (2004), Grabe and Stoller (2011), Farrell (2009), Nation (2009), and my own experience with teaching ESL and EFL students to read.

14 Grabe and Stoller (2011:15).

15 Similar activities are in Coxhead (2014), Day (2015), and Farrell (2009).

16 I first learned about having students create their own dictionaries from John Fanselow (personal communication) in the early 1980s. Folse (2004) uses the term *vocabulary log* to express the same idea.

17 Ur (2016) discusses arguments for and against using grammar to teach English.

18 Nation (2009).

19 Nation (2009:40).

20 See Celce-Murcia and Larson-Freeman (2015) for a full list of subordinate conjunctions.

21 Halliday and Hasan (1976) discuss comparison in English.

22 Nation (2009:45).

23 I wrote this passage. My source for the content was wikipedia.org, List of U.S. States by Population Growth Rate.

24 See Kelley and Clausen-Grace (2007).

25 This activity is an adaptation from Pritchard and Van Vleet (2012).

26 See Boon (2012:92–93).

27 This is my own original activity.

28 See Day (2012a).

29 See Kitao (2012).

30 N.J. Anderson (2014) elaborates on the intermediate-level slump and characteristics of engaged readers. I highly appreciate his knowledge.

31 See N.J. Anderson (2014:171).

32 See N.J. Anderson (2014:172).

33 The three ways are also discussed in my article "Teaching Reading through Assumptions about Learning" (Gebhard 1985).

34 See Stevick (1978, 40).

12

Since writers do not seem to know beforehand what it is they will say, writing is a process through which meaning is created. This suggests composition instruction that recognizes the importance of generating, formulating, and refining one's ideas. It implies that revision should become the main component of this instruction, that writing teachers should intervene throughout the process, and that students should learn to view their writing as someone else's reading.

—Zamel, 1982, 195

Teaching Students How to Process Writing

▌ *What does writing include?*

▌ *How do EFL/ESL teachers teach beginners to write?*

▌ *What kinds of writing activities do EFL/ESL teachers use with post-beginners?*

▌ *Why should grammar be part of teaching writing at an advanced level?*

▌ *What problems do some EFL/ESL teachers have as writing teachers?*

What Does Writing Include?

The usual things associated with writing are word choice, use of appropriate grammar (such as subject-verb agreement, tense, and article use), syntax (word order), mechanics (such as punctuation, spelling, and handwriting), and organization of ideas into a coherent and cohesive form. However, writing also includes a focus on audience and purpose, as well as a recursive process of discovering meaning.

AUDIENCE AND PURPOSE

When we put pen to paper or fingers to keyboard, we usually have a specific audience in mind who will read what we wrote. On a personal level, we write tweets, emails, and text messages to friends, relatives, and lovers.

228

We also write diary entries to ourselves. As teachers, we write emails to colleagues, notes to students, and reports to parents and administrators. We might also write articles and newsletter items about teaching and learning for other teachers; conference papers to deliver at professional meetings; reading materials for students; and grant proposals to government agencies, corporations, or a private funding source.

A RECURSIVE PROCESS OF CREATING MEANING

When we write, especially something that is fairly complex, we do not ordinarily write a perfect letter, email, essay, or proposal in a single draft. Rather, we go through a process of creating and recreating this piece of writing until we discover and clarify within ourselves what we want to say and until we are able to express this meaning in a clear way.

To prepare to write, some of us make lists, sketch, cluster our related ideas, or outline our thoughts. Some of us prefer to think about our topic, create mental notes and images, then begin to write. As we write, we put ideas into draft form, and as we do this, we create meaning.

As we write, we also take breaks to read the draft, reflecting on whether our writing reveals our intended meaning. We might also consider our purpose and audience, and as we read what we wrote, we cross out paragraphs, sentences, and words; reorder the way we present ideas; and make notes about how to revise our writing. We continue to write and read and draft changes until we are satisfied with the piece of writing. If the piece of writing is important enough, we ask a trusted friend to read it and give us feedback. We then use this feedback as a way to further revise our writing.

How Do EFL/ESL Teachers Teach Beginners to Write?

Teachers generally agree that beginning-level EFL/ESL writers need to learn the basic conventions of writing. This includes being able to identify and write letters, words, and simple sentences, as well as learning to spell and punctuate. Teachers use a variety of activities to teach these conventions.[1]

One basic activity is tracing letters, words, and sentences. Although such a task may seem trivial, it can teach students letter recognition and discrimination; word recognition; and basic spelling, punctuation, and capitalization rules. Students, for example, can use pencils to trace letters and words written in an appropriate size and shape on tablet-style sheets used to teach American children. In addition, students can use their index finger to trace letters and words cut from felt. This can be especially useful for those whose learning modality is more kinesthetic than visual. Some students also benefit from saying the letters and words aloud as they trace them.

Another widely used activity is called Copy and Change. Students are given a passage and asked to copy it. But they are also required to change one aspect of the passage—for example, to change the subject from *he* to *she* and make accompanying changes (for instance, all references to *him* need to be changed to *her*). This activity can be done using other grammatical features, such as changing verb tense from present to past time and changing the subject from singular to plural form.

A similar activity involves teaching students a grammatical pattern and functional rules. For example, we can teach students that we use simple present tense to describe everyday routines, and we can provide a model sentence pattern, such as this one:

Subject + Adverb + Pres. Tense Verb + Object + Preposition + Time

I   usually   eat   lunch   at   noon.

Based on this pattern, students make up new sentences by exploring different grammatical conventions, such as investigating the use of other adverbs of frequency *(never, rarely, seldom, sometimes, often, frequently, always)*, as well as changing the verb *(have, go out for, make)*, object *(breakfast, dinner, a snack)*, or time *(3:00 AM, 8:30 PM)*.

Another beginning-level activity is to have students unscramble muddled sentence parts. For example, students are given a list of words—such as *school, goes, friend, everyday, my, to*—and they are asked to form a sentence.

After students gain some of the conventions of grammar, mechanics, spelling, and punctuation, they can take on more demanding tasks. One idea is to have students plan a party by making two lists: Things to Do and Things to Buy. Students work in groups or pairs to create their two lists and practice related tasks, such as writing invitation notes and addressing envelopes.

Another activity for advanced beginners is to read and write public notices, such as the ones on supermarket, dormitory bulletin boards, or Craigslist. I have had ESL students in beginning-level classes practice with reading notices I bring to class and copy notices they see on bulletin boards or online and bring them to class. We also prepare for and role-play telephone conversations to practice asking questions related to a notice. Based on their reading, copying, and conversation experience, students write their own notices. It is interesting that some students have been able to make connections with the larger community outside the classroom through actual use of their notices, thus expanding their language learning opportunities. For example, one student started a haircutting business, another found a job doing lawn care, and another found a free ride to a distant city.

As the grammar activities in my discussion illustrate, grammar-focused writing lessons are a pertinent way for beginning (and beyond) students to learn English and develop their writing. With this in mind, I have added a new chapter question to this third edition on why and how teachers use grammar to teach writing. I ask and answer this question after discussing the kinds of writing activities ESL/EFL teachers use with post-beginners.

What Kinds of Writing Activities Do EFL/ESL Teachers Use with Post-Beginners?

After students have gained some control over the conventions of writing, they can focus more easily on communicating their ideas through writing. There are a variety of writing activities students can do.

COMPOSITION WRITING

As writing teachers, we have students write short stories, descriptions, arguments, and more. Quite often we find ourselves giving a composition assignment, such as to write about the character of a person we know, and we immediately focus on vocabulary and grammar that can be used to complete this assignment. When the composition is completed, we read each student's work and mark the errors with red ink. We might also write comments in the margins, such as *Very interesting* or *Good use of the present tense*. But is it enough to give an assignment, to let the students write, and then to evaluate the product of their work? No, it is not. In fact, as writing teachers, we are advised to take students through a nonlinear process whereby, as writers, they can discover and rediscover their ideas as they attempt to put meaning into prose.

Our role is to provide chances for students to develop workable strategies for getting started (finding topics, generating writing ideas, focusing, planning content and organization), for drafting (working through multiple drafts), for revising (deleting, adding, reorganizing, modifying), and for editing (working out problems with word choice, grammar and mechanics, and sentence structure). To accomplish this, we are encouraged to have students work through a process of pre-writing, drafting, revising, and editing.[2] In addition, students can benefit from peer review feedback. Although each of these activities does not have to take place in a linear fashion, let's look at each separately.

Pre-Writing

Brainstorming begins with the introduction of a topic by the teacher or students, after which students call out ideas associated with the topic while the teacher (or a student or two) writes the ideas on the board (see Figure 12.1). Although there is no right or wrong association in this activity, some EFL/ESL students will shy away from calling out their ideas. As such, some teachers have students brainstorm first in small groups individually and then as a whole class. Brainstorming can also be done by the writer. Similar to brainstorming is an activity called **clustering** (or word mapping), in which students' associations are clustered together and stem off of the central word.[3]

Another pre-writing activity is **strategic questioning**, where students consider their topic through a series of questions, such as *What do you know about your topic?* and *What do you still need to learn?* Students consider what they know and need to learn about their writing topic. **Sketching** is a visual idea-generating strategy, useful, for example, when visualizing descriptions or showing the plot of a story. When **free-writing**, students put their ideas into writing,[4] then write continuously for a set amount of time (e.g., eight minutes) and do not stop writing. They write whatever comes to mind, even if it's *The teacher is crazy!* Then students read and consider what they wrote, after which they free-write again. Freed from worrying about grammar and word choice, students generate lots of raw material for their essays.

FIGURE 12.1: **Pre-Writing: Ways to Get Started**

Brainstorming: Based on a topic of interest, students call out as many associations as possible while the teacher (or students) jots them down.

Clustering: Using a key word placed in the center of a page (or board), a student (or teacher) jots down all the free associations students give related to the word, clustering similar words.

Strategic Questioning: Students answer a set of questions designed to guide their writing, such as *What do you want to write about? What is your goal? What do you know about this topic? What do you need to find out? What interests you or surprises you about this topic? Who might want to read what you are about to write?*

Sketching: Students draw a series of sketches that represent ideas for an essay—for example, the plot of a short story.

Free-writing: Students write nonstop on a topic for a set time (e.g., eight minutes). They stop to read and consider what they wrote and then write nonstop again for another set amount of time.

Exploring the Senses: Suitable for generating ideas for descriptive essays, the teacher guides students through their senses by asking them to visualize, hear, smell, and feel a person or place.

Interviewing: Students interview each other or go outside the classroom to interview people on a particular topic.

Information-gathering: Students collect information about a topic through library and online research.

I developed a prewriting activity, Exploring the Senses, to facilitate idea gathering for descriptive essays on a place or person.[5] I begin by having students relax (sometimes doing deep-breathing exercises). I then take them through a series of "daydreaming" experiences by guiding them to see, hear, smell, touch, and feel a place or to see, listen to, smell, and have feelings about a particular person. As I do this, I do not get too specific but rather act as a guide and create an opportunity for the students to capture their own descriptions: "See the person. Zoom in on this person's face. Study the face. (Silence.) Now back away from the person. Look at this person from different positions, as if you are walking around the person." (Silence.) For example, after several minutes as a visual guide, I switch the students' experience to another sense: "Now, sense what it is like to be with this person. What feelings do you have when you are with this person?" I also guide students through smelling, touching, and listening experiences.

Teachers can have students experience a combination of prewriting activities. For example, after taking students though the activity exploring the senses, I have students list their visual, auditory, kinesthetic, tactical, and other sensual experiences. If students are willing, I then have them meet in groups, each taking turns describing their person or place, after which I take them through a free-writing experience.

Drafting

After students have generated ideas, they start writing. This can be done in a number of ways. One way is to have students do component writing in which they write different sections of their texts within a certain period of time. Another way is to have students do one-sitting writing in which they are encouraged to write a draft of their entire essay, from beginning to end, in one sitting. Another way is through leisurely writing in which students begin a draft in class and finish it at their leisure at home.

Revising

Once students have generated a draft, they can consider revision of the content and organization of their ideas. However, this is not necessarily easy for students to do. Some students have a limited understanding about what revision includes, and some lack the patience needed to go through a time-consuming and sometimes frustrating revision process. However, there are things teachers can do to teach students the concept of revision.

In the university ESL writing courses I have taught, I have made revision a required part of the students' essay-writing experience, but I also teach them how they can explore the revision process. Here are the instructions I use when I teach narration:

1. Write and hand in three versions of your essay. Mark the essay you like the most with an asterisk (*) next to the title. Add a note explaining why you like it the most.

2. Here are some ways you can revise. Consider changing one or a combination of the following: (a) the beginning, (b) the climax, (c) the events in the steps that build up to the climax,

(d) the sex of the main character, (e) the "person" in which the story is told (e.g., from first person, *I,* to second person, *he* or *she*), (f) the setting in which the study takes place (for instance, from an inner-city high school to a summer camp), (g) the time when the story takes place (for example, from the past to 100 years in the future), and (h) any major content or organization change you would like to make.

Editing

Editing requires recognizing problems in grammar (e.g., subject-verb disagreement, improper pronoun use, incorrect verb tense), syntax (e.g., fragments and run-on sentences), and mechanics (e.g., spelling and punctuation errors). Editing is not problematic in the way that revision is because most students are willing to work hard at editing their work. However, it does take much time, knowledge, experience, and commitment to become a good editor; some students (and teachers) can become so preoccupied with editing that they equate good writing with correct grammar, syntax, word choice, and mechanics rather than with the expression of meaning, of which editing is simply a part.

Nonetheless, teaching students how to edit their work is important, and teachers approach this task in a variety of ways. Some teachers go through each student's paper, circling errors and writing notes, such as "wrong tense" or "awkward sentence." Although we teachers have good intentions and spend hours marking papers, students do not always appreciate our efforts and can even be confused by many corrections and comments. Realizing this, some teachers select one or two aspects of the student's work, such as a particular grammatical error and punctuation problem, and mark only these errors. There are, of course, other ways to respond to students' work, and these are discussed in the problem section at the end of this chapter. For ways teachers can respond to grammar errors, see pages 250–251.

Getting Feedback

A part of the process of developing an essay (and other kinds of writing) is to get feedback, and there are different approaches to doing this. Some teachers read student essay-drafts and give jot down directives on how to improve the essay. Although students use the feedback to change their essay, and some likely learn something about writing from doing this, I prefer to get students more engaged in the feedback process by having them do peer responses of each others' work.[6]

Here is a set of procedures for conducting a **peer-group response session.**[7]

1. Provide students with written guidelines.

2. Model appropriate responses to students' drafts.

3. Group students.

4. Ask students to post essay drafts on a group wikisite or coursesite before coming to class.

5. Ask students to read each other's drafts. Ask them to comment on the draft and/or complete a peer review sheet.

6. Ask students to discuss each other's drafts.

Guidelines include advice for the draft reader and the author. For example, my guidelines for readers are fairly simple: "Read the complete essay. Feel free to write questions and thoughtful comments on the essay. Then, complete the Peer Review Sheet (Figure 12.2). After reading all of your group's essays, discuss each using the sheet.

FIGURE 12.2: Sample Peer Review Sheet

1. I think the best part of your paper is _____.

2. You could reorganize your ideas by _____.

3. You could omit _____.

4. You could change _____.

5. You could add _____.

6. You have a talent at _____.

A more elaborate way for students to get feedback on their writing is to have them join an ongoing peer feedback group of five or six students in which the writing teacher also joins. I have found that by joining each group, the students will better understand the goals, procedures, and value of these writing group conferences. When I teach a writing course with 15–20 students, I ask each group of students to meet with me in my office every other week for an hour. As is evident from the guidelines shown in Figure 12.3, it is imperative for the students to prepare for these conferences.

LANGUAGE-PLAY WRITING

Some EFL/ESL teachers use language-play activities in writing classes. I consider such activities as "play" because they can be fun and still engage students in writing. There are, of course, a great number of language-play writing activities, and here I only provide two examples.

One activity is called the How Does It End? activity. The teacher has students read the first part of a short story, preferably something that builds suspense but is not very long, and then asks them to complete the story. For example, I use an English translation of a German short story by Kurt Kusenberg called "Odd Tippling."[8] In this story a hiking traveler stops at a tavern to have a glass of wine. After ordering the first glass, the town mayor shows up and tells the traveler he has to pay a fortune for the wine. The traveler is surprised and argues with the mayor, but to no avail. Frightened and confused, the traveler decides to order a second and then a third glass, and to his amazement, he discovers that the third glass had created a totally new situation, that he was no longer in debt but rather owned the tavern and inn. Surprised, the traveler decides to have a fourth glass of wine.

I cut the end of the story off, and having students read all but the ending, I give a homework assignment, to write their own ending to the story, telling what happens to the traveler after ordering the fourth glass of wine. During the next class I have students read each other's endings, as well as write a group ending to the story. After having students read their group ending to the class, we read the author's ending, sometimes amazed at how close some individuals and groups came to matching the author's ending, as well as appreciating the creative, playful, and sometimes more interesting, endings of the students.

FIGURE 12.3: Bi-Weekly Writing Conferences: Guidelines

1. Select an essay you want to have writing group members read. At the top of the first page or on the back of the essay, write at least 6 questions you would like the readers to answer. Here are some questions you might consider asking. If you have other questions that are not listed, feel free to ask them!

   a. Is my introduction interesting? How can I possibly change it?

   b. Is my conclusion powerful enough? How can I possibly change it?

   c. Is my purpose/assertion/thesis clear? If not, how might I rewrite it?

   d. Do I adequately support my thesis? If not, what are ways I might do this?

   e. Do I offer enough detail? Where and how might I add more detail?

   f. What do you think of the organization of my essay ideas?

   g. Is there anything in this essay I could delete?

   h. Is there anything in this essay I could add?

   i. Does my essay flow logically from one idea to the next (cohesion)? What might I do to strengthen the cohesion? Use transition sentences?

   j. What do you think of my word choice? Are there any places I might consider using different words?

   k. What do you think of my use of dialogue? Is it appropriate? Add quality to the essay?

   l. What do you think of my punctuation and spelling? Correct?

   m. What do you think of my paragraphing? Do I have one topic in each paragraph?

   n. What do you think of my grammar? Do you see any problems?

   o. What do you think about redundancy in the essay? Do I repeat myself too much? At the sentence level, do I use more words than I need to use? Can you point out some places I use too many words?

   p. What do you think of my title? Is it interesting? Capture your attention? Indicate what my essay is about?

   q. Is there any way you can think of to make my essay more creative?

2. A week before the conference, give a printout of your essay to each person in your group.

FIGURE 12.3: Bi-Weekly Writing Conferences: Guidelines (continued)

---

3. Study each essay and prepare to comment on the essay and answer the writer's feedback questions. As we will talk about each essay for ten minutes, it is important to come prepared! Here is how you can prepare: Read each essay at least twice.

    ■ The first time read to understand the content. Then think about your first impression. Ask yourself, "What do I like? Find interesting? Do I see anything that the writer might further develop?

    ■ Next, read for the purpose of answering the writer's questions. Write down your answers on the essay. Point to specific places in the essay that support your response to each question.

Another play activity aims at challenging students to communicate descriptions of people in writing. Students are divided into pairs and are given a picture that has lots of people in it. Each pair is asked to select one person in the picture to describe. After describing the person's physical appearance, the pairs exchange their pictures and written descriptions. The objective is to identify the person in the picture who the students described.

DIGITAL WRITING

As with other language skills, digital technology has opened up new ways for teachers and students to process writing. To begin, many teachers and students now have access to email, including chat rooms, and some teachers have made creative use of this technology. Nancy Krooenberg, for example, wanted to increase students' thinking and communicative writing skills by using chat room technology. She linked two classes of multinational students and involved them in a one-topic discussion through a chat-mode where students used the computer simultaneously to discuss the topic. She let students come up with a topic to discuss, after which she had them discuss the opposing sides to the issue.[9]

An activity the whole class can do is a chain-story activity in which the teacher emails a partial sentence, such as *It was a dark, stormy night and* . . . to one of the students in the class. Then, that student completes the line and begins a new one, then sends the emails to a classmate. The story continues to move from student to student until it is complete.

Some teachers have students keep electronic portfolios of their writing. The content of the portfolios are often similar to traditional portfolios and include a variety of different writing by the student—short stories, letters, essays, book critiques, poetry, academic papers, jokes, dialogues, short plays. However, the electronic medium offers chances for students to add sound, images, video clips, graphics, or other multimedia.[10]

As discussed in Chapter 7, both blogs and wikis are ways to provide students with opportunities to use English, especially writing. Blogs give students chances to write for a real audience on a great variety of topics. Classmates, the teacher, and possibly a wider reading audience can provide comments, making the writing process more interactive. Wikis can provide students with chances to work on group writing projects, which teach them how to collaborate, share ideas, edit, and see a writing project through from start to finish. WordPress (wordpress.com) is a popular free blogging tool, and www.wikispaces.com is learner-friendly website.

Why Should Grammar Be Part of Teaching Writing at an Advanced Level?

One reason to include grammar is to have a meta-language (a language to talk about language) during discussions about writing. Throughout my teaching career I have discovered that many students can "speak grammar" as I like to call it, and some are relieved and happy that their teacher can speak it, too. I have also found that students who have little background in grammar, such as beginning students, can quickly learn the basics and build on these basics as they continue to develop their writing.[11]

An especially important reason to use grammar in our writing classes is because, as Dana Ferris, a leading expert on teaching writing and grammar, points out: Students will make grammar errors, and without expert intervention through feedback and instruction, they could end up with fossilized English.[11] In other words, they will make errors a deeply rooted part of their written English. Although some teachers believe that through exposure to lots of English, students will acquire the correct English in time, we now know that this is not necessarily true. We also have learned that error feedback and instruction can provide a means for students to advance their written English.[12]

As Dana Ferris also points out, another reason to use grammar in our writing classes is that ESL/EFL writers tend to write more simply than their native-speaker peers, indicating less complexity and range in their written work.[13] As such, this undeveloped writing style can be seen as being a lower quality than it deserves.[14] As Ferris emphasizes, students recognizably need to continue to develop and apply a more refined range of grammatical features to their writing, especially for academic and professional reasons. In short, "students will be empowered if they have knowledge of and control over a broad range of language structures so that they can make appropriate choices for the specific rhetorical situation in which they are writing."[15]

Let's move on to how teachers can use grammar as a part of teaching writing. First, there is a grammar-based relationship between teaching students to read and write. By this I mean that the grammar activities in Chapter 11 on teaching students to comprehend what they read are as relevant to **learning to write** as they are to **learning to read**. For example, Chapter 11 discussed how reading teachers can help students to comprehend the meaning of a text by teaching them how ideas are connected through transition words and their meaning—for instance, *but*, *although*, and *nevertheless* show contrast, and *therefore*, *so*, *as a result*, and *as such* show consequence. Such concepts are also useful to students who are working on improving their writing skills. What the writing teacher needs to do is help students to make use of such grammatical concepts in their writing.

To illustrate how grammatical concepts can be taught, I provide an example lesson from one of my high-beginner writing classes. This activity was developed to complement a required textbook chapter section on describing a daily routine. The students first studied the meaning of the grammatical structures:

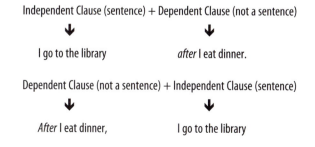

Independent Clause (sentence) + Dependent Clause (not a sentence)

↓ ↓

I go to the library   *after* I eat dinner.

Dependent Clause (not a sentence) + Independent Clause (sentence)

↓ ↓

After I eat dinner,   I go to the library

We then made up sentences using different subordinate conjunctions that indicate time (e.g., *when, before, after, as soon as, whenever, while*) and condition (*if, even if*). I wrote them on the board while highlighting that when the dependent clause (not a sentence) goes before the independent clause (a sentence that can stand alone), then they are required to use a comma to separate the two clauses. However, when the independent clause (sentence) comes first, there is no comma. I then asked the students to start their writing assignment as I moved from student to student to check work and answer questions (see Figure 12.4). I then asked the students to finish their essays outside class and send them to me the next day.

During the next class, I gave them feedback and asked for volunteers to read their essays aloud. Because the students said the assignment was a little boring, during a later class I asked them to meet in small groups and to create a daily routine of a scary monster, an animal, a hero, or someone else who might have an interesting life. As I can clearly recall, they had a lot of fun, and appeared to have made progress on writing grammatically accurate sentences with subordinate clauses.

In addition to using grammar-focused writing activities, such as this one, we can also give feedback to students on their grammatical errors. A usual way is for the teacher to identify and mark errors students make. However, this can be an endless time-consuming endeavor if not done in a systematic way. For example, Dana Ferris uses a three-step process.[16] On the first draft of a paper, she focuses on identifying the most major of the problems and limits her feedback to only two or maybe three of them. In a summary note to the writer, in addition to feedback on content and organization, she will point out these grammatical problems (e.g., "Check

---

FIGURE 12.4: Writing Practice Using Subordinate Conjunctions

My Daily Routine

Instructions: Write about your daily routine. Use simple present tense. Try to use all the subordinate conjunctions on this page.

after before when whenever while even though because as soon as if even if

---

your writing for subject-verb agreement") and highlights a few places these errors are made. Some teachers use different colored highlight for each error pattern. The second step is to highlight all occurrences of errors throughout the paper on the previously selected error patterns. The third step, before the student turns in the paper for a grade or to be included in a portfolio, Ferris marks any remaining errors and possibly corrects "untreatable" errors, such as word choice and preposition errors.

As a writing teacher, I have taken pride in locating or creating the right grammar explanations, exercises, and websites to teach my students different grammatical concepts. I also have explored different ways to provide feedback to students on their grammar errors. However, I also have learned that these classroom activities and feedback techniques are only a part of grammar accuracy. As Ferris points out, students also need to develop solid self-editing strategies because they shift the responsibility for grammar development to the students.[17]

One self-editing strategy I have taught students to use is to read their writing aloud. This can help them to notice missing words, redundancy, and some grammar problems. Some students have also found reading their essay backwards by beginning with the last sentence to be useful. This editing technique takes their focus off of meaning and onto grammar rules and word choice.[18]

Another strategy is to encourage students to "add another pair of eyes."[19] I have encouraged students at all levels, from beginning IEP students to doctoral students and accomplished professionals, to ask others to proofread their writing and point out grammatical and organization problems. When students are fully engaged in this proofreading process, they can learn much about their writing and use of grammar.

However, some students understand asking others to proof their papers as a free pass to have others do their work for them instead of a way for them to further develop their writing. Knowing that attitudes toward using this grammar development strategy can vary, I agree with Dana Ferris who provides rules for students. She instructs students that as writers, they must participate actively in the proofing process, not allow the proofreader to use any writing instruments, make their own changes, and thank or reward the proofreader for his or her help.[20]

What Problems Do Some EFL/ESL Teachers Have as Writing Teachers?

Problems some EFL/ESL teachers face include:

- The "teaching the less-proficient writer" problem
- The "teacher response" problem
- The "essay grading" problem
- The "serving generation 1.5 learners with their writing" problem
- The "I am expected to teach grammar in my writing class, and I don't know what I'm doing" problem

THE "TEACHING THE LESS-PROFICIENT WRITER" PROBLEM

To teach less-proficient writers, it helps to identify how they process writing differently from the proficient writer (see Figure 12.5).[21] Unlike proficient writers, less-proficient writers tend to jump right into the writing task without using prewriting strategies to generate ideas and organize thoughts. In addition, rather than quickly getting organized thoughts onto paper, they might take much time to write down their ideas, as well as focus primarily on surface level aspects of writing, struggling with form over meaning.

Unlike proficient writers, less-proficient writers will revise primarily at the word and sentence level, using the revision process to edit grammar, syntax, spelling, and punctuation. Their revisions do not usually show many additions, deletions, substitutions, or reordering of ideas; when revision is done, it occurs primarily on the first draft. Perhaps this is because there is often confusion associated with revision, and unlike proficient writers, less-proficient writers seem to lack patience to work through the confusion in the process of clarifying meaning.

Understanding the writing behaviors of proficient and less-proficient writers is a start. The question then becomes how teachers can provide opportunities for less-proficient writers to improve their writing skills. We need to give less-proficient writers more of everything—"More time, more opportunity to talk, listen, read, and write; more instruction and practice in generating, organizing, and revising ideas; more attention to the rhetori-

FIGURE 12.5: The Composing Behaviors of EFL/ESL Writers

Proficient writers . . .

- Think about the task and use a variety of prewriting strategies.
- Have a sense of audience and will consider audience while composing.
- Once organized, get ideas onto paper quickly.
- At drafting stage, pay attention to meaning over form.
- Are concerned with higher levels of meaning as well as at the surface level.
- Will revise at all levels (word, sentence, paragraph, entire text).
- Will revise by adding, deleting, or reordering ideas.
- Generate several drafts, each with some revision.

Less-proficient writers . . .

- Start off confused, without using pre-writing strategies.
- Have a vague or little awareness of audience.
- Take too much time to get ideas onto paper.
- Work primarily at the sentence level and struggle with form.
- Are concerned with vocabulary choice and sentence structure.
- Will revise primarily at the word and sentence level and at the surface level (spelling, grammar, punctuation, etc.).
- Are bothered by confusion over revision and tend to avoid adding, deleting, and reordering ideas.
- Revise primarily only the first draft.

cal options available to them; and more emphasis on editing for linguistic form and style."[22] In short, we need to do more than simply take less-proficient writers through a process of producing a piece of writing. We also need to give our full attention to them, to show them how to plan a piece of writing through prewriting activities (discussed earlier in this chapter), how to draft and revise (discussed later in this chapter under The Teaching Response Problem), and how to edit their writing.

THE "TEACHER RESPONSE" PROBLEM

Writing teachers often spend many hours reading and marking students' papers, offering revision suggestions and feedback on language errors. We correct, circle, underline, and write notes like "preposition problem."

But students quite often do not pay attention to our comments and corrections. When what we do does not seem to work, or when we simply want to explore new ways of responding to students' work, we can try out alternative ways to respond to students' writing. In this section, I offer some of the ways that EFL/ESL writing teachers can respond to students' writing.

Writing teachers need to recognize if they treat an initial draft as if it were a final draft, applying a prescriptive, grammar-focused stance, the response is likely to fail. A grammar-focused teacher should respond to student drafts in ways that are appropriate to the development of a piece of writing. One way to do this is to require students to hand in two or three drafts of their writing. The teacher can then respond to each draft of writing in different ways.[23] For example, on some students' early drafts, the teacher can comment on how the students can revise their work, using such remarks as, "Did your topic change here? You need to add a transition." "What are ways to capture the reader's attention at the start of your essay?" and "I like the content of the five points. But try reordering them. See if you like the change." The teacher can also point out two or three grammatical pattern errors for the student to work on. On a later draft, the teacher can respond to other surface-level errors, such as spelling, punctuation, and syntactical errors. It is worth pointing out that students say they appreciate and gain something from the teacher's responses, especially if these responses are clear in their intent.

In addition to written responses, teachers can work with students on developing their written work through one-to-one conferences. Teachers and students often point out the value of such conferences, especially when the teacher and student focus on specific aspects of the student's writing and the student has chances to negotiate meaning. One way to provide focus is to have the student prepare for the conference by writing questions, comments, and explanations before the conference. The teacher can also prepare by reading the student's draft before the conference while taking side notes on problems (e.g., with revision) that can be addressed during the conference. A way to encourage students to negotiate meaning is to let the student begin the conference (rather than the teacher) by describing what he or she wants to accomplish in the piece of writing and the noticeable problems in doing this. As the student talks, the teacher can paraphrase, thus providing a recognized version of what the student has said and a way for the student to reflect and discover new things in his or her writing. If the student does not react well to a paraphrasing approach, which is the case for some students, another way to engage the student in negotiation is through collaboration. For example, the teacher and student can take turns generating ways to revise the student's paper. The teacher might suggest the student rewrite the essay in first person, the student might suggest writing a new conclusion, the teacher might suggest that the student use the final paragraph to begin the essay, and so on. At any point in this turn-taking process, the student should feel free to ask questions, add details, and explore additional ideas.

THE "ESSAY GRADING" PROBLEM

Some teachers struggle with grading essays. Some provide guidelines that outline how the paper will be graded. Some teachers follow the guidelines to the letter, while others try to relate them to each student and evaluate the progress each student has made. Either way, grading is often subjective, and it is not always fair to the students. Further, some teachers, either by requirement or by choice, grade one essay at a time throughout a semester or year.

An alternative way, which I believe is much more fair to the students, is not to grade any essays until the end of the semester or a designated period of time. At that time the teacher can require students to hand in a *portfolio* of their best work. This does not mean the teacher ignores students writing until the portfolio is due. Throughout the semester students can work on specific assignments, such as a research paper, a short story, a descriptive essay, a film critique, haiku, and more. Writers can read essays to get ideas, participate in peer review sessions, have group and teacher conferences on their writing, and hand in essays to the teacher for feedback. However, these essays are not graded. When students complete one assignment, perhaps having worked through two drafts of a film critique or an academic research paper, they simple set it aside, saving the drafts, feedback, prewriting, and notes from working through the process to create the document. Then, when the deadline for handing in the portfolio approaches, the students can review their work and decide which essays they will further work on and include in their graded portfolio. The teacher (and students) can decide how many essays should be included.

I have used this portfolio system for about 25 years, which I have changed over time based on my teaching experience and student feedback, and I try not just to focus on the portfolio itself but also on how it fits into my writing course as a whole. Through this progression there are two things I still find especially useful. First, I require students to turn in a letter that informs me (the reader) about what is included in the portfolio, why they selected the particular essays they include in the portfolio, which essay is their favorite and why, and what they have learned about processing their writing. One reason I ask them to do this is because I want a to read a preview and gain knowledge about the portfolio before I read it. Another reason is that this kind of letter writing is what we might find in a professional portfolio (not necessarily a writing portfolio) that is being handed in to be evaluated, for example, to get a job or enter some competitive graduate programs. Another reason is it is a test. I want to see if a student rushed the letter without really processing it or if a student really processed the letter with the same thought and creativeness that I have been emphasizing throughout the semester. I don't hide this reason. I tell students that the letter is as important as any other piece of writing in the portfolio.

The second especially useful part of the portfolio is that I only count it as 50 percent of their grade. This is because I believe the process is as important as the process. As such, the other 50 percent is on a **writing journal** students are asked to keep throughout the semester. To illustrate what I mean, here is a description taken from one of my syllabi:

> Students are expected to keep a writing journal. This journal should include each piece of writing we have worked on during the semester, including all prewriting (notes, mapping, free writing, and any other pre-writing you did), early partially written handwritten or word processed drafts, peer review sheets, the first complete essay draft, as well as at least one revised draft of each. The journal should be organized and each essay section clearly marked.

The journal is useful because it places focus on the process of their writing. For hardworking students, some with a lot of talent, the journal is a place for them to shine. They can show how they understand what revision actually means, how they learned to edit, and more. Admittedly though, some students have problems being organized. Some even throw away parts of their process without thinking, mainly because they have never really had to keep track of or think about their writing process. Other students include too much. They try to impress or fool me with the thickness of their journal by including multiple drafts with only small changes to each one. A few students even attempt to hide the fact that they have plagiarized by including multiple drafts of each essay with almost no substantial changes. In short, a pattern does emerge in regard to how each student has processed their work and even how some students changed their process to become a more engaged writer who is on a path to more fully realizing the importance of knowing how to process his or her own writing.

THE "SERVING GENERATION 1.5 LEARNERS WITH THEIR WRITING" PROBLEM

Some ESL high school and university composition teachers in the United States have expressed frustration with teaching composition to Generation 1.5 students. Many of these long-term U.S. residents and English learners are fluent, even native-like in their use of spoken English, but they still have ESL-type language errors in their writing. Depending on their previous experiences with learning to compose in English, many have a rather negative attitude toward writing, believing that they will never master writing in English.

My response to those teachers who want to know how to work with Generation 1.5 learners is fairly basic and is based on my experience as a college composition teacher, as well as on the experiences of other teachers who have taught 1.5 learners.[24]

1. Recognize that Generation 1.5 learners have long-term experience in the United States. Learn about what experience they have had in school and in their personal lives, including their cultural heritage.

2. Draw from their experience. Can you help them to tap into their cultural heritage? Include assignments that allow these 1.5 writers to draw on the familiar. (For example, many African cultures keep historical records through storytelling; many Hmong enjoy storytelling and song writing.)

3. Recognize that although the student's spoken English might sound close to a native speaker, the student likely does not have native-like intuition as a writer.

4. Work one-to-one with the student; conference with the student over his or her writing.[25]

5. Teach the student how to write; don't simply show the student how to get through an assignment. This means explaining the process of developing an essay through prewriting, composing, revising, and editing stages, as well as offering constructive feedback as the student works through the process.

6. Spend time working with the student on both grammar and rhetoric (for example, how to organize sections in an essay; how to make smooth transitions from one idea to the next).

THE "I AM EXPECTED TO TEACH GRAMMAR IN MY WRITING CLASS, AND I DON'T KNOW WHAT I AM DOING" PROBLEM

Some teachers, especially those new to teaching, are concerned that they do not have much experience with grammar. Some ask questions like, "I can recognize when a student makes an error in his or her writing, but how do I explain the error to the student?" "How do I recognize a grammatical pattern error? I have no experience doing that?" and "I am afraid the students know more about grammar than me. What should I do if I can't answer a student's question about grammar?" With such questions in mind, ESL/EFL teachers do need to learn and continually develop their knowledge about grammar and abilities to teach it.

To begin, teachers can learn a lot simply by taking a basic grammar course. Most certification and BA and MA TESOL programs require students take at least one pedagogical grammar or structure class. Personally, I am happy that I took a few grammar classes, especially those that were taught as a tool for ESL/EFL teachers to use in the classroom. I ended up building on my basic courses and texts, and through the many student-questions I have answered and concepts I have taught throughout my career, I have expanded my grammatical knowledge and have found that an understanding of grammar when teaching writing (and other skills) is very useful.

Teachers can also learn a lot by studying student grammar textbooks. These books are usually written in easy to understand English. For example, Keith Folse, in his *Clear Grammar* book series, provides a grammar mini lesson, kinds of errors students might make (in his Be Careful! Section) and exercises, such as editing and fill in the blank.[26] As teachers, we can also study grammar handbooks such as Keith Folse's *Keys to Teaching Grammar to English Language Learners* or Marianne Celce-Murcia and Diane Larsen-Freeman's *The Grammar Book*.[27] Although it is not a teacher reference or manual, I also recommend a classic book, *English Sentence Structure* by Robert Krohn.[28] Krohn's book is very basic, and although it is more than four decades old, it is still used and in print.

We can also learn a lot from our classroom teaching experience. I know that my students have given me many opportunities to learn grammar! When I was new to teaching, and a student asked me a question I couldn't answer, I would tell them I would answer that question during the next class, and I knew it was important to keep my word and the students' trust. So, off I would go in search of an answer either from a colleague, a reference book, or both. More recently there are, of course, many online websites and search engines that can be very useful. In addition, I have learned much over the years from analyzing grammar problems in students' writing and creating handouts on grammatical concepts based on my analysis.

In short, if you are a little intimidated by the thought of teaching grammatical concepts and answering students grammar questions, don't be. Be willing to develop your knowledge as a teacher, to build trust with the students by searching out answers to their grammar questions, and to expand your abilities to use grammar as a tool to help students improve their writing. If you have teaching experience but have thought grammar is not useful to teaching writing (and other skills), reconsider your position with an open mind. You just might surprise yourself!

TEACHER SELF-DEVELOPMENT TASKS

Talk Tasks

1. What do writing experts mean when they say, "writing is a recursive process of creating meaning"? Ask other teachers this question.

2. What activities do I suggest writing teachers use with beginning writers? Meet with another teacher. Add an additional three activities that a teacher might use to teach beginners.

3. Study the list of prewriting activities I suggest teachers use to provide a genuine writing experience for students. Which have you used, or which would you like to use? Find out what prewriting activities other teachers have used.

4. Study the kinds of activities I suggest teachers use to provide a genuine writing experience for students. Which have you used, or which would you like to use? Find out what activities other teachers use or would like to use.

5. I listed a few ways teachers can use digital technology to give students practice with writing. What other ways can you think of to do this?

6. Why is grammar an important part of writing?

Observation and Talk Tasks

1. Interview a writing teacher. Find out what his or her beliefs are about teaching students to write. Then observe his or her class. Are this teacher's beliefs reflected in the classroom writing activities?

2. Ask a writing teacher if you can observe his or her class. Take detailed descriptive notes that focus on the activities the teacher has students do in class. After the class, consider what you saw this teacher do that you would like to do in your own teaching.

3. Locate an EFL or ESL student. Ask this student to describe how he or she composes. It might help to ask, "How do you write an essay from beginning to end?" Keep the student talking by paraphrasing what he or she says, adding comments like "Very interesting! Tell me more!" and showing interest with facial and other nonverbal expressions. After talking with the student,

consider what he or she told you. Does he or she consider the audience? Pay attention to expressing meaning in early drafts? Reorganize, delete, and add? Generate several drafts? Does the student see writing as a developmental process? Interpret what the student said. Would you classify him or her as a proficient writer? What advice (if any) would you give to this writer?

Journal Writing Tasks

1. Write about you own experiences in learning to write. Did your teachers treat writing as a process of development? Why or why not?

2. Reflect on how you compose. Do you do the kinds of things writing experts say proficient writers do?

3. Write about your observation and interviewing experiences from doing the observation and talk tasks.

4. Write about your comfort level teaching grammar. If you don't feel comfortable, develop a plan to learn more about grammar and how to teach it in a writing class.

RECOMMENDED TEACHER RESOURCES

Select Recommended Writing Textbooks

Beaumont, J. *Focus on Writing 4*. New York: Pearson Education ESL, 2011. (One of a series of five books.)

Blanchard, K. and C. Root. *Ready to Write 1: A First Composition Text, 3rd ed.* New York: Pearson Education, 2010.

Carlock, J., M. Eberhardt, J. Horst, and L. Menasche. *The ESL Writer's Handbook*. Ann Arbor: University of Michigan Press, 2010.

Lockwood, R.B. and K. Sippell. *Four Point: Reading and Writing English for Academic Purposes, Intro*. Ann Arbor: University of Michigan Press, 2012.

Swales, J.M. and C.B. Feak. *Academic Writing for Graduate Students: Essential Skills and Tasks, 3rd ed.* Ann Arbor: University of Michigan Press, 2012.

Resources on Teaching Writing

Casanave, C.P. *Controversies in Second Language Writing: Dilemmas and Decisions in Research and Instruction, 2nd ed.* Ann Arbor: University of Michigan Press, 2017.

Crusan, D. *Assessment in the Second Language Writing Classroom*. Ann Arbor: University of Michigan Press, 2010.

de Oliveira, L.C. and T. Silva, eds. *L2 Writing in Secondary Classrooms: Student Experiences, Academic Issues, and Teacher Education.* New York: Routledge, 2013.

Ferris, D.R. "Promoting Grammar and Language Development in the Writing Class: Why, What, How, and When." In *Teaching English Grammar to Speakers of Other Languages,* ed. E. Hinkel, 5485–6016 (Kindle pages). New York: Routledge, 2016.

Ferris, D.R. *Treatment of Error in Second Language Student Writing, 2nd ed.* Ann Arbor: University of Michigan Press, 2011.

Ferris, D.R. and J.S. Hedgcock. *Teaching L2 Composition: Purpose, Process, and Practice.* New York: Routledge, 2014.

Liu, J. and J.G. Hansen Edwards. *Peer Response in Second Language Writing Classrooms, 2nd ed.* Ann Arbor: University of Michigan Press, in press.

Matusda, P.K., M. Cox, J. Jordon, and C. Ortmeier-Hooper. *Second Language Writing in the Composition Classroom: A Critical Source Book.* New York: Bedford St. Martins, 2010.

Ortmeier-Hooper, C. and T. Ruecker, eds. *Linguistically Diverse Immigrant Writers: Transitions from High School to College.* New York: Routledge, 2017.

Reid, J., ed. *Writing Myths: Applying Second Language Research to Classroom Teaching.* Ann Arbor: University of Michigan Press, 2008.

Reynolds, D.W. *One on One with Second Language Writers: A Guide for Writing Tutors, Teachers, and Consultants.* Ann Arbor: University of Michigan Press, 2009.

Tannacito, D. J. *A Guide to Writing in English as a Second or Foreign Language: An Annotated Bibliography of Research and Pedagogy.* Alexandria, VA: TESOL, 1995.

Weigle, S.C. "Considerations for Teaching Second Language Writing." In *Teaching English as a Second or Foreign Language, 4th ed.,* eds. M. Celce-Murcia, D.M. Brinton, and M.A. Snow, 222–37. Boston: Heinle Cengage, 2014.

ENDNOTES

1   Olshtain (2014), Raimes (1983), and White (1995) describe and illustrate a number of activities for beginning EFL/ESL writers.

2   See Matsuda et al. (2010), Raimes (1985), and Silva (2010).

3   These prewriting strategies are discussed in Kroll (2001) and Richards (1990). The Sketching and Exploring the Senses activities are created out of my own experience as a writing teacher.

4   Freewriting was originally discussed by Elbow (1973).

5   I created the Exploring the Senses prewriting activity while studying Neurolinguistic Programming (NLP). NLP offers a way to guide people through hypnotic trance states that can, with regard to prewriting, offer writers new ways to understand their own experience. Introductory books include Bandler and Grinder (1979) and Lankton (1980).

6   See Liu and Hansen (in press) for their second edition on peer response in ESL/EFL classrooms. See Ferris (2011) for ideas about treating writing errors.

7   These procedures based on my experience as a writing teacher and Nelson and Murphy (1992–93).

8   "Odd Tippling" by Kusenberg can be found in Lewis and Jungman's 1986 collection, *On Being Foreign: Culture Shock in Short Fiction.*

9   See Krooenberg (1994–95).

10 Kahtani (1999), whose ideas I use here, elaborates on the use of electronic portfolios. Also see Bloch and Wilkinson (2014).

11 See McCarthy (2016). He provides a strong case for and practical ideas on using grammar in the advanced writing class.

12 See Ferris (2016).

13 See Ferris (2006, 2016), Hartshorn et al. (2010), and Russell and Spada (2006).

14 See Ferris (2016). See cites Hyland (2002) and Silva (1993).

15 See Hamp-Lyons (1991, 2003); discovered in Ferris (2016).

16 Ferris (2016: Kindle Locations 5560-5562).

17 Ferris (2008, 2011).

18 Ferris (2008).

19 Ferris (2008) also discusses this editing strategy.

20 Ferris (2008:100).

21 I have realized the power of participating in a proofing process with my own writing. I have learned much about my writing, including my use of grammar, by asking colleagues, friends, and sometimes students to proof my writing in this way.

22 The characteristics I assign to less-proficient (and proficient) writers are based on research done by Raimes (1985), and Zamel (1982, 1983), as well as on my own experience.

23 See Raimes (1985, 248).

24 The idea of treating writing from a developmental point of view and responding to writing in ways appropriate to the development of the piece of writing is most convincingly made by Zamel (1985) and Ferris (1995, 2011).

25 I talked with several high school and college teachers who consistently work with K–12 learners and have read the work of experienced K–12 teachers. I especially draw from de Oliviera and Silva (2013), Harklau, Losey, and Siegal (1999), and Thonus (2003), and I especially thank Agnes Malicka for sharing her experience with teaching Generation 1.5 learners.

26 See Thonus (2003) for detailed suggestions about how to conference with Generation 1.5 students over their writing.

27 I used Folse's *Clear Grammar 3* (2015) as my analysis of his book sections.

28 See Azar (2009), Folse (2016), and Celce-Murcia and Larson-Freeman (2015).

29 Krohn (1971).

Appendixes

Appendix A
A Selection of Professional Journals

ANNUAL REVIEW OF APPLIED LINGUISTICS (ARAL)

Published annually, this journal provides a comprehensive, up-to-date review of research in key areas in the broad field of applied linguistics. Each issues is thematic, covering the topic by means of critical summaries, overviews, and bibliographic citations. Every fourth or fifth issue surveys applied linguistics broadly, offering timely essays on language learning and pedagogy.

Cambridge University Press: www.journals.cambridge.org

APPLIED LINGUISTICS

This journal promotes principled and multidisciplinary approaches to research on language and language-related concerns by encouraging enquiry into the relationship between theoretical and practical studies. It publishes research in language with relevance to real-world problems.

Oxford University Press: http://applij.oxfordjournals.org

ASIAN EFL JOURNAL

Published quarterly, this free electronic journal examines issues within the Asian EFL linguistic context and considers how traditional educational approaches are integrated with or contrasted against what is new in the field. It seeks new insights into key issues that are emerging and of contemporary interest.

TESOL Asia: http://asian-efl-journal.com

ELT JOURNAL

Published quarterly, this English language teaching journal maintains an international scope. Practical articles are written by experienced EFL/ESL teachers and teacher educators. Article titles, abstracts, and key concepts appear free online through the ELT Journal website.

Oxford University Press (in association with the British Council): http://eltj.oxfordjournals.org

ENGLISH FOR SPECIFIC PURPOSES JOURNAL

Published three times a year, this journal includes articles that address language teaching and learning within specific contexts.

ELSEVIER: www.journals.elsevier.com/english-for-specific-purposes

ENGLISH TEACHING FORUM

Published quarterly, this journal includes practical articles on teaching EFL/ESL. Articles focus on the theory and practice of teaching English and include methods, techniques, and ideas useful in the classroom.

U.S. Department of State: http://exchanges.state.gov/englishteaching/forum-journal.html

FOREIGN LANGUAGE ANNALS

Published quarterly, this journal serves the interests of teachers, administrators, and researchers in foreign language teaching.

American Council on the Teaching of Foreign Languages (ACTFL): www.actfl.org

INTERNATIONAL JOURNAL OF INNOVATION IN ENGLISH LANGUAGE TEACHING AND RESEARCH

This journal is a refereed scholarly publication that focuses on ELT curriculum and materials design, teaching methodology, testing assessment in ELT, computer assisted learning, teacher education, and teacher professional development.

NOVA Science Publishers: http://novapublishers.com

JALT JOURNAL

Published semiannually, this journal includes articles on teaching and learning EFL and prides itself on applied research with the aim of linking theory to practice.

Japan Association of Language Teachers (JALT): http://jalt-publications.org/jj

JOURNAL OF SECOND LANGUAGE WRITING

Published quarterly, this journal includes articles on topics related to teaching writing in the second language classroom, especially theoretically grounded research reports on implications of teaching on writing with the aim of understanding current issues in second and foreign language writing and writing instruction.

ELSEVIER: www.journals.elsevier.com/journal-of-second-language-writing

LANGUAGE TEACHING

Articles in this journal focus on research in the field of second language teaching and learning. It provides an overview of current research and offers a critical survey of recent research on specific topics and related to second and foreign languages and countries.

Cambridge University Press: http://journals.cambridge.org/jid_LTA

LANGUAGE TESTING

Published quarterly, this peer-reviewed journal includes articles on language testing and assessment, including EFL and ESL and child second language acquisition.

Sage Publications: http://ltj.sagepub.com

STUDIES IN SECOND LANGUAGE ACQUISITION

Published quarterly, this refereed journal includes articles related to second language acquisition and foreign language learning and teaching. Being international in scope, it aims to contribute to the scientific discussion of issues in second and foreign language acquisition of any language.

Cambridge University Press: http://journals.cambridge.org/jid_SLA

TESL CANADA JOURNAL

Published twice yearly, this journal publishes articles on diverse aspects of teaching and learning EFL/ESL for graduate students, teachers, teacher educators, and researchers.

TESL Canada: www.tesl.ca

TESOL QUARTERLY

Published quarterly, this journal represents contemporary thinking in the field and includes original research, reviews of research, and practical applications of theory and research to teaching EFL/ESL.

TESOL International: www.tesol.org

Appendix B
List of Publishers

Berty Segal Cook, Inc.
www.tprsource.com

Cambridge University Press
www.cambridge.org
www.cambridgeenglish.org

Delta Systems Co, Inc.
www.deltapublishing.com

Intercultural Press
www.Nicholasbrealy.com

Multilingual Matters
www.multilingual-matters.com

National Geographic Learning – Cengage
www.ngl.cengage.com

Oxford University Press
http://elt.oup.com?cc=us&selLanguage=en

Pro Lingua Associates
www.prolinguaassociates.com

Routledge Publishing
Taylor & Frances Group
www.routledge.com

TESOL (Teachers of English to Speakers of Other Languages)
www.tesol.org

The University of Michigan Press ELT
www.press.umich.edu/elt
esladmin@umich.edu

| REFERENCES

Adler, P. S. "Culture Shock and the Cross-Cultural Learning Experience." In *Toward Internationalism*, eds. L. F. Luce and E. C. Smith. Rowley, MA: Newbury House.

Allwright, D. and K. M. Bailey. *Focus on the Language Classroom*. Cambridge, U.K.: Cambridge University Press.

Alrashidi, O. and H. Phan. "Education Context and English Teaching and Learning in the Kingdom of Saudi Arabia: An Overview." *Language Teaching* 8, no. 5 (2015): 32–94.

Anderson, N. J. "Developing Engaged Second Language Readers." In *Teaching English as a Second or Foreign Language, 4th ed.*, eds. M. Celce Murcia, D. M. Brinton, and M. A. Snow, 170–85. Boston: Heinle Cengage, 2014.

———. "L2 Strategy Research." In *Handbook of Research in Second Language Teaching and Learning*, ed. E. Hinkel, 757–72. Mahwah, NJ: Lawrence Erlbaum, 2005.

Anderson, P. A. "In Different Dimensions: Nonverbal Communication and Culture." In *Intercultural Communication: A Reader*, eds. L. A. Samovar, R. E. Porter, E. R. McDaniel, & C. S. Roy, 229–41. Belmont, CA: Wadsworth, 2015.

Andrade, M. S. *Language Games: Innovative Activities for Teaching English*. Alexandria, VA: TESOL, 2009.

Aoki, S. "Potential of Voice Recording Tools in Language Instruction." *Working Papers in TESOL and Applied Linguistics* (14, no. 2). Teachers College, Columbia University, 2014.

Arcario, P. "Post-Observation Conferences in TESOL Teacher Education Programs." Doctoral dissertation, Teachers College, Columbia University, 1994.

Asher, J. *Learning Another Language through Actions*. Los Gatos, CA: Sky Oaks, 1982.

Atkinson, J. M. and J. Hertiage, eds. *Structures of Social Action: Studies in Conversation Analysis*. Cambridge, U.K.: Cambridge University Press, 1984.

Azar, B.S. and S. Hagen. *Understanding and Using English Grammar*. New York: Pearson-Longman, 2009.

Bailey, K. M. *Language Teacher Supervision: A Case-Based Approach*. New York: Cambridge University Press, 2006.

Bailey, K. M., A. Curtis, and D. Nunan. *Pursuing Professional Development*. Boston: Heinle Cengage, 2001.

———. "Undeniable Insights: The Collaborative Use of Three Professional Development Practices." *TESOL Quarterly* 32, no. 3 (1998): 546–56.

Bailey, K. M. and L. Savage, eds. *New Ways in Teaching Speaking*. Alexandria, VA: TESOL, 1994.

Bandler, R. and J. Grinder. *Frogs into Princes*. Boulder, CO: Real People Press, 1979.

Barnlund, D. C. *Public and Private Self in Japan and the United States*. Boston: Intercultural Press, 1975.

Barns, D. *From Communication to Curriculum*. Harmondsworth, U.K.: Penguin, 1975.

Becker, H. *Teaching ESL K–12: Views from the Classroom*. Boston: Heinle Cengage, 2001.

Begley, P. A. "Sojourner Adaptation." In *Intercultural Communication: A Reader*. eds. L. A. Samovar, R.E. Porter, and E. R. McDaniel, 387–93. Belmont, CA: Wadsworth, 2003.

Bennett, G.R. *Using Corpora in the Language Learning Classroom: Corpus Linguistics for Teachers*. Ann Arbor: University of Michigan Press, 2010.

Bèrubè, B. *Managing ESL Programs in Rural and Small Urban Schools*. Alexandria, VA: TESOL, 2000.

Bleistein, T, M. K. Smith, and M. Lewis. *Teaching Speaking*. Alexandria, VA: TESOL, 2013.

Bloch, J. *Technologies in the Second Language Composition Classroom*. Ann Arbor: University of Michigan Press, 2007.

Bloch, J. and M. J. Wilkinson. *Teaching Digital Literacies*. Alexandria, VA: TESOL, 2014.

Bohlke, D. "Fluency-Oriented Second Language Teaching." In *Teaching English as a Second or Foreign Language*, 4th ed., eds. M. Celce Murcia, D. M. Brinton, and M. A. Snow, 121–35. Boston: Heinle Cengage, 2014.

Bonn. S. "Prediction Practice through Internet News Headlines." In *New Ways in Teaching Reading*, ed. R. R. Day, 91–93. Alexandria, VA: TESOL, 2012.

Brenner, K. "Oral Journals: A Journey from Analog to Digital." *Essential Language Teacher* 5, no. 4, (2008): 23–26.

Brinton, D. "Tools and Techniques of Effective Language Teaching." In *Teaching English as a Second or Foreign Language*, 4th ed., eds. M. Celce Murcia, D. M. Brinton, and M. A. Snow, 340–61. Boston: Heinle Cengage, 2014.

Brinton, D. and C. Holten. "What Novice Teachers Focus on: The Practicum in TESL." *TESOL Quarterly* 23, no. 3 (1989): 343–50.

Brislin, R. W. et al. *Intercultural Interactions: A Practical Guide*. Beverly Hills, CA: Sage Publications, 1986.

Brock, C. A. "The Effects of Referential Questions on ESL Classroom Discourse." *TESOL Quarterly* 20, no. 1 (1986): 47–59.

Brown, G. and G. Yule. *Teaching the Spoken Language.* Cambridge, U.K.: Cambridge University Press, 1983.

Brown, H. D. *Principles of Language Learning and Teaching, 6th ed.* White Plains, NY: Longman, 2014.

Brown, H. D. and H. Lee. *Teaching by Principles: An Interactive Approach to Language Pedagogy, 4th ed.* New York: Pearson, 2015.

Brown, S. *Listening Myths: Applying Second Language Research to Classroom Teaching.* Ann Arbor: University of Michigan Press, 2011.

Bueffel, E. G. and C. T. Hammett, prods. *It's Toddler Time.* Long Branch, NJ: Kimbo Educational Record, 1982.

Bullough, R.V. and K. Baughman. "Continuity and Change in Teacher Development: First Year Teachers after Five Years." *Journal of Teacher Education* 44, no. 2 (1993): 86–93.

Burns, A. "Action Research." In *Handbook of Research in Second Language Teaching and Learning*, ed. A. Burns and J.C. Richards, 241–56. Mahwah, NJ: Lawrence Erlbaum Publishers, 2004.

———. "Collaborative Action Research and Curriculum Change in the Australian Adult Migrant English Program." *TESOL Quarterly* 30 (1996): 591–98.

———. *Collaborative Action Research for English Language Teachers.* Cambridge, U.K.: Cambridge University Press, 1998.

———. *Doing Action Research in English Language Teaching: A Guide for Practioners.* New York: Routledge, 2011.

Bygate, M. *Speaking.* Oxford, U.K.: Oxford University Press, 1987.

Calderhead, J., ed. *Teachers' Professional Learning.* London: The Falmer Press, 1988.

Canale, M. and M. Swain. "Theoretical Bases of Communicative Approaches to Second Language Teaching and Testing." *Applied Linguistics* 1, no. 1 (1980): 1–47.

Carrrell, P. L., J. Devine, and D. Eskey, eds. *Interactive Approaches to Second Language Reading.* New York: Cambridge University Press.

Celce-Murcia, M. and D. Larson-Freeman. *The Grammar Book, 3rd ed.* Boston: Heinle ELT, 2015.

Celce-Murcia, M., D. M. Brinton, and M. A. Snow, eds. *Teaching English as a Second or Foreign Language, 4th ed.* Boston: Heinle Cengage, 2014.

Chang, B. M. "Korea's English Education Policy Innovations to Lead the Nation into the Globalized World." *Journal of Pan-Pacific Association of Applied Linguistics* 13, no. 1 (2009): 83–97.

Clarke, M. A. *A Place to Stand: Essays for Educators in Troubled Times*. Ann Arbor: University of Michigan Press, 2003.

———. "On Bandwagons, Tyranny, and Common Sense." *TESOL Quarterly* 16, No. 4 (1982): 437–48.

Clarke, M. A. and S. Silberstein. "Problems, Prescriptions, and Paradoxes in Second Language Teaching." In *Enriching ESOL Pedagogy*, eds. V. Zamel and R. Spack, 3–16. Mahwah, NJ: Lawrence Erlbaum, 2002.

Clarke, N. and H. Park. "Education in South Korea." *Asia Pacific*, June 2013.

Compoy-Cubillo, M., B. Bellés-Fortuno, and M. Gea-Valdor. *Corpus-Based Approaches to English Language Teaching*. New York: Continuum International Publishing, 2010.

Conrad, K. B. and T. Conrad. "Creating an ESL Computer-Mediated Class Memory Book." *TESOL Journal* 11, no. 3 (2002): 47–48.

Conrad, T. "An Exploration of Transformative Intercultural & Intracultural Interaction among Middle-School Dual Language Spanish/English Class." Doctoral dissertation, Indiana University of Pennsylvania.

Coxhead, A., ed. *New Ways in Teaching Vocabulary*. Alexandria, VA: TESOL, 2014.

Crookes, G. "Action Research for Second Language Teachers: Going beyond Teacher Research." *Applied Linguistics* 14, no. 2 (1993): 130–44.

Crystal, D. *English as a Global Language, 2nd ed.* Cambridge, U.K.: Cambridge University Press, 2003.

Curran, C.. *Counseling-Learning in Second Languages*. Apple River, IL: Apple River Press, 1976.

———. *Understanding: A Necessary Ingredient in Human Belonging*. Apple River, IL: Apple River Press, 1978.

Day, L. P. "Letter to a Character." In *New Ways in Teaching Reading*, ed. R. R. Day, 9–10. Alexandria, VA: TESOL, 2012.

Day, R. R. "Jigsaw Reading." In *New Ways in Teaching Reading*, ed. R. R. Day, 213–14. Alexandria, VA: TESOL, 2012a.

———. "Later…" In *New Ways in Teaching Reading*, ed. R. R. Day, 12–13. Alexandria, VA: TESOL, 2012b.

———, ed. *New Ways in Teaching Reading*. Alexandria, VA: TESOL, 2012c.

———. *Teaching Reading*. Alexandria, VA: TESOL, 2015.

Day, R. R. and J. Bamford. *Extensive Reading in the Second Language Classroom*. New York: Cambridge University Press, 1998.

Delaney, T. "Putting Names to Faces Together: Using Digital Photo Sheets to Manage Large Classes." In *Classroom Management*, ed. T. S. C. Farrell, 89–96. Alexandria, VA: TESOL, 2008.

de Oliveira, L.C. and T. Silva, eds. *L2 Writing in Secondary Classrooms: Student Experiences, Academic Issues and Teacher Education.* New York: Routledge, 2013.

Dobbs, J. *Using the Board in the Language Classroom.* New York: Cambridge University Press, 2001.

Doi, T. *The Anatomy of Dependence.* Tokyo: Kodansha International, 1973.

Doughty, C. J. and M. H. Long. "Optimal Psycholinguistic Environments for Distance Foreign Language Learning." *Language Learning and Technology* 7, no. 3 (2003): 50–80.

Dwyer, M. A. "Creating and Sustaining Change for Immigrant Learners in Secondary Schools." *TESOL Journal* 7, no. 5 (1998): 6–11.

Eamer, A. and J. Hughes. "Mediating Identity Projects in an ESL Classroom." In *ESL Digital Video Integration: Case Studies*, ed. J. Li, N. Gromik, and N. Edwards, 47–62. Alexandria, VA: TESOL, 2012.

Edge, J. *Continuing Cooperative Development: A Discourse Framework for Individuals and Colleagues.* Ann Arbor: University of Michigan Press, 2002.

Eisenman, G. and H. Thorton. "Telementoring: Helping New Teachers through the First Year." *T.H.E. Journal* 26, no. 9 (1999): 79–82.

Elbow, P. *Writing without Teachers.* New York: Oxford University Press, 1973.

Ellis, R. *The Study of Second Language Acquisition, 2ⁿᵈ ed.* Oxford, U.K.: Oxford University Press, 2008.

———. *Task-based Language Learning and Teaching.* Oxford, U.K.: Oxford University Press, 2003.

Fanselow, J. F. "Beyond Rashomon: Contextualizing and Observing the Teaching Act." *TESOL Quarterly* 11, no. 1 (1977): 17–41.

———. *Breaking Rules: Generating and Exploring Alternatives in Language Teaching.* White Plains, NY: Longman, 1987.

———. *Contrasting Conversations: Activities for Exploring our Beliefs and Teaching Practices.* New York: Longman, 1992.

———. "Let's See: Contrasting Conversations about Teaching." *TESOL Quarterly* 22, no. 1 (1988): 113–30.

———. "Over and Over Again." In *GURT 83: Applied Linguistics and the Preparation of Second Language Teachers: Toward a Rationale*, ed. J. E. Alatis, H. H. Stern, and P. Strevens, 168–76. Washington, DC: Georgetown University Press, 1983.

———. "Post Card Realities." In *Becoming a Language Educator: Personal Essays on Professional Development*, ed C. P. Casanave and S. R. Schecter, 157–72. Mahwah, NJ: Lawrence Erlbaum, 1997.

———. *Try the Opposite.* Amazon: Book Surge Publishing, 2010.

Farrell, T. S. C. "Anxiety: The Hidden Variable in the Korean EFL Classroom." *Language Teaching* 1, no. 1 (1993): 16–18.

——. "ESL/EFL Teacher Development through Journal Writing." *RELC Journal* 29, no. 1 (1998): 92–109.

——. *Language Teacher Professional Development.* Alexandria, VA: TESOL, 2015a.

——. *Promoting Teacher Reflection in Second Language Education.* New York: Routledge, 2015b.

——. *Reflecting on Classroom Communication in Asia.* White Plains, NY: Longman, 2004.

——. *Teaching Reading to English Language Learners: A Reflective Guide.* Thousand Oaks, CA: Corwin Press, 2009.

Ferris, D.R. "Does Error Feedback Help Student Writers? New Evidence on the Short- and Long-Term Effects of Written Error Correction." In *Feedback in Second Language Writing: Contexts and Issues,* eds. K Hyland and F. Hyland, 81–104. Cambridge, U.K.: Cambridge University Press, 2006.

——. "Myth 5: Students Must Learn to Correct Their Writing Errors." In *Writing Myths,* ed. J. Reid, 90–114. Ann Arbor: University of Michigan Press, 2008.

——. "Promoting Grammar and Language Development in Writing Class: Why, What, How, and When." In *Teaching English Grammar to Speakers of Other Languages,* ed. E. Hinkel, 2016.

——. "Student Reactions to Teacher Response in Multiple-Draft Composition Classrooms." *TESOL Quarterly* 29, no. 1 (1995): 33–53.

——. *Treatment of Error in Second Language Writing, 2nd ed.* Ann Arbor: University of Michigan Press, 2011.

Flowerdew, J. and L. Miller. *Second Language Listening: Theory and Practice.* New York: Cambridge University Press, 2005.

Folse, K.S. *Clear Grammar 3, 2nd ed.* Ann Arbor: University of Michigan Press, 2015.

——. *Keys to Teaching Grammar to English Language Learners, 2nd ed.* Ann Arbor: University of Michigan Press, 2016.

——. *Vocabulary Myths. Applying Second Language Research to Classroom Teaching.* Ann Arbor: University of Michigan Press, 2004.

Folse, K. and J. Ivone. *First Discussion Starters: Speaking Fluency Activities for Lower-Level ESL/EFL Students.* Ann Arbor: University of Michigan Press, 2002a.

——. *More Discussion Starters: Activities for Building Fluency.* Ann Arbor: University of Michigan Press, 2002b.

Forest, T. "Shooting Your Class: The Videodrama Approach to Language Acquisition." In *Video in Second Language Teaching,* ed. S. Stempleski and P. Arcario. Alexandria, VA: TESOL, 1992.

Frake, C. *Language and Cultural Description.* Palo Alto, CA: Stanford University Press, 1980.

Fruend, B. "Young Radio Amateurs Speak English." *English Teachers Journal* 51 (1997): 70–71.

Fuller, F. F. "Concerns of Teachers: A Developmental Characterization." *American Educational Research Journal* 6 (1969): 207–26.

Fuller, F. F. and O. H. Brown. "Becoming a Teacher." In *Teacher Education: The Seventy-Fourth Yearbook of the National Society for the Study of Education*, ed. K. Ryan, 25–51. Chicago: The National Society for the Study of Education, 1975.

Garber, C. A. and G. Holmes. "Video-Aided Written/Oral Assignments." *Foreign Language Annals* 14 (1981): 325–31.

Gebhard, J. G. "Reflective Development of Teaching through Self-Observation: Learning To See our Teaching Differently." *International Journal of Innovation in English Language Teaching and Research* 3, no. 1 (2014): 105–122.

———. "EFL Learners Studying Abroad: Challenges and Strategies." *The Asian EFL Journal* 15, no. 2 (2013).

———. "International Students' Adjustment Problems and Successes." *Journal of International Students* 2, no. 2 (2012): 184–193.

———. *What Do International Students Think and Feel? Adapting to U.S. College Life and Culture.* Ann Arbor: University of Michigan Press, 2010.

———. "Awareness of Teaching through Action Research: Examples, Benefits, Limitations." *JALT Journal* 27, no. 1 (2005a): 53–69.

———. "Teacher Development through Exploration: Principles and Activities." *TESOL EJ* 9, no. 2 (2005b): 1–15.

———. "Reflecting through a Teaching Journal." In *Language Teaching Awareness: A Guide to Exploring Beliefs and Practices*, eds. J. G. Gebhard and R. Oprandy, 78–98. New York: Cambridge University Press, 1999.

———. "Interaction in a language teaching practicum." *Second language teacher education*, eds. J. C. Richards and D. Nunan, 118–31. New York: Cambridge University Press, 1990.

———. "Awareness of Teaching: Approaches, Benefits, and Tasks." *English Teaching Forum* 30, no. 4 (1992): 2–7.

———. "Teaching Reading through Assumptions about Learning." *English Teaching Forum* 23, no. 3 (1985): 16–20.

Gebhard, J. G. and A. Ueda-Motonaga. "The Power Of Observation: Make a Wish, Make a Dream, Imagine All the Possibilities." In *Collaborative Language Learning and Teaching*, ed. D. Nunan, 178–91. New York: Cambridge University Press, 2003.

Gebhard, J. G. and E. Han. "What Korean Students Gain from Studying Abroad: English Proficiency and Cultural Awareness." *Studies in English Education* 19, no. 2 (2014): 1–22.

Gebhard, J. G., J. M. Fodor, and M. Lehmann, "Teacher Development through Exploration: Principles, Processes, and Issues in Hungary." In *Studies in English Theoretical and Applied Linguistics*, eds. J. Andor, J. Horvàth, and M. Nikolov, 250–61. Pècs, Hungary: Lingua Franca Csoport, 2003.

Gebhard, J. G., S. Gaitan, and R. Oprandy. "Beyond Prescription: The Student Teacher as Investigator. *Second Language Teacher Education*, eds. J.C. Richards and D. Nunan, 83–95. New York: Cambridge University Press, 1990.

Gebhard, J. G. and T. Nagamine. "A Mutual Learning Experience: Collaboration between a Non-Native Speaker Intern and Native-Speaker Cooperating Teacher." *Asian EFL Journal 7*, no. 2 (2005).

Gebhard, J. G. and R. Oprandy. *Language Teaching Awareness: A Guide to Exploring Beliefs and Practices*. New York: Cambridge University Press, 1999.

Gershon, S. *Present Yourself 2: Viewpoints, 2nd ed*. New York: Cambridge University Press, 2015.

———. *Present Yourself 1: Experiences, 2nd ed*. New York: Cambridge University Press, 2014.

Giannotti, J. *Voices of Experience: How to Manage Student-Centered ESL Classes*. Ann Arbor: University of Michigan Press, 2015.

Gibson, R. "The Strip Story: A Catalyst for Communication." *TESOL Quarterly* 9 (1975): 149–54.

Gilbert, J. *Clear Speech: Pronunciation and Listening Comprehension in North American English*. New York: Cambridge University Press, 2014.

———. *Nonverbal Tools for Teaching Pronunciation*. University of California, Davis, n.d. Unpublished.

Goh, C. C. M. "Second Language Listening Comprehension: Process and Pedagogy." In *Teaching English as a Second or Foreign Language, 4th ed.*, eds. M. Celce-Murcia, D. M., Brinton and M. A. Snow, 72–89. Boston: Heinle Cengage, 2014.

Goodwin, J. "Teaching Pronunciation." In *Teaching English as a Second or Foreign Language, 4th ed.*, eds. M. Celce-Murcia, D. M. Brinton, and M. A. Snow, 136–51. Boston: Heinle Cengage, 2014.

Grabe, W. "Reflections on Second Language Reading." In *Reading: Research and Instruction*, eds. Z-H Han and N. Anderson, 192–205. Ann Arbor: University of Michigan Press, 2009.

Grabe, W. and F.L. Stoller. *Teaching and Researching Reading, 2nd ed*. New York: Pearson Education ESL, 2011.

Graham, C. *Holiday Jazz Chants*. New York: Oxford University Press, 1999.

———. *Jazz Chants*. New York: Oxford University Press, 1978.

———. *Jazz Chants Old and New*. New York: Oxford University Press, 2003.

Graves, K. *Designing Language Courses*. Boston: Heinle Cengage, 1999.

Grellet, F. *Developing Reading Skills: A Practical Guide to Reading Comprehension Exercises*. New York: Cambridge University Press, 1981.

Gromik, N. "Female Arab Students' Production of Cell Phone Videos." In *ESL and Digital Video Integration: Case Studies*, eds. J. Li, N. Gromik, and N. Edwards, 117–34. Alexandria, VA: TESOL, 2012.

Hall, E. T. *The Silent Language*. New York: Anchor Books, 1966.

Halliday, M. A. K. and R. Hasan. *Cohesion in English*. London: Longman, 1976.

Hamp-Lyons, L. "Writing Teachers as Assessors of Writing." In *Exploring the Dynamics of Second Language Writing*, ed. B. Kroll, 162–89. Cambridge, U.K.: Cambridge University Press, 2003.

Harklau, L. "ESL versus Mainstream Classes: Contrasting L2 Learning Environments." In *Enriching ESOL Pedagogy*, eds. V. Zamel and R. Spack, 127–57. Mahwah, NJ: Lawrence Erlbaum, 2002.

Harklau, L., K. M. Losey, and M. Siegal, eds. *Generation 1.5 Meets College Composition: Issues in Teaching Writing to U.S.-Educated Learners of English*. Mahwah, NJ: Lawrence Erlbaum, 1999.

Hartshorn, J.K., N.W. Evans, P.F. Merrill, R.E. Strong-Krause, and N.J. Anderson. "The Effects of Dynamic Corrective Feedback on ESL Writing Accuracy." *TESOL Quarterly* 44, no. 1 (2010): 84–109.

Heinze, R. L. *Tham Khwan: How to Contain the Essence of Life*. Kent Ridge, Singapore: Singapore University Press, 1982.

Holten, C. A. and D. M. Brinton. "You Shoulda Been There: Charting Novice Teachers Growth Using Dialogue Journals." *TESOL Journal* 4, no. 4 (1995): 23–26.

Hull, G. et al. " Remediation as Social Construct: Perspectives from an Analysis of Classroom Discourse." In *Enriching ESOL Pedagogy*, eds. V. Zamel and R. Spack, 159–91. Mahwah, NJ: Lawrence Erlbaum, 2002.

Hyland, K. *Teaching and Researching Writing*. Harlow, U.K.: Pearson Education, 2002.

Hymes, D. "On Communicative Competence." In *Sociolinguistics: Selected Readings*, eds. J. Pride and J. Holmes. Harmondsworth, U.K.: Penguin, 1972.

Institute of Higher Education. *Open Doors: 2014: International Students in the United States at an All Time High*, www.iie.org, 2014.

Jacobs, J. "Learning English." *Education Next* 16, no. 2 (2016).

Jersild, A. T. *When Teachers Face Themselves*. New York: Teachers College Press, 1955.

Johnson, K. E. "Portfolio Assessment in Second Language Teacher Education." *TESOL Journal* 6, no. 2 (1996): 11–14.

Jones, T. *Pronunciation in the Classroom: The Overlooked Essential*. Alexandria, VA: TESOL, 2016.

Jung, S. K. and B. Norton. "Language Planning in Korea: The New Elementary English Program." In *Language Policies in Education: Critical Issues*, ed. W. Tollefson. Mahwah, NJ: Lawrence Erlbaum, 2002.

Kachru, B. *The Alchemy of English*. Oxford, U.K.: Oxford University Press, 1989.

———. "Teaching World Englishes." *Indiana Journal of Applied Linguistics* 15, no. 1 (1986): 85–95.

Kahtani, S. "Electronic Portfolios in ESL Writing: An Alternative Approach." *Computer Assisted Language Learning* 12, no. 3 (1999): 261–68.

Kelly, M. J. and N. Clausen-Grace. *Comprehension Shouldn't Be Silent: From Strategy Instruction to Student Independence*, 2nd ed. Newark, DE: International Reading Association, 2013.

Kim, Y.Y. "Adapting to a New Culture." In *Intercultural Communication*, 14th ed., eds. L. Samovar, R.E. Porter, E.R. McDaniel, and C.S. Roy, 385–97. Independence, KY: Cengage Learning, 2015.

Kitao, K. S. "Teaching Transitions." In *New Ways in Teaching Reading*, ed. R. R. Day, 102–3. Alexandria, VA: TESOL, 2012.

Klausner, W. J. *Reflections on Thai Culture*. Bangkok: The Siam Society.

Kluge, D. E. "Your Turn at the Mike." In *New Ways in Teaching Reading*, ed. R. R. Day, 9–11. Alexandria, VA: TESOL, 1993.

Knagg, J. "TESOL President Award Speech." Portland, OR: International TESOL Convention, 2014.

Korean Ministry of Education. *Chodeung Hakgyo Yeong-eo Gyoyuk Jeongchaek Jaryjip (The English Education Policies in Elementary Schools)*. Seoul, Korea: Ministry of Education, 2010.

Krashen, S. D. "Do We Learn by Reading? The Relationship between Free Reading and Reading Ability." In *Linguistics in Context: Connecting Observation and Understanding*, ed. D. Tannen, 269–98. Norwood, NJ: Ablex, 1988.

———. *The Power of Reading: Insights from the Research*. Englewood, CO: Libraries Unlimited, 1993.

Krohn, R. *English Sentence Structure*. Ann Arbor: University of Michigan Press, 1971.

Kroll, R. "Considerations for Teaching an ESL/EFL Writing Course." In *Teaching English as a Second or Foreign Language*, 3rd ed., eds. M. Celce-Murcia, D.M. Brinton, and M.A. Snow, 219–32. Boston: Heinle and Heinle, 2001.

Kroonenberg, N. "Developing Communicative and Thinking Skills via Electronic Mail." *TESOL Journal* 4 (1994–95): 24–27.

Kusenberg, K. "Odd Tippling." In *On Being Foreign: Culture Shock in Short Fiction*, eds. T. Lewis and R. Jungman, 51–53. Boston: Intercultural Press.

Lankton, S. *Practical Magic: A Translation of Basic Neuro-Linguistic Programming into Clinical Psychotherapy*. Cupertino, CA: Meta Publications, 1980.

Larson-Freeman, D. "Teaching Grammar." In *Teaching English as a Second or Foreign Language, 4th ed.*, eds. M. Celce-Murcia, D. M. Brinton, and M. A. Snow, 256–70. Boston: Heinle Cengage, 2014.

Larson-Freeman, D. and M. Anderson. *Techniques and Principles in Second Language Teaching, 3rd ed.* New York: Oxford University Press, 2011.

Lazaraton, A. "Second Language Speaking." In *Teaching English as a Second or Foreign Language, 4th ed.*, eds. M. Celce Murcia, D. M. Brinton, and M. A. Snow, 106–121. Boston: Heinle Cengage, 2014.

Lessow-Hurley, J. *The Foundations of Dual Language Instruction, 6th ed.* New York: Pearson, 1212.

Lewis, T. J. and R. E. Jungman. *On Being Foreign: Culture Shock in Short Fiction*. Boston: Intercultural Press, 1986.

Li, J., N. Gromik, and N. Edwards, eds. *ESL and Digital Video Integration: Case Studies*. Alexandria, VA: TESOL, 2012.

Lieberman, A. Foreword to *Contrasting Conversations: Activities for Exploring our Beliefs and Teaching Practices* by John F. Fanselow. White Plains, NY: Longman, 1992.

Littlewood, W. *Communicative Language Teaching*. Cambridge, U.K.: Cambridge University Press, 1981.

———. *Teaching Oral Communication: A Methodological Framework*. Oxford, U.K.: Blackwell, 1992.

Liu, J. and J. G. Hansen Edwards. *Peer Response in Second Language Writing Classrooms, 2nd ed.* Ann Arbor: University of Michigan Press, in press.

Llurda, E., ed. *Non-native Language Teachers: Perceptions, Challenges and Contributions to the Profession*. New York: Springer, 2006.

Lonergan, J. *Video in Language Teaching*. Cambridge: Cambridge University Press, 1981.

Lotherington, H. and J. Jenson. "Teaching Multimodal and Digital Literacy in L2 Settings." *Annual Review of Applied Linguistics* 31 (2011): 226–46.

Long, M. H. "A Role for Instruction in Second Language Acquisition: Task-Based Language Teaching." In *Modeling and Assessing Second Language Development*, eds. K. Hyltenstam and M. Pienemann, 77–99. Clevedon, U.K.: Multilingual Matters, 1985.

Long, M. H. and C. Sato. "Classroom Foreigner Talk Discourse: Forms and Functions of Teachers' Questions." In *Classroom Oriented Research in Second Language Acquisition*, eds. H. Seliger and M. Long, 268–86. Rowley, MA: Newbury House, 1983.

Lorayne, H. and J. Lucas. *The Memory Book*. New York: Dorset Press, 1974.

Maley, A. and A. Duff. *Drama Techniques in Language Learning*. New York: Cambridge University Press, 1982.

Mann, S. and F. Copeland. *Materials Development*. Alexandria, VA: TESOL, 2015.

Marshall, T. *The Whole World Guide to Language Learning*. Boston: Intercultural Press, 1989.

Martire, J. *Small Group Discussion Topics for Korean University Students*. Busan, South Korea: Pusan National University Press, 2001.

———. *Small Group Discussion Topics for Korean University Students, 2ⁿᵈ ed*. Busan, South Korea: Pusan National University Press, 2011.

Marzio, M. "Getting 'Real' with Video and CD-ROM: Real English at the Marzio School." In *Technology-Enhanced Learning Environments*, ed. E. Hanson-Smith, 67–81. Alexandria, VA: TESOL, 2000.

Matsuda, P. K., M. Cox, J. Jordon, and C. Ortmeier-Hooper. *Second Language Writing in the Composition Classroom: A Critical Resource Book*. New York: Bedford St. Martins, 2010.

McCarthy, M.J. "Teaching Grammar at the Advanced Level." In *Teaching English Grammar to Speakers of Other Languages*, ed. E. Hinkel, 203–21. New York: Routledge, 2016.

McCarthy, M. and A. Okeefe. "Spoken Grammar." In *Teaching English as a Second or Foreign Language, 4ᵗʰ ed.*, eds. M. Celce Murcia, D. M. Brinton, and M. A. Snow, 271–87. Boston: Heinle Cengage, 2014.

McDaniel, E. R. "Japanese Nonverbal Communication: A Reflection of Cultural Themes." In *Intercultural Communication: A Reader, 14ᵗʰ ed.* eds. L. A. Samovar, R.E. Porter, and E. R. McDaniel, 242–56. Belmont, CA: Wadsworth, 2015.

McKay, S. L. *Teaching English Overseas: An Introduction*. New York: Oxford University Press, 1992.

Medgyes, P. "Native or Non-native: Who's Worth More?" *ELT Journal 46*, no. 4 (1991): 340–49.

Melvin, B. S. and D. F. Stout. "Motivating Language Learners through Authentic Materials." In *Interactive Language Teaching*, ed. W. Rivers, 44–56. New York: Cambridge University Press, 1987.

Mendelsohn, D. *Learning to Listen: A Strategy-based Approach for the Second-Language Learner*. San Diego, CA: Dominie Press, 1994.

Mikulecky, B. S. *A Sort Course in Teaching Reading: Practical Teaching Techniques for Building Reading Power, 2ⁿᵈ ed*. White Plains, NJ: Pearson Education, 2011.

Minh, N. T. T. *Textbook Evaluation: The Case Currently Used in Vietnam's Upper-Secondary Schools*. Singapore: RELC SEAMEO, 2007.

Ministry of Education and Training of Vietnam. *The English Curriculum for the Secondary School*. Hanoi: Education Publishers, 2006.

Morley, J. ed. *Current Perspectives on Pronunciation*. Alexandria, VA: TESOL, 1987.

Munby, J. *Communicative Syllabus Design: A Sociolinguistic Model for Designing the Content of Specific Language Programs*. Cambridge, U.K.: Cambridge University Press, 1981.

Nam, K. *A Critical Look at Interaction in a Korean Middle School Classroom: Its Role in Development of Students' Communicative Abilities*. Ph.D. dissertation, Pusan National University, 2011.

Nation, I. S. P. "Second Language Speaking." In *Handbook of Research in Second Language Teaching and Learning, Vol II*, ed. E. Hinkel, 444–54. New York: Routledge, 2011.

———. *Teaching ESL/EFL Reading and Writing*. New York: Routledge, 2009.

Nation, I. S. P. and J. Newton. *ESL/EFL Listening and Speaking*. New York: Routledge, 2009.

Nelson, G. L. "Narratives of Classroom Life: Changing Conceptions of Knowledge." *TESOL Quarterly* 45, no. 3 (2011): 463–485.

Nemtchinova, E. *Teaching Listening*. Alexandria, VA: TESOL, 2013.

Nelson, G. L. and J. M. Murphy. "Writing Groups and the Less Proficient ESL Student." *TESOL Journal* 2, no. 2 (1992–1993): 23–25.

Nicholson, P. and R. Sakuno. *Explain Yourself: An English Conversation Book for Japan*. Kyoto, Japan: PAL, 1982.

Numrich, C. "On Becoming a Language Teacher: Insights from Diary Studies." *TESOL Quarterly* 30, no. 1 (1996): 131–53.

Nunan, D. *Task-Based Language Teaching*. Alexandria, VA: TESOL, 2013.

———. "Task-Based Teaching and Learning." In *Teaching English as a Second or Foreign Language*, 4th ed., eds. M. Celce Murcia, D. M. Brinton, and M. A. Snow, 455–70. Boston: Heinle Cengage, 2014.

Nunan, D. and K. M. Bailey. *Exploring Second Language Classroom Research: A Comprehensive Guide*. Boston: Heinle Cengage, 2009.

Nydell, M. K. *Understanding Arabs: A Guide for Westerners*, 2nd ed. Boston: Intercultural Press, 2002.

Ogami, N. prod. *Cold Water*. Yarmouth, ME: Intercultural Press, 1988. Videotape.

Ohata, K. "Cultural and Personal Aspects of Language Learning Anxiety: A Case Study of Seven Japanese Individuals' Reflective Accounts of Language Learning Anxiety." Doctoral dissertation, Indiana University of Pennsylvania, 2004.

Olshtain, E. "Functional Tasks for Mastering the Mechanics of Writing and Going Just Beyond." In *Teaching English as a Second or Foreign Language*, 4th ed., eds. M. Celce Murcia, D. M. Brinton, and M. A. Snow, 208–21. Boston: Heinle Cengage, 2014.

Orlando, R. *Teaching English in U.S. University IEP Programs*. Alexandria, VA: TESOL, 2016.

Oxford, R. "Anxiety and the Language Learner." In *Affect in Language Learning*, ed. J. Arnold, 58–67. New York: Cambridge University Press, 1999.

Parks, M. "Internet Scavenger Hunt." In *New Ways in Teaching Reading*, ed. R. R. Day, 74–75. Alexandria, VA: TESOL, 2012.

Pèregoy, S. and O. F. Boyle. *Reading, Writing and Learning in ESL: A Resource Book for K–12 Teachers*, 7th ed. New York: Pearson, 2017.

Pitts, L. *ESL Role Plays*. North Charleston, SC: ECQ Publish, 2016.

Platt, J., H. Webber, and H. M. Lian. *The New Englishes*. London: Routledge, 1984.

Porter, D. and J. Roberts. "Authentic Listening Activities." In *Methodology in TESOL*, eds. M. L. Long and J. C. Richards, 177–87. Rowley, MA: Newbury House, 1987.

Prensky. M. "Digital Native, Digital Immigrant." *On the Horizon* 9, No. 5 (2001).

Pritchard, R. and R. VanVleet. "Using Think-Alouds to Teach Reading Strategies." In *New Ways in Teaching Reading*, ed. R. R. Day, 142–43. Alexandria, VA: TESOL, 2012.

Raimes, A. *Techniques in Teaching Writing*. New York: Oxford University Press, 1983.

———. "What Unskilled ESL Students Do as They Write." *TESOL Quarterly* 19, no. 2 (1985): 229–58.

Ramirez, S. and K. L. Savage. "Video-Based Distance Education for Adult English Language Learners." Center for Applied Linguistics, ED 99-CO-0008, 2000.

Reppen, R. *Using Corpora in the Language Classroom*. New York: Cambridge University Press, 2010.

Reyes, S. H. and T. Kleyn. *Teaching in Two Languages: A Guide for K–12 Bilingual Educators*. Thousand Oaks, CA: Sage, 2010.

Richards, J. C. "Beyond the Textbook: The Role of Commercial Materials in Language Teaching." *RELC Journal* 24, no. 1 (1993): 1–14.

———. *The Language Teaching Matrix*. New York: Cambridge University Press, 1990.

Richards, J. C. and A. Burns. *Tips for Teaching Listening: A Practical Approach*. White Plains, NY: Pearson, 2012.

Richards, J. C. and T. S. C. Farrell. *Professional Development of Language Teachers: Strategies for Teacher Learning*. New York: Cambridge University Press, 2005.

Richards, J. C. and T. Rodgers. *Approaches and Methods in Language Teaching*, 3rd ed. New York: Cambridge University Press, 2011.

Rinvolucri, M. *Grammar Games*. Cambridge, U.K.: Cambridge University Press, 1984.

Rivers, W., ed. *Interactive Language Teaching*. New York: Cambridge University Press, 1987.

Rose, G. *Perspectives on Teaching Adults in the Digital World*. Alexandria, VA: TESOL, 2015.

Rosen, S. *My Voice Will Go with You: The Teaching Tales of Milton H. Erickson*. New York: W. W. Norton, 1991.

Rowe, M. "Wait Time: Slowing Down May Be a Way of Speeding Up." *Journal of Teacher Education* 37, no. 1 (1986): 43–50.

Rost, M. *Teaching and Researching Listening*, 2nd ed. Harlow, U.K.: Longman, 2011.

Russell, J. and N. Spada. "The Effectiveness of Corrective Feedback for the Acquisition of L2 Grammar: A Meta-Analysis of the Research." In *Synthesizing Research on Language Learning and Teaching*, eds. J. Norris and L. Ortega, 133–64. Amsterdam: John Benjamins, 2006.

Ryan, P. "Exploring Elementary Teachers' Experiences with English Language Learners." Doctoral dissertation, Indiana University of Pennsylvania, 2004.

Savignon, S. "Communicative Language Teaching in the Twenty-First Century." In *Teaching English as a Second or Foreign Language*, 3rd ed. ed. M. Celce-Murcia, 13–28. Boston: Heinle & Heinle, 2001.

Schenkein, J., ed. *Studies in the Organization of Conversational Interaction*. New York: Academic Press, 1978.

Schmitt, N. *Vocabulary in Language Teaching*. New York: Cambridge University Press, 2000.

Schön, D. A. *The Reflective Practioner: How Professionals Think in Action*. New York: Basic Books, 1983.

Scovel, T. "The Effect and Affect on Foreign Language Learning: A Review of Anxiety Research." *Language Learning* 28, no. 1 (1978): 129–42.

Segal, B. prod. *Teaching English through Action*. Brea, CA: Berty Segal, 1983. Video.

Segal, B. and H. Sloan, prods. *TPR and the Natural Approach*. Brea, CA: Berty Segal, 1983. Video.

Sharma, D. "Second Language Varieties of English." In *The Oxford Handbook of the History of English*, eds. T. Nevalainen and E. C. Traugott, 654–66. Oxford, U.K.: Oxford University Press, 2012.

Sherman, J. *Using Authentic Video in the Language Classroom*. New York: Cambridge University Press, 2003.

Silberstein, S., B. K. Dobson, and M. A. Clarke. *Reader's Choice*, 5th ed. Ann Arbor: University of Michigan Press, 2008.

Silva, T. *Practice and Theory in Second Language Writing*. Anderson, SC: Parlor Press, 2010.

Smith, F. *Understanding Reading*. New York: Holt, Rinehart, and Winston, 1994.

Smith, L. "Some Distinctive Features of EIL vs. ESOL in English Education. In *Readings In English as an International Language*, ed. I. Smith. Oxford, U.K.: Pergamon Press, 1983.

Sokolik, M. "Digital Technology in Language Teaching." In *Teaching English as a Second or Foreign Language, 4th ed.*, eds. M. Celce Murcia, D. M. Brinton, and M. A. Snow, 409–21. Boston: Heinle Cengage, 2014.

Stempleski, S. "Teaching Communication Skills with Authentic Video." In *Video in Second Language Teaching*, eds. S. Stempleski and P. Arcario, 7–14. Alexandria, VA: TESOL, 1992.

Stevick, E. W. "Control, Initiative, and the Whole Learner." In *Collected Papers in Teaching English as a Second Language and Bilingual Education*. New York: NYSTESOL, 1978.

———. *My Understanding of Teaching Languages: A Way and Ways*. Paper presented at the TESOL Convention, Honolulu, HI, 1982.

———. *Teaching Languages: A Way and Ways*. New York: Newbury House, 1980.

Storti, C. *The Art of Crossing Cultures*. Boston: Intercultural Press, 1989.

———. *The Art of Crossing Cultures, 2nd ed.* Boston: Intercultural Press, 2007.

———. *Figuring Foreigners Out: A Practical Guide*. Boston: Intercultural Press, 2011.

Thomas, M. and H. Reinders, eds. *Contemporary Task-Based Language Teaching in Asia*. New York: Bloomsbury Publishing, 2015.

Thonus, T. "Serving Generation 1.5 Learners in University Writing Centers." *TESOL Journal* 12, no. 1 (2003): 17–24.

Trudgill, P. and J. Hannah. *International English: Guide to the Varieties of Standard English*. New York: Routledge, 2008.

Ur, P. "Grammar Practice." In *Teaching English Grammar to Speakers of Other Languages*, ed. E. Hinkel, 109–27. New York: Routledge, 2016.

Ur, P. *Teaching Listening Comprehension*. New York: Cambridge University Press, 1984.

Uzunboylu, H., N. Carvus, and E. Ercag. "Using Mobile Learning to Increase Environmental Awareness." *Computers and Education* 52 (2009): 381–89.

Vandergrift, L. and C. Goh. *Teaching and Learning Second Language Listening: Metacognition in Action*. Malden, VA: Wiley-Blackwell, 2012.

Vernon, S. A. *176 ESL Games for Children, 3rd ed.* Seattle: Amazon Publishing, 2015.

Via, R. "'The Magic If' of Theater: Enhancing Language Learning through Drama." In *Interactive Language Teaching*, ed. W. Rivers, 110–23. New York, 1987.

Wallace, M. J. *Action Research for Language Teachers*. Cambridge, U.K.: Cambridge University Press, 1998.

Wallender, D. *The Bridge, Fall*. Excerpts from a volunteer's journal, 1997.

Wang, M. M. et al. *Turning Bricks into Jade*. Boston: Intercultural Press, 2000.

Warschauer, M. "The Changing Global Economy and the Future of English Teaching." *TESOL Quarterly* 34, no. 3 (2012): 511–35.

White, A. ed. *New Ways in Teaching Writing*. Alexandria, V: TESOL, 1995.

White, D., prod. *Action Songs for Indoor Days*. Los Angeles: Tom Thumb Recordings, 1978.

Wong, J. and H. Z. Waring. *Conversation Analysis and Second Language Pedagogy: A Guide for ESL/EFL Teachers*. New York: Routledge, 2010.

Wong, L. A. "The Descriptive Analysis of the Varieties of Singapore English as Recreated by Singapore Writers of Fiction." Doctoral dissertation, Indiana University of Pennsylvania, 1992.

Wright, A., D. Betteridge, and M. Buckly. *Games for Language Learning*. Cambridge, U.K.: Cambridge University Press, 1994.

Yahya, N. "Keeping a Critical Eye on One's Own Teaching Practice: EFL Teachers' Use of Reflective Teaching Journals." *Asian Journal of English Language Teaching* 10 (2000): 1–18.

Yeh, A. "English Learning through Arts, Music, and Digital Media: A Photostory Project." In *ESL and Digital Video Integration: Case Studies*, eds. J. Li and N. Edwards, 63–82. Alexandria, VA: TESOL, 2012.

Zamel, V. "The Composing Processes of Advanced ESL Students: Six Case Studies." *TESOL Quarterly* 17, no. 2 (1983): 165–90.

——. "Writing: The Process of Discovering Meaning." *TESOL Quarterly* 16, no. 2 (1982): 195–209.

Zohrobi, M., M. Yaghoubi-Notash, and S. Y. Khiabani. "Teachers Use of Display vs. Referential Questions." *International Journal of Applied Linguistics & English Literature* 3, no. 2 (2014): 96–100.

Zukerman, E. "The Cute Cat Theory Talk at Etech." EthanZukerman.com, 2003.

INDEX